Theatre History Studies

2019 Volume 38

Edited by

SARA FREEMAN

PUBLISHED BY THE MID-AMERICA THEATRE CONFERENCE
AND THE UNIVERSITY OF ALABAMA PRESS

Template Design: Todd Lape / Lape Designs

Essays appearing in this journal are abstracted and indexed in *Historical Abstracts* and *America: History and Life*.

MEMBER
CELJ
Council of Editors of Learned Journals

Cover Art
Macbeth at Fort Point (2014). John Hadden as Macbeth, Jack Halton as Banquo; photo by Jamie Lyons. Courtesy of We Players.

Cover Design
Todd Lape / Lape Designs

Please note: there was no issue published in 2013.

Theatre History Studies is an official journal of the Mid-America Theatre Conference, Inc. (MATC). The conference is dedicated to the growth and improvement of all forms of theatre throughout a twelve-state region that includes the states of Illinois, Iowa, Nebraska, Kansas, Missouri, Minnesota, North Dakota, South Dakota, and Wisconsin. Its purposes are to unite people and organizations within this region and elsewhere who have an interest in theatre and to promote the growth and development of all forms of theatre.

Theatre History Studies is devoted to research in all areas of theatre studies. Manuscripts should be prepared in conformity with the guidelines established in the most recent edition of the *Chicago Manual of Style* and emailed to Lisa Jackson Schebetta at lisajschebetta@gmail.com. Consulting editors read the manuscripts, a process that takes approximately four months. The journal does not normally accept studies of dramatic literature unless there is a focus on actual production and performance. Authors whose manuscripts are accepted must provide the editor with an electronic file, using Microsoft Word. Illustrations are welcomed and should conform to the instructions listed in the style guide on the website: http://matc.us/theatre-history-studies-4/theatre-history-studies-the-matc-journal.

This publication is issued annually by the Mid-America Theatre Conference and the University of Alabama Press.

Subscription rates for 2019 are $25.00 for individuals, $35.00 for institutions, and an additional $10.00 for foreign delivery. Subscription orders and changes of address should be directed to Allie Harper, The University of Alabama Press, Box 870380, Tuscaloosa, AL 35487; (205) 348-1564, phone; (205) 348-9201, fax.

Any single current-year issue or back issue is $34.95 each if ordered through the Chicago Distribution Center. (Please note: there was no issue published in 2013.)

Theatre History Studies is indexed in *Humanities Index*, *Humanities Abstracts*, *Book Review Index*, *MLA International Bibliography*, *International Bibliography of Theatre & Dance*, *Arts & Humanities Citation Index*, *IBZ International Bibliography of Periodical Literature*, and *IBR International Bibliography of Book Reviews*, the database of the *International Index to the Performing Arts*. Full texts of essays appear in the databases of both *Humanities Abstracts Full Text* and *SIRS*. The journal has published its own index, *The Twenty Year Index, 1981–2000*. It is available for $10 for individuals and $15 for libraries from Sara Freeman, associate professor, Theatre Arts CMB 1084, University of Puget Sound, 1500 N. Warner St., Tacoma, WA 98416; (253) 879-2438.

CONTENTS

CONTENTS

CONTENTS

ILLUSTRATIONS

Introduction

—SARA FREEMAN

This issue is the final one for which I will serve as the editor of the *Theatre History Studies* journal, and it is my pleasure to welcome Dr. Lisa Jackson-Schebetta as the incoming editor. This hand off naturally puts me in a retrospective mood. Surveying the articles for this, my last, issue, I find myself thinking about the tension between teaching theatre history and writing it. This tension feels acute because I write this introduction as I compile the final grades for my fall semester undergraduate theatre history class. Theatre History I has been on my teaching docket almost every fall for fifteen years. This is my first time teaching theatre history since a sabbatical in 2017. Returning to teaching reminds me that on a fundamental level I don't know what I'm doing. I'm trying to distill the huge sweep of human performance activity from antiquity to the sixteenth century for a 300-level seminar, while at the same time I have amassed a storehouse of what my graduate school professor James Moy would have called "cranky" details about events and patterns from the past that I seem to want my undergraduates to notice and remember. In class, I am always navigating the tensions between understanding historical events, engaging with the dramaturgical logics (to use a phrase that motivates the investigations in the special section) of performances during certain periods, and framing the historiographical questions that propel the scholarship in our field and distinguish its insights.

For theatre history, the devil is in the details. While I'm afraid I get bogged down in them with my students, details are what I most thrill to in the articles in this issue and the writing of theatre history. I appreciate how Elizabeth Coen's descriptions of two actors from Stranitzky's company mooning the Viennese audience in 1717 accompanies her masterful narration of the careful political maneuvering across the next seventy years by Empress Maria Theresa and her successors to contain critique from the stage. And I admire how Bridget McFarland's thorough reconstruction of the 1791 town meeting where revolutionary-war-hero-turned-elder-statesman Samuel Adams makes a losing case for maintaining the ban on theatres in Boston stands alongside her vivid rereading of pamphlets from the era debating the utility and morality of theatre. McFarland's and Coen's articles provide dimensional discussions of censorship, politics, and comedy on the eighteenth-century stage, detailing in parallel moments from points across the world how popular forms like pantomime that use improvisation are modes of dynamic negotiation over representation and rights. Then there's how Ryan Tvedt's accounts of Vladimir Mayakovsky and his band of brother cubo-futurists parading through the towns on their 1913–1914 provincial tour of Russia—wearing radishes as boutonnieres, painting their faces, and dying their hair wild colors—sets up his analysis of how deftly the avant-gardists both antagonized and expertly negotiated authorities at each stop. And how Daniella Vinitski Mooney records through artist interviews what working in a warehouse in DUMBO in New York was like in the 1990s as part of establishing the context and impact of GAle GAtes et al.'s theatre of images in a continuous experimental theatre lineage and as an under recognized precursor of the commercial upsurge in immersive and site-based theatre in the twenty-first century.

These articles are also strong on concepts. Coen makes the particularly important distinction between *a* public and *the* public, something authorities often fail to differentiate between, just as historians can miss the difference between the *literary* public and the *theatregoing* public when trying to reconstruct what was at stake in different skirmishes about the censorship of satire and the comic performances of Hanswurst onstage. In this vein, McFarland's treatment of controversy about the role of theatre in conceptions of early American self-governance delves deeply into anxieties around the ridicule of authority, explicating the way the early republic came to license pantomimes, since people must be able to imagine challenging leaders in a system where they assert self-rule. Conceptually, Tvedt provides an important frame about industrial-age travel and its relationship to the avant-garde project of shaking up perception. Mooney, for her part, posits an inverse relationship between site-bound performance and its immediate geographic landscape, distinguishing between how GAle GAtes's obscure, site-specific locale supported work that could not be reproduced or commodified but that was not necessarily "opposed to the mainstream nor working from an ideological vantage point." Current immersive theatre also sits on this paradox, mobilizing disruptive aesthetics but creating commercial and symbolic cachet.

By documenting antecedents to a contemporary trend, Mooney's article serves as a useful precursor to this issue's special section, which focuses on the dramaturgy and ethics of site-based theatre. Mooney demonstrates what it means to record the work of a site-based practitioner and put it in historical context. Section editors Penelope Cole and Rand Harmon conceived the special section not just as an attempt to document manifestations of site-based performances but also as an effort to delve into the dilemmas of audience experience in this mode of work. The articles they collected—by Cole herself, as well as by Sean Bartley, David Bisaha, and Colleen Rua—are both theatre histories and ethical inquiries. As Cole's introduction describes, these articles are records of participant-observation on the part of the scholars as well as theorizations about the way the properties of storytelling operate in site-based work. They are also probing critiques of artistic assumptions about spectatorship, ability, politics, and mobility. The theoretical and critical work of this special section culminates with an expansive curated discussion between Cole, Harmon, Erin B. Mee, and Guillermo Aviles-Rodriguez that provides documentation of several more site-based works of the last decade and pushes intimately into the ethical implications of audience experience in site-based work. It is fitting that a special section about theatre methods that challenge formal expectations and highlight exchange and participation closes with an article in a format this journal does not usually use, namely, the curated discussion, and does so to maximize exchange and participation. The special section provides history and historiography about contemporary work; the details about production and reception in it are matched by a conceptual framing that I know would compel my students' understanding of the theatrical landscape they inhabit, especially since large-scale immersive productions like Punchdrunk's *Sleep No More* have become the first theatre that many of them encounter beyond community productions or a Broadway tour.

The issue is capped by Michelle Granshaw's Schanke Award-winning conference paper about the comic tramp figure on the nineteenth-century variety stage. Granshaw contrasts the whiteface/Irish tramp to blackface tramps, noting that the mobility of the tramp produces opposite depictions on the variety stage depending on the racialized identity of the character. Like her other articles and book projects, Granshaw's article provides an informed reading of race and representation on the variety stage, both through close readings of sketches and afterpieces and through discussion of the "visual vocabulary" tied to "ethnic and racial comic stereotypes." The Schanke Award exists to honor an exemplary conference paper from the Mid-America Theatre Conference annual meeting, and Granshaw's work shows how it should be done, with a level of detail that makes a conference paper an education unto itself.

As I close my tenure as editor, I am reflecting on the education I've sought and received. Another of my teachers, my colleague and most revered advisor, Geoff Proehl, has for years had a small sign on his office door that reads "god is in the details." It is in simple typeface, all lowercase, and quietly sits posted on the corkboard on the door. Perhaps this is it: For artists, for teachers, and for historians, it is not the devil but god who is in the details. Geoff is retiring this year, but the teaching, and the history, and the dramaturgy will go on. There are many details still to relish. I have enjoyed every article I supervised for this journal because I learned so much from each of them. I wish the same for Lisa and look forward to enjoying how her editorial focus advances the theatre historical conversations of our field.

Part I

STUDIES IN THEATRE HISTORY

Hanswurst's Public

Defending the Comic in the Theatres of Eighteenth-Century Vienna

—ELIZABETH COEN

> I flatter myself in being a necessary and agreeable citizen in the best comic world, and therefore hope I shall not be banished from thence, as so many fools are suffered to appear therein for the service of the wisest philosophers.
>
> JUSTUS MÖSER, HARLEQUIN: OR, A DEFENCE OF GROTESQUE COMIC PERFORMANCES

In the Age of Enlightenment, a sausage-loving prankster named Hanswurst tormented bourgeois reformers of the German theatre with his exceptional ability to charm audiences.[1] Determined to replace extemporized performances with a literary repertoire, these reformers harnessed the press to argue that the harlequin's plays were "without choice, regularity, unity, or harmony" and that they functioned "without plan or design." Moreover, they asserted in a litany of rants recounted by the eighteenth-century historian Justus Möser that such material was "low, creeping, indecent, and foolish!—full of obscene language, filthy allusions, poor flashes of empty wit, and proverbs without number!"[2] These invectives helped Hanswurst's detractors curry favor with the literary public, a bourgeois readership from cities across Austria, Prussia, and the German Reich.[3] Nevertheless, they failed to persuade the theatregoing public, a populace much larger and more socioeconomically diverse than their own literate circles. Hanswurst's frequent banishments from the stage were almost always followed by reappearances. This was especially true in Vienna. From 1748 until the 1770s, the Viennese debated the cultural legitimacy of Hanswurst and the merits of German-language comedy in a controversy known as the *Hanswurststreit*.[4]

Pointing to the emergence of the bourgeois public sphere, the rise of nations, and the general fervor for moral education in Europe, theatre historians have long perpetuated the narrative that Hanswurst's exile was inevitable. To that end, the writings of bourgeois reformers aptly illustrate what sociologist Norbert Elias calls the "civilizing process." Striving for upward mobility, they cast off the priapic Hanswurst (in English, the name is Jack Sausage) to introduce gentility to the German stage.[5] However, this historiography has engendered an unintended consequence. Scholars commonly assume that eighteenth-century publics engaged with cultural and political issues only in the literary public sphere. By expanding the scope of evidence to include the defense of Hanswurst, one finds a significant if neglected story of actors who used the stage to also actuate a public sphere. To take a case in point, Justus Möser contended in his satiric treatise *Harlequin: Or, a Defence of Grotesque Comic Performances* (1761) that the comic fool was, in fact, a citizen of the theatre and a productive member of society, targeted foolishly by enlightenment devotees. Comic performers in Vienna echoed this argument when they used the city's municipal theatre to not only mock their detractors in operas and plays but also proffer a reasoned defense of their work. They maintained, for example, that Hanswurst's silly form of dress allowed him to say things about Viennese society that otherwise could not be said. Much like the interlocutors of Aristophanic Old Comedy, Hanswurst was a purveyor of "truth" who could speak frankly about issues that directly affected the city. As such, he encouraged laughter at the expense of his bourgeois critics, the aristocracy, and the imperial family. Many of the great German intellectuals of the eighteenth century—Gotthold Ephraim Lessing, Johann Wolfgang von Goethe, Ludwig Tieck—were not indifferent in their writings to the cultural significance of Hanswurst and his ability to offer a social critique.[6] Their work has garnered a significant amount of scholarly attention. Still, we know little about the intellectual pursuits of the actors who regularly depicted Hanswurst in repertoires of improvised entertainments.[7] With few of their plays and libretti to draw from, scholars bypass the modes and conditions of public engagement encouraged by the German popular stage, to focus instead on the dramatic theories, acting treatises, and plays of bourgeois writers determined to change the conventions of the time. This essay examines the Hanswurst controversy in Vienna and the defense of an art form typically viewed as sociopolitically regressive. I suggest otherwise. Through an analysis of repertory records, performances, and plays, I demonstrate that the comedians' ludic theatrical practices created a public sphere that directly engaged residents of the city as well as the Austrian heads of state.

The Promotion of German-Language Comedy in Vienna

In 1766, the playwright Christian Gottlob Klemm assumed the post of secretary at the Kärntnertor Theatre in Vienna and committed himself to the task of putting Viennese comedies to paper. Klemm's reasoning for this endeavor is published in the preface to his collection of plays (1767): "I live and write in Austria, and I have had to strive to please the Viennese audience since the larger plays of this collection were performed at the Viennese theatres. Therefore, it was impossible to avoid the local character and language of the city."[8] Klemm appealed to his readership by distinguishing himself as a patriot of Austria and as an admirer of Viennese custom. The city's theatrical institutions served as a source of pride for residents. In the smaller German states, few princes had established public theatres, so access to an ongoing repertory was limited. By contrast, the Habsburgs of Austria recruited artists from across Europe, and the public could attend several genres of entertainment, including opera and ballet, at either the Burg or Kärntnertor Theatre. But the Viennese loved the German comedy most of all. It had been that way from the beginning.

When the Holy Roman Emperor Joseph I approved plans for the Kärntnertor Theatre in 1708, he perhaps envisioned a public venue not unlike the Hôtel de Bourgogne, which once housed the Comédie-Italienne in Paris, France. In keeping with other European rulers, the Habsburgs sponsored commedia dell'arte troupes at court, and the Italian comedians proved equally at home performing for crowds in Vienna's market squares. Yet these troupes were not immune to competition. German-speaking companies such as the *Teutsche Komödianten* (German Comedians) also attracted spectators to their temporary outdoor stages. Thus, when the Italians failed to sustain financial losses in the Kärntnertor Theatre, they quickly found themselves displaced by their local competitors. In 1711, the German Comedians' principle performer, Joseph Anton Stranitzky, assumed the lease to the venue.

Before Stranitzky became a star of the Viennese stage, he trained as a puppeteer. Born the son of a footman in Graz, he left home early to find his fortune as an entertainer and toured the cities of Bavaria with his marionettes. Later, when he came to Vienna and joined the German Comedians, he become famous for his portrayal of Hanswurst. Like other Hanswurst actors, who commanded makeshift stages in the German territories, Stranitzky spoofed some ubiquitous elements of German custom (a predilection for sausage, for instance); although, in his signature jacket, ruffled shirt collar, and pointed green hat, he distinguished himself as a character that directly appealed to Viennese humor and sensibility. His mannerisms as a Salzburg peasant were instantly recognizable, as was his Viennese dialect, and he mixed these qualities with a style that borrowed from commedia dell'arte troupes, especially the gestures and slapstick of the Italian-born trickster Arlecchino. Yet above all, Stranitzky's level of success was most certainly contingent upon his ability to capitalize on the public's interest in operatic works. At least five of the fourteen surviving Stranitzky plays are parodies of popular Habsburg operas.[9]

During Stranitzky's tenure as manager of the Kärntnertor Theatre, German comedy thrived in the imperial capital. His company wooed the city's "*mittelständischen Publikum*," a "public" composed of the middle-class or rising bourgeoisie. As the theatre historian Hilde Haider-Pregler writes, this class distinguished themselves from the masses by means and stature and thus could frequent operatic or theatrical works in formal venues.[10] Stranitzky likewise won the benefaction of the Viennese court. Both strata of Viennese society appeared to share a common affection for the genre. At least that is what Lady Mary Wortley Montagu observed when she visited Vienna in 1717. In a letter to Alexander Pope, she recounted her experience watching a German language comedy.[11] "I understand enough of that language to comprehend the greatest part of it," she wrote. And after describing the play's numerous comic scenarios, she professed, "I never laughed so much in my life." However, Lady Montagu found another aspect of the production rather confounding. In one scene, two of the actors had "let down their breeches in the direct view of the boxes, which were full of people of the first rank"; yet despite this gross display of indecency, she wrote, the audience "seemed very well pleased with their entertainment and assured me this was a celebrated piece."[12]

In the eyes of a foreign visitor, this crass gesture before the nobility pointed to Austria's slow progress toward a more civilized theatre and, by extension, a more civilized society. Lady Montagu often suggested that her Austrian hosts were a bit boorish, and when the English musicologist Charles Burney came to Vienna in 1772, he concurred, recounting her story as evidence of German "ribald taste."[13] Still, putting the superior view of the English aside, her account reveals something more about audience reception in early-eighteenth-century Vienna. On the one hand, such a performance style evoked what literary theorist Mikhail Bakhtin calls the "carnival-grotesque," an "artistic, heuristic, and unifying force" of temporary liberation and convention for both spectators and performers.[14] In an auditorium occupied by people of "first rank"—which at various times included the imperial family—the comedians actuated a public space without order and class hierarchy. By extension, their "mooning" of the aristocracy, an otherwise intolerable offense outside of the theatre, had no repercussions. Yet, on the other hand, this fictional world was not wholly detached from the *real*. The Habsburgs condoned these actions because the crudities of a profession defined by rogues and vagabonds posed no obvious threat to the social order. Subsequently, this bawdy form of German comedy remained a popular mainstay in Vienna, and the absence of legislative censorship suggests that the Habsburgs did not share Lady Montagu's misgivings.

The ruling family's laissez-faire attitude toward the stage changed in the late 1740s, and the reason for this cultural shift can be attributed to the growing influence of what the philosopher Jürgen Habermas describes as "the public sphere in the world of letters" or "*literarische Öffentlichkeit*." This arena of discourse, he writes, "preserved a certain continuity with the publicity involved in the representation enacted at the prince's court," for "the bourgeois avant-garde of the educated middle class learned the art of critical-rational public debate through its contact with the 'elegant world.'"[15] Yet notably, this society separated itself over time to counterbalance the influence of the court in civil matters. Their discursive practices, Habermas argues, served as the "literary precursor of the public sphere operative in the political domain."[16] For the theatre historian interested in tracing the development of bourgeois theatre in eighteenth-century Austria, the growing influence of the literary public sphere assumes visibility within the moral weeklies, journals, and literary treatises of the *Bildungsbürgertum* (educated bourgeoisie). The figure of Hanswurst obviously featured prominently in the discourse, though his eradication was first discussed as part of a much larger cultural project.

In the 1730s and 1740s, German philologists and literary scholars waged a campaign not only to promote the teaching of German, as opposed to French and Latin, but also to purify the language by eliminating regional dialects. As those presumed to speak "proper German" largely originated from Saxony and other Protestant regions, these grammarians targeted Austria for allowing the "nonstandard" and "common" qualities of the German language to proliferate with damaging effect. With an aim to homogenize the language, they promoted the use of literary German, writing and publishing a series of their own instructional primers. Some literary scholars, such as Johann Christoph Gottsched, also turned to the theatre to advance their ideas. With the presentation of a well-written drama, one did not need to be literate to benefit from literary instruction. He or she only required the capacity to listen and see the actors speak in a dignified manner. In Vienna, Gottsched's theories received a significant amount of consideration from members of learned societies. Additionally, they garnered attention from the Austrian empress Maria Theresa. In 1750, she addressed the concerns of bourgeois scholars by establishing a professorship of German eloquence in her own Theresian Academy. Then, by imperial decree, she prescribed the use of Gottsched's primer *Grundlegung einer deutschen Sprachkunst* (*Foundations of the Art of German Speaking*).[17]

The reach of Gottsched's reformist program in the early to mid-eighteenth century cannot be overstated. He facilitated the movement to replace extemporized dramas, especially the plays of Hanswurst, with a literary repertoire; several prominent German acting troupes had incorporated his plays and theories of elocution into their performances. In 1737, his most famous partner, the actress-manager Caroline Neuber, even staged a ceremonial banning of the harlequin in Leipzig. And while many aspects of the scholar's work proved controversial, for example, his distaste for Hanswurst and his sycophancy toward the French, erudite circles of his peers generally agreed that he had elevated the cultural caliber of German theatre. It follows then that several representatives of German and Austrian literary societies hoped to implement Gottsched's reforms in Vienna.

Led by the actor-playwright Friedrich Wilhelm Weiskern, the Kärntnertor Theatre underwent its first transformation. Repertory records reveal that from 1748 through much of the year 1752, the resident company presented a series of French plays in German translation.[18] Many of these plays were written by Gottsched, who had recently published a six-volume collection called *Die Deutsche Schaubühne* (*The German Stage*). But the new repertoire failed to attract audiences, so it became obvious that Hanswurst and his comic peers would return to the Kärntnertor Theatre.

Despite their critical and reasoned appeals, members of the literary societies failed to win the favor of the public. The incongruity thus serves to elucidate Habermas's observation that "wherever the [literary] public established itself institutionally as a stable group of discussants, it did not [and could not] equate itself with *the* public but at most claimed to act as its mouthpiece, in its name, perhaps even as its educator—the new form of bourgeois representation."[19] This means that another kind of public, that is, the theatregoing public, could counter the opinions of the literary public in another arena of discourse, the "theatrical public sphere."[20] In some respects, these two forums of discursive exchange overlapped. Indeed, Habermas asserts that the theatre obtained a bourgeois public, much in the same way as literature, when theatrical venues attached to court and palace became "public."[21] However, by acknowledging that two spheres of discourse made the opinions of a larger heterogeneous population publicly visible, one can see that the cultural issues debated during the *Hanswurststreit* were far more nuanced than historians often lead us to believe and, moreover, had real political stakes. Consider, for instance, that when Viennese theatregoers showed their support for the miscreant German comedians, they defied the men of letters who claimed the mouthpiece of the public, as well as the empress, who coopted that mouthpiece as her own.

Haider-Pregler observes that in the first years of the controversy, the character of Hanswurst symbolized a genre of theatre that obstructed the implementation of Gottsched's model repertoire.[22] Much of the literary discourse focuses on the edifying qualities of a reformed German stage. Within a short time, however, the general condemnation of Hanswurst became markedly specific. The success of the comedians prompted greater scrutiny from both bourgeois critics and the Viennese court. Soon, these factions of society redirected much of their vitriol for the character of Hanswurst toward the performers themselves, especially the actor who portrayed the comic role of Bernardon.

The Players Played

In the 1750s, the Hanswurst-performer Stranitzky no longer managed the Kärntnertor Theatre. He had died in 1726. Instead, a new generation of performers took up the mantle of German comedy in Vienna, adapting the genre to reflect the customs and cultural sensibilities of their own time. The actor Gottfried Prehauser, for example, donned Stranitzky's jacket and pointed green hat but portrayed a version of Hanswurst described as less vulgar than that of his predecessor. In *Theatererinnerungen eines alten Burgschauspielers* (*An Old "Burg" Actor's Memories of the Theatre*, 1802), fellow actor Johann Friedrich Müller noted that Prehauser "stayed true to nature" and "was restrained and cleverly tempered when compelled to use parody."[23] Prehauser's closest associate, Joseph Felix von Kurz, assumed the comic guise of Bernardon. Known for his wit and talent for mimicry, Kurz also specialized in machine plays that burlesqued the conventions of baroque opera, a courtly genre that typically represented the feats of Greek and Roman heroes using stage machinery to spectacular effect.

For more than a century, the Habsburgs commissioned baroque operas to glorify the religiosity of their dynastic rule and the history of their empire, so when Kurz burlesqued the art form, he subverted the representative symbols of a divinely ordained power structure. The historian James van Horn Melton offers a colorful description of these techniques, which is worth quoting at length here. It demonstrates that Kurz and his comedic partner, Prehauser, often teetered on the edge of profanity. Van Horn Melton writes, "Kurz and Prehauser disjoined baroque effect from its sacred matrix, transforming the miraculous into a vehicle of comical slapstick. The fire and smoke simulated on

Figure 1. Gottfried Prehauser as Hanswurst. © KHM-Museumsverband.

the Habsburg stage depicted the burning of martyrs; in a Kurz burlesque, they portrayed a hapless Bernardon with his trousers afire. The machinery in a Jesuit drama that enabled, say, an angel to descend from the heavens to rescue a repentant sinner was, under Kurz's direction, employed to transport a live donkey across the stage, fly Bernardon through the air atop a mechanical rooster, or dangle Hanswurst from a cloud as he converses with the devil."[24] In imagining the actors in these comic scenarios, one can see how this genre of comedy could ignite political outrage. By commandeering the emblems of the dynastic sovereign as state, the actors reminded audiences of the artificiality of ruling power.

Given that composers and playwrights of the seventeenth and eighteenth century regularly incorporated commedia-styled entertainments and intermezzi into Habsburg baroque operas and plays, one could argue that the genre's historical framework offset the incendiary nature of the material. However, it is crucial to acknowledge that with the rise of the bourgeois public sphere and the increased circulation of philosophical tracts, which challenged the fiction of divine kingship, governing aristocracies developed an increased sensitivity to topical jokes and carnivalesque ridicule in the theatre.[25] Moreover, because these performances took place in a public rather than a private venue, the court found themselves vulnerable to criticism before an audience of their perceived inferiors. Perhaps that is why the empress could not ignore the comedians' jests as her family had done previously with the plays of Stranitzky. In fact, she attempted to ban their work from the theatre entirely.

One account of this censorship is discussed in an early biography of Kurz-Bernardon's most famous collaborator, the composer Joseph Haydn. According to Haydn's biographer, the duo's first comic opera *Der krumme Teufel* (*The Lame Devil*) was "performed twice to great acclaim" and "then was forbidden because of offensive remarks in the text."[26] The reason for this act of censorship remains a subject of speculation. Some historians believe that Kurz ridiculed one of the city's Italian impresarios.[27] Yet unquestionably, the performer's antics pushed the limits of satire, inviting the censor's attention as well as the attention of the empress. Because Kurz and Prehauser extemporized so much of their work, it became increasingly difficult for the ruling family to control the content of their performances. As masters of pantomime and pun, the two men pressed upon the margins of lawful speech and ridiculed their critics using the public forum of the stage.

It is useful to employ public sphere theory to examine the reasons that motivated these governmental acts of censorship. Empress Maria Theresa's struggle to suppress the performers illustrates her perception that *a public*, that is, an audience gathered together in a particular space for a particular theatrical event, had assumed the characteristics of *the public*, an imagined social body that was formed independently of the Austrian state. To put it another way, when the players ridiculed the Viennese court inside of the theatre, the audience expressed their approval as *a public*. But when their opinions escaped onto the streets, into private residences, and then reached the chambers of Hofburg palace, home to the empire's highest representatives, it became impossible to quantify just how large the actors' audience had grown. The discursive exchange between players and a theatrical public seemed to represent the interests of *the public*, and thus posed a threat to the political order. Because Maria Theresa could do nothing to stymie the opinions of this elusive social body, she obstructed the source, criminalizing the actions of the theatre's beloved performers.[28]

In the winter of 1752, she issued a directive to prohibit extemporization and formally endorsed an administrative system to review and censor plays written for the Viennese stage. At that time, she also relegated the German performers to the Kärntnertor Theatre (figure 2) and reserved the newly constructed Burg Theatre for the presentation of Italian opera and French plays, genres that appealed mainly to the Viennese court. Her instructions evoked the rhetoric of bourgeois reformers, who argued that the leading men of the popular stage embodied the worst models of decorum: "The German theatre must remain completely separate from the other [theatre]. . . . The comedy should give no pieces other than those coming from the French, Italian, or Spanish theatres [i.e., in translation]; locally produced pieces by Bernardon and others are to be completely discontinued; however, should there be some good ones by Weiskern, these should carefully be read through in advance and no *équivoques* or filthy language tolerated in them, nor should the actors be allowed to use them with impunity."[29] Aware that an outright ban on German plays would facilitate the appearance of despotism—Austria, after all, was a German-speaking country—the empress outlined a rather vague plan to censor the comedic performers. First, she condoned the presentation of comedies in translation so that she could benefit from the distancing effects of foreign referents and still appear in support of German-language entertainments. Then, she asserted that the comedies of Bernardon, who critiqued local matters using "filthy language" and "*équivoques*," would not be tolerated; although, she made exceptions for actor-playwrights like Weiskern. As I noted earlier, Weiskern played an instrumental role in bringing Gottsched's reformist repertoire to the Kärntnertor Theatre and had a talent for translation and adaptation. In sum, she hoped to exert greater control over the genres of entertainment presented in Vienna and therefore discourage the German actors from recommencing their extemporized style of performance.

Unfortunately for the empress, that is not what happened. Records from the Kärntnertor Theatre's performance register indicate that the German comics continued to perform their pantomimes, plays, and comic operas.[30] Additionally, there is evidence to suggest that they may have parodied the French players, who occupied the court-favored Burg Theatre. As the musicologist Bruce Alan Brown observes in his study of the repertories: "Regnard's *Le Joueur* given in the Burgtheater in 1752, and revived several times during the next year, inspired the German comedians to produce *Hannswurst der Spieler* on 3 December 1753.

Figure 2. Image of Hanswurst and other comic figures in front of the Kärntnertor Theatre. "Die Deutsche Schaubühne zu Wienn, nach alten und neuen Mustern," Wien 1756. © KHM-Museumsverband.

When the French piece was given again in 1761 (on 16 July), the parody followed only two weeks later. The adroit German authors could move even faster: in 1753 *Hanns Wurst Herr und Knecht* was being played a mere eight days after *Arlequin maître et valet* (by Moissy) in the French theater."[31] These patterns of production indicate that even after the empress took actions to diminish the publicity of the German actors, they still commanded the public's attention.

Scholars have suggested that by mandating reforms in the theatre, the empress elevated the importance of the Viennese stage and stimulated the progress of German literary theatre. However, she also used this directive to shield herself from public criticism, a common strategy for European autocrats. For example, the French King Louis XIV notoriously exiled his own commedia dell'arte troupe in 1697, when he learned that the actors had ridiculed Madame de Maintenon, his second wife by an unsanctioned private marriage. "So long as the Italians had simply allowed their stage to overflow with filth or impiety, they only caused laughter," reported the Duke of Saint-Simon. "But they set about playing a piece called *The False Prude*, in which Madame de Maintenon was easily recognized. Everybody ran to see the piece; but after three or four representations, given consecutively on account of the gain it brought, the Italians received orders to close their theatre and to quit the realm in a month."[32] Similarly, in Vienna, the pronouncement of "filthy" remarks and the use of obscene gestures proved an embarrassment to the empress. Crude behavior on the public stage could perhaps be justified, so long as it did not undermine or ridicule royal authority.

Empress Maria Theresa's concerns with public perception reflected the unique difficulties of being a female leader in a governing patriarchy. As a woman, she could not legally inherit the Holy Roman Empire after the death of her father Charles VI. Officially, she could be called the Archduchess of Austria and the Queen of Hungary, among other designations. The title of empress was strictly an honorary distinction. Given this state of affairs, it is no wonder that she found the rulers of Europe eager to claim Habsburg lands and a European readership, who delighted in the political intrigue surrounding her disinheritance. "In cartoon after cartoon, from England to Hungary," writes the historian Andrew Wheatcroft, "she was displayed as being robbed of her clothing (her territories) by her lascivious neighbors."[33] Much to her credit, after marrying Francis Stephen of Lorraine, crowned Holy Roman Emperor in 1745, Maria Theresa informally assumed many of his duties as ruler and managed the publicity of her reputation by putting the discourse associated with her sexualized female body to good political use.[34] In royal portraits, she often posed with her eldest son, Joseph II, surrounded by the insignia of the imperial court, to emphasize both her fecundity and her natural role in preserving the paternal strength of the empire.[35] Moreover, these depictions promoted her image as a mother to both the subjects of her imperial dynasty and her own children.

The institution of theatre supported this maternal persona. For her children, she advised that the stage provide a space for learning the speech and gesture of a ruler. These lessons authenticated the aura of what Habermas calls "representative publicness," a display of authority that represented lordship "not for, but 'before' the people."[36] Naturally, the public theatres of mid-eighteenth-century

Vienna could not endorse the same pedagogical mission; however, they did need to embrace the values of the bourgeoisie. In the literary public sphere, the theatre was viewed as an educational tool that could raise up the lower classes. Maria Theresa alluded to this potential in her directives, although her chief concern was to maintain the status quo and remind spectators of their proper place in society, in terms not only of rank or class but also of political agency.

Some monarchs from the period demonstrated an affinity for the ideals of the Enlightenment through their support of German literature. The Prussian King Frederick II, for instance, was beloved for allowing the publication of literary journals such as Friedrich Nicolai's *Allgemeine deutsche Bibliothek* (*German General Library*) in the country's capital.[37] Because the people in Berlin enjoyed "a republican freedom of thought and writing," wrote one German critic, they were "the fittest for the recording of German literature, and drama in particular."[38] Maria Theresa too attempted to style herself as an enlightened ruler, though her reformist efforts, which were shared and then sustained by her son, the emperor Joseph II, did not *dismantle* the existing structure of Habsburg institutions. As historian R. J. W. Evans writes, "Rather they sought to *redirect* it, maintaining their alliance with Church, nobles, and intelligentsia, but turning it from a conservative-universalist hierarchy [of the Catholic baroque] into an enlightened-absolutist one."[39] Empress Maria Theresa publicized this redirection by reforming the imperial capital's theatrical institutions. It is debatable whether she found success or not. As I have demonstrated, the reformist decrees encouraged by the bourgeoisie did not win the support of Vienna's theatregoers. This public pledged their loyalty to the German comedians. Therefore, the controversy over the fate of Hanswurst continued.

The Critics Criticized

In the 1760s, the bourgeois intellectual Gotthold Emphraim Lessing famously pioneered the German national theatre movement, an initiative to advance dramatic literature by native-born playwrights and unify the German people, despite the disparate nature of the German sovereign territories. Yet, he acknowledged in his critical journal *Hamburgische Dramaturgie* (*Hamburg Dramaturgy*) that the formation of a common national identity was incredibly difficult to achieve.[40] The German people found themselves divided not only geopolitically but also religiously and culturally. Consequently, the project to replace local theatrical traditions with a national genre of German dramatic literature was not always popularly received, especially in Vienna. Writing in 1768, Leopold Mozart, father to young Wolfgang and a musician himself, noted rather begrudgingly, "That the Viennese, generally speaking, do not care to see serious and sensible performances, have little or no idea of them, and only want to see foolish stuff, dances, devils, ghosts, magic, clowns, Lipperl, Bernardon, witches and apparitions is well-known; and their theatres prove it every day."[41] The elder Mozart considered himself a sophisticate and viewed the German comedy as an impediment to the development of serious German arts and perhaps more importantly, the court's recognition of serious German artists, like his son.[42]

Clearly, the controversial work of the German actors still incited polarizing responses. In Mozart's opinion, it needed to be abolished, and his letter evinced an argument that was already prevalent in the literary public sphere. Nevertheless, other genres of performance struggled to compete with the German comedy, and so reformists confronted the same issues of the previous decade. As one local in Vienna wrote, "these two vulgar buffoons," meaning Hanswurst and Bernardon, "degraded the theatre" and "it was agreed that the characters should be suppressed." Yet if the local magistrates pursued this course, he observed, "the theatre would then no longer be frequented," which would in turn generate a substantial loss of income. For this reason, he reported that the jesters were not banished but instead forbidden to utter "dirty equivocations"—a necessity as "their Majesties or the imperial family will often attend the *Tudesque* [i.e., Germanic] theatre."[43] In light of these circumstances, many men of letters harnessed the press to make further appeals to the public. For instance, in his critical journal *Briefe über die wienerische Schaubühne* (*Letters on the Viennese Stage*, 1767–1769), an advisor to the imperial court and professor of cameral science named Joseph von Sonnenfels targeted the German actors and the characters that they portrayed with new fervor. Dubbing the comedians' work as the scourge of a potentially decorous German stage, he implored theatregoers to support his reforms.[44] These vitriolic attacks on Hanswurst garnered considerable attention, both positive and negative, from notable men of letters, members of the theatre community, and eventually the Holy Roman Emperor Joseph II.

A self-appointed *Kunstrichter* (art critic) and chair of Vienna's German literary society, Sonnenfels served as both the chosen representative of local literary affairs as well as the principal correspondent for several German periodicals published outside of Austria.[45] In occupying these positions, he kept abreast of theatrical innovation in the German Empire and published an ongoing critique of works presented in Vienna. It follows, then, that Sonnenfels had a unique understanding of the German national theatre movement and was keenly aware of its significance in an Austrian context.[46] For example, in learning that Lessing had joined the first national theatre in Hamburg, Sonnenfels contended that Vienna should have its own national institution but that the gross indignities of the city's beloved harlequin would undermine such efforts and cripple the appearance and interests of Austria within the German Empire. By abolishing German-language comedy and adopting a national repertoire, the emperor could thus transform the dignity of German authorship and manners, paving the way for lesser German courts to follow his lead.[47] His criticisms of the popular stage earned him few friends in Vienna as well as abroad. Even Lessing observed in a letter to his wife Eva König that "Herr von Sonnenfels's all too severe zeal against the burlesque is not at all the right way to win the public."[48]

One of Sonnenfels's severest detractors was the aforementioned playwright Christian Gottlob Klemm, who asserted that the local character of his comedies reflected Austria's rich theatrical traditions.[49] Accordingly, in February 1767, he staged a baroque apotheosis play that ridiculed the critic and elevated the Hanswurst actor Prehauser to the proscenium heavens. In *Der auf den Parnass versetzte grüne Hut* (*The Green Hat Has Been Moved onto Parnassus*), Klemm utilized the conventions of a baroque spectacle, which typically glorified the leadership and virtues of a commissioning prince, to show Prehauser as the people's true representative.

To see how Hanswurst came to the fore of cultural politics in this performance, let us consider an overview of the production's dramaturgy.[50] The play opens with Apollo and the muse of comedy, Thalia, at home on Mount Parnassus. Troubled, Thalia reveals that she fears her empire is imperiled by someone who conspires against her. This enemy, however, is not armed with weapons or grandiose ambition but rather a propensity for loquacious moralizing. In an obvious reference to Sonnenfels, Apollo questions how the Critic should have degraded into such a "horrifying fury."[51] Sonnenfels's fervent condemnation of the harlequin had clearly proven wearisome. So, in response, Thalia and Apollo decide to orchestrate an elaborate test of Hanswurst's moral character and abilities. Disguised as mortals, they recruit the actor Prehauser to don his signature green hat and enter a play that paid homage to the archetypes of the commedia dell'arte and the comedic stylings of French playwrights like Molière.

Tasked with uniting lovers and fixing the misdeeds of a miserly father named Lysimon, Hanswurst, who plays a trickster servant, shows an aptitude for deception aimed at righting all wrongs. However, within these scenes, we also see how the actor Prehauser asked his audience to evaluate the larger cultural and political implications of the Hanswurst controversy. Midway through the play, for example, he arrives at the father's house disguised as a theatre critic, most likely doing his best Sonnenfels impression, and offers his authoritative views on Hanswurst and the subject of "good taste." Yet much to his dismay, he finds in this discussion that his audience is unfamiliar with the comic figure who wears the green hat. Prehauser as Hanswurst (playing a servant who is playing a theatre critic) explains:

HANSWURST. That is the person of the theatre that chooses to wear a peculiar and silly form of dress, because in that costume he can tell truths that would be unacceptable were they uttered by a servant in livery.
LYSIMON. Is it not funny then?
HANSWURST. No, it is against good taste.
LYSIMON. What, then, is good taste?
HANSWURST. What I declare it to be! Nothing funny, just long moral treatises that one can write out in peace without the need to further exercise oneself, and with which one can put the people to sleep by sheer laziness.[52]

Hanswurst's appeal not only justifies a place for the ludic comedian within a well-functioning government—remember that at the start of the play Thalia intimates that the critic poses a threat to her empire—but also activates the critical faculties of the audience. He makes a clear distinction between engagement through laughter and passivity out of boredom to encourage audience members to arbitrate a debate that would impact the future of their city. At the end of the play, they must decide whether an actor who wears the costume of a harlequin can be heralded as a great man of the people.

In the final scenes, Apollo reveals his scheme and confesses his interest in assessing the true nature of Hanswurst. He declares, "The voice of the people, or of Nature, decides alone in *comic* works."[53] Then, he invites Prehauser, the Hanswurst-actor, to preserve the spirit of Thalia's empire. "My dear Prehauser, for forty-four years you have given pleasure to the very highest court, a high nobility, and an enlightened public. . . . Give me your hand, my friend, and continue to broaden our empire and amuse our virtuous people."[54] Prehauser, however, has the last word. And I would like to suggest that in looking out upon the audience during the first performance, the actor acknowledged the unwavering power of the Holy Roman Empire's multinational court as well as the German bourgeoisie gathering strength as a nation. His lines are as follows: "As long as my gray head can still collect thoughts, and as long as this old body can still stand upright, I will utilize all my strength to dedicate my comic performances to the greatest of European courts and the best nation."[55] In the twilight of Prehauser's career, these two factions of society vied for the people's favor. So, rather than choose a side, Prehauser played to both.

The Ruler Ruled

Within two years of this performance, the actor Prehauser died. In response, Sonnenfels suggested that it was an apt time to reinstate mandates for reform and seize upon the bourgeoisie's growing interest in German national theatre.[56] He made his appeals to Joseph II, who had assumed purview over matters related to Vienna's theatrical institutions. Together, they changed the culture of theatregoing and put an end to the Hanswurst controversy. In 1770, after a decade of what the emperor viewed as a rather lackadaisical approach to the control of discourse emanating from the Burg and Kärntnertor Theatres, he appointed Sonnenfels as censor. The critic quickly got to work. Exiling Hanswurst and other comic figures from the stage, he vowed to banish from the theatre all "that offends in the slightest against religion, the state, or good manners, all obvious nonsense and coarseness" and "everything unworthy of a capital city and the seat of a court."[57]

With Vienna's municipal theatres purged of offensive material, the emperor formally endorsed an institution that would present a new bourgeois sensibility to Vienna's theatregoing public. In the spring of 1776, he declared that the Burg Theatre be called the German National Theatre, a political strategy that proved its worth before the turn of the century. By establishing a national stage, Joseph II maintained cultural alliances with the German Empire and appeared to embrace the values of the bourgeoisie's imagined German nation. This political strategy was one of many that sustained his powers during the French Revolution. For as the historian T. C. W. Blanning argues, "Of all the manifold failings of the French monarchy in the eighteenth century, the most serious was its inability to sense the growing authority of the nation."[58] With the harlequin gone from Vienna's Burg Theatre and a national repertoire put into place, the Austrian emperor ensured that the bourgeois class found themselves represented in a more dignified form of entertainment. In the end, Joseph II had won the public by playing the role of an enlightened prince.[59]

Notes

1. In the epigraph, the author assumes the voice of a German harlequin to wage a rational argument in the harlequin's defense. Justus Möser, *Harlequin: Or, a Defence of Grotesque Comic Performances*, trans. Joachim Warnecke (London, 1776), 10. I reproduce Warnecke's translation and spelling of "defense" in rendering the title.
2. Möser, *Harlequin*, 69.

3. The term *Reich* in the eighteenth century referred to the *Heilige Römische Reich Deutscher Nation* (the Holy Roman Empire of the German Nation). Historians refer to the area both as the German Empire and the Holy Roman Empire.
4. For an overview of the history, see W. E. Yates, *Theatre in Vienna: A Critical History, 1776–1995* (New York: Cambridge University Press, 1996). For descriptions of the key players involved in the Hanswurst controversy, see Hilde Haider-Pregler, *The Theatre in Austria* (Vienna: Federal Press Service, 1973). Karen Jürs-Munby addresses the discourse in her article on the development of bourgeois representation and the censorship of Hanswurst on German stages, "Hanswurst and Herr Ich: Subjection and Abjection in Enlightenment Censorship of the Comic Figure," *New Theatre Quarterly* 23, no. 2 (2007): 124–35. Relevant scholarship in the Germanophone tradition includes Helmut G. Asper's comprehensive history of Hanswurst in *Hanswurst: Studien zum Lustigmacher auf der Berufsschauspielerbühne in Deutschland im 17. und 18. Jahrhundert* (Emsdetten, Germany: Lechte, 1980). See also Karl von Görner's *Der Hans Wurst-streit in Wien und Joseph von Sonnenfels* (Charleston, SC: BiblioLife, 2009), Beatrix Müller-Kampel, *Hanswurst, Bernardon, Kasperl: Spaßtheater im 18. Jahrhundert* (Paderborn, Germany: Ferdinand Schöningh, 2003), and Hilde Haider-Pregler, *Des sittlichen Bürgers Abendschule* (Vienna: Jugend und Volk, 1980). Haider-Pregler analyzes the history and historiography of eighteenth-century German theatre and offers a compelling and detailed study of the *Hanswurststreit*; see Haider-Pregler, *Des sittlichen Bürgers Abendschule*, especially 269–350.
5. Norbert Elias, *The Civilizing Process: Sociogenetic and Psychogenetic Investigations*, trans. Edmund Jephcott (Malden, MA: Blackwell, 2000). For a good overview of Elias's work and its application in theatre scholarship, see Erika Fischer-Lichte's essay "Theatre and the Civilizing Process: An Approach to the History of Acting," in *Interpreting the Theatrical Past: Essays in the Historiography of Performance*, ed. Thomas Postlewait and Bruce A. McConachie, 19–36 (Iowa City: University of Iowa Press, 2000). See also Jürs-Munby, "Hanswurst and Herr Ich," 126–29.
6. Lessing discussed the banishment of Hanswurst in his *Literaturbriefe* (*Letters on Literature*, Letter 16, February 1759). Johann Wolfgang von Goethe found inspiration from the German puppet plays of his youth in writing *Hanswursts Hochzeit oder der Lauf der Welt* (*Hanswurst's Marriage or the Way of the World*, 1775). Hanswurst is also a character in Ludwig Tieck's dramatic satire *Der gestiefelte Kater* (*Puss in Boots*, 1797).
7. The philosophies of reformist actors serve as a notable exception. For example, Gustav Zechmeister discusses Friedrich Wilhelm Weiskern's efforts to alter the repertoire of Vienna's public theatre in *Die Wiener Theater Nächst der Burg und Nächst dem Kärntnerthor: Von 1747 bis 1776* (Vienna: Hermann Böhlaus, 1971), 29. Haider-Pregler also addresses Weiskern's ambitions in *Des sittlichen Bürgers Abendschule*, 282–302.
8. "Ich lebe und schreibe in Österreich, ich habe mich bestreben müßen dem wienerischen Publikum zu gefallen, denn die größern Stücke dieser Sammlung sind auf dem Wienertheater aufgeführt worden. Ich habe also unmöglich das Locale in Charaktern und in der Sprache vermeiden können, das der Stadt gemäß ist." Christian Gottlob Klemm, *Beyträge zum Deutschen Theater* (Vienna: 1767), preface.
9. For further discussion of these parodied operas, see Otto Rommel, *Die Alt-Wiener Volkskomödie; Ihre Geschichte vom barocken Welt-Theatre bis zum Tode Nestroys* (Vienna: A. Schroll, 1952), 231, and James Van Horn Melton, "School, Stage, Salon: Musical Cultures in Haydn's Vienna," *Journal of Modern History* 76, no. 2 (2004): 268.

10. Haider-Pregler, *Des sittlichen Bürgers Abendschule*, 270–71.
11. When Lady Mary Wortley Montagu attended the theatre, she saw a German language production of *Amphitryon*, which was most likely adapted from the play by Molière.
12. Lady Mary Wortley Montagu to Alexander Pope, Vienna, September 4, 1717. Lady Mary Wortley Montagu, *The Letters of Lady Mary Wortley Montagu*, ed. Mrs. Hale (Boston, 1876), 127.
13. Charles Burney, *Dr. Burney's Musical Tours in Europe Volume II: An Eighteenth-Century Musical Tour in Central Europe and the Netherlands*, ed. Percy A. Scholes (London: Oxford University Press, 1959), 75.
14. Mikhail Bakhtin, *Rabelais and His World*, trans. Hélène Iswolsky (Bloomington: Indiana University Press), 34.
15. Jürgen Habermas, *The Structural Transformation of the Public Sphere: An Inquiry into a Category of Bourgeois Society*, trans. Thomas Burger (Cambridge: MIT Press, 1991), 29.
16. Habermas, *The Structural Transformation of the Public Sphere*, 29.
17. For an overview of Empress Maria Theresa's efforts to bring Gottsched's language reforms to Vienna, see Anna D. Havinga, *Invisiblising Austrian German: On the Effect of Linguistic Prescriptions and Educational Reforms on Writing Practices in 18th-Century Austria* (Berlin: Walter de Gruyter GmbH, 2018), section 2.3.
18. While these records are not entirely complete, they are still quite comprehensive. I refer to the chronological register compiled by Zechmeister, *Die Wiener Theater Nächst der Burg und Nächst dem Kärntnerthor*, 401–17.
19. Habermas, *The Structural Transformation of the Public Sphere*, 37.
20. I borrow this phrase from Christopher Balme. Balme describes the eighteenth-century theatrical public sphere as a forum for expressions of taste and pressing issues that manifested both inside and outside of the auditorium. *The Theatrical Public Sphere* (Cambridge: Cambridge University Press, 2014), 22.
21. Habermas, *The Structural Transformation of the Public Sphere*, 38.
22. Haider-Pregler, *Des sittlichen Bürgers Abendschule*, 295.
23. "Er blieb stets der Natur treu. Wurde er genötigt zu übertreiben oder zu parodieren, so geschah es mit Verstand und Kluger Mäßigung." As quoted in Asper, *Hanswurst*, 58.
24. Melton, "School, Stage, Salon," 269.
25. In 1751, Empress Maria Theresa developed a centralized system for the censorship of printed books. Her legislation prohibited the publication and circulation of books by authors including Blaise Pascal, Voltaire, Montesquieu, John Locke, John Milton, and Edward Gibbon. As noted in Oszkár Jászi, *The Dissolution of the Habsburg Monarchy* (Chicago: University of Chicago Press, 1961), 64.
26. Christoph Dies, *Biographische Nachrichten von Joseph Haydn* (Vienna 1810), 41.
27. Georg August Griesinger suggests in his biography *Biographische Notizen über Joseph Haydn* (Leipzig, 1810), 18, that the opera satirized Count Guisippe Affligio. However, Eva Badura-Skoda notes that Affligio did not reside in Vienna at the time of the opera's production; see Eva Badura-Skoda, "The Influence of the Viennese Popular Comedy on Haydn and Mozart," *Proceedings of the Royal Musical Association* 100 (1973–1974): 192. The anecdote is examined further in Tom Beghin's and Sander M. Goldberg's *Haydn and the Performance of Rhetoric* (Chicago: University of Chicago Press, 2007), 94.
28. In analyzing how "a public" became "the public," I owe a significant debt to Michael Warner, whose scholarship on public sphere theory and queer studies has provided

ample space for further reflection about the constructions and functions of social formations. See Michael Warner, *Publics and Counterpublics* (New York: Zone, 2005), 66–68.

29. As quoted in Bruce Alan Brown, *Gluck and the French Theatre in Vienna* (Oxford: Clarendon, 1991), 65.
30. Zechmeister, *Die Wiener Theater Nächst der Burg und Nächst dem Kärntnerthor*, 399–562.
31. Brown, *Gluck and the French Theatre in Vienna*, 102.
32. Louis de Rouvroy duc de Saint-Simon, *The Memoirs of the Duke of Saint-Simon on the Reign of Louis XIV and the Regency*, trans. Bayle St. John (New York: James Pott, 1901), 130.
33. Andrew Wheatcroft, *The Habsburgs: Embodying Empire* (London: Penguin, 1996), 219.
34. I echo Regina Schulte in her book *The Body of the Queen: Gender and Rule in the Courtly World, 1500–2000* (New York: Berghahn, 2006), 10.
35. Michael Elia Yonan, *Empress Maria Theresa and the Politics of Habsburg Imperial Art* (University Park: Pennsylvania State University Press, 2011), 27.
36. Habermas, *The Structural Transformation of the Public Sphere*, 8.
37. Ironically, King Frederick II preferred French theatre and made no secret of his aversion to the German language.
38. Johann Friedrich Löwen, *Johann Friedrich Löwens Geschichte des Deutschen Theaters (1766) und Flugschriften über das Hamburger National-Theater (1766 und 1767)*, ed. Heinrich Stümcke (Berlin: E. Frensdorff, 1905), 69.
39. R. J. W. Evans, *The Making of the Habsburg Monarchy: 1550–1700* (Oxford: Clarendon, 1979), 449.
40. In his last essays, Lessing suggested that the founding of a German national theatre was a well-intended but flawed idea. Gotthold Ephraim Lessing, *The Hamburg Dramaturgy by G.E. Lessing: A New and Complete Annotated English Translation*, trans. Wendy Arons and Sara Figal, ed. Natalya Baldyga (Oxford: Routledge, 2018). *Media Commons Press Online*, Essay 101–4.
41. Leopold Mozart to Lorenz Hagenauer, Vienna, 30 January–3 February, 1768, in Emily Anderson, *The Letters of Mozart and His Family* (London: W. W. Norton), 80.
42. In another letter to Lorenz Hagenauer (Vienna, July 30, 1768), Leopold Mozart voices his frustration with the Viennese court's preference for foreign composers. He writes, "All sensible people must with shame agree that it is a disgrace to our nation that we Germans are trying to suppress a German [his son Wolfgang], to whom foreign countries have done justice by their great admiration and even by public acknowledgements in writing." See Anderson, *The Letters of Mozart and His Family*, 90.
43. Thomas Abbt, *Vermischte Werke: Freundschaftliche Correspondenz, Dritter Theil* (Berlin, 1771), 63–64. My thanks to Guillaume Tourniaire for assisting me with the translation of a letter from Herrn von Barr, nd.
44. Joseph von Sonnenfels, *Briefe über die wienerische Schaubühne* (Vienna, 1884), 316.
45. Representative publications include the *Bibliothek der schönen Wissenschaften und der freyen Künste*, *Der neue Teutsche Merkur*, and the *Berlinische Monatsschrift*.
46. Sonnenfels monitored activities at the Hamburg National Theatre quite closely. For example, in July 1768, he observed that the Hamburg institution recently presented four artful plays and that authorial genius burgeoned in Germany. Sonnenfels, *Briefe über die wienerische Schaubühne*, 204.
47. Sonnenfels argues these points in his critical treatise "Über die Nothwendigkeit, das Ex-

temporieren Abzustellen" (1770). This work is quoted at length in Heinz Kindermann, *Theatergeschichte Europas*, vol. 5 (Salzburg, Germany: Otto Müller, 1962), 70.

48. "Schon des Herrn von Sonnenfels allzu strenger Eifer gegen das Burleske ist gar nicht der rechte Weg, das Publicum zu gewinnen." As quoted in Kindermann, *Theatergeschichte Europas*, 72.

49. Interestingly, both Klemm and Sonnenfels critiqued the vulgarities of the popular Viennese stage in the early 1760s. However, Klemm came to challenge Sonnenfels's zealous crusades against the harlequin later in the decade.

50. Christian Gottlob Klemm, *Der auf den Parnass versetzte grüne Hut* (North Charleston, SC: CreateSpace, 2013). Thanks to Jasmin Krakenberg and Viktoria Harms for assisting me with translations.

51. "Critic" is spelled with a capital C to denote the name of the character as listed in the dramatis personae.

52. HANSWURST. Das ist eine Person auf dem Theater, die deßwegen eine sonderbare einfältige Kleidung gewählet hat, weil sie in der Tracht Wahrheiten sagen kann, die man einem Lakey in der Livree niemals verzeihen würde.
    LYSIMON. Ist denn das nicht lustig?
    HANSWURST. Nein, es ist wider den guten Geschmack.
    LYSIMON. Was ist denn der gute Geschmack?
    HANSWURST. Was ich davor ausgebe. Nichts lustiges, aber lange moralische Abhandlungen, wobey man ruhig ausschreiben kann, ohne daß man sich weiter weh zu thun braucht, und wodurch man recht mit Bequemlichkeit die Leute einschläfert.
    Klemm, *Der auf den Parnass versetzte grüne Hut*, 29.

53. "Die Stimme des Volks, oder der Natur entscheidet allein in komischen Werken." Klemm, *Der auf den Parnass versetzte grüne Hut*, 39.

54. "Schon seit vier und vierzig Jahren vergnügen sie einen allerhöchsten Hof, einen höchsten Adel, und ein erleuchtetes Publikum. . . . Geben sie mir ihre Hand, meine Freunde, und fahren sie fort, unser Reich zu erweitern, und rechtschaffene Leute zu vergnügen." Klemm, *Der auf den Parnass versetzte grüne Hut*, 40–41.

55. "Ja, das will ich auch thun, so lange mein grauer Kopf noch Gedanken sammeln kann, so lange dieser alte Körper noch aufrecht steht, so lang werde ich alle meine Kräfte anwenden, dem größten Hofe Europens, und der besten Nation meine komischen Vorstellungen zu widmen." Klemm, *Der auf den Parnass versetzte grüne Hut*, 41.

56. Yates, *Theatre in Vienna*, 9.

57. As quoted in Yates, *Theatre in Vienna*, 9–10.

58. T. C. W. Blanning, *The Culture of Power and the Power of Culture: Old Regime Europe, 1660–1789* (Oxford: Oxford University Press, 2002), 4.

59. Notably this form of performance continued outside of the court. For more on Joseph II's reforms, see Rudolf Payer von Thurn, *Joseph II. als Theaterdirektor: Ungedruckte Briefe und Aktenstücke aus den Kinderjahren des Burgtheaters* (Vienna: Heidrich, 1920).

"This Affair of a Theatre"

The Boston Theatre Controversy and the Americanization of the Stage

—BRIDGET MCFARLAND

> I declare firmly, that this affair of a Theatre, was not managed with coolness and candor; and that some of the advocates for it, did take advantage of their number to silence and bear down their opponents. Among those, thus silenced and borne down, was Mr. Samuel Adams.
>
> ABRAHAM BISHOP, *Argus*, Boston, 1791

> Jests may be represented as realities.
>
> *INDEPENDENT CHRONICLE*, Boston, 1791

On October 26, 1791, during a town meeting at Faneuil Hall, Samuel Adams rose to debate the legality of the ban on the theatre in Boston and was silenced. The theatre ban, in effect since 1750, was supported by a vocal and powerful minority, including Adams and Governor John Hancock; however, the majority of Bostonians no longer supported it. As a result, the ban became a point of political contention during the highly partisan 1790s, so much so that when "Samuel Adams rose to speak in the midst of his fellow-citizens, [he] was silenced!" exclaimed the Democratic-Republican newspaper the *Argus*.[1] Moral, economic, and political factors, as theatre historians such as Peter A. Davis and Heather S. Nathans have shown, motivated the debate over the ban, a debate that was waged not only in town meetings but also in newspapers and pamphlets.[2] The conflict over theatre's legalization offered an uneasy reminder of the conflicts over governance in the new republic. The success of self-governance seemed tied to the legality and promotion of theatre, yet neither side of the debate directly articulated the troublesome intertwining of governance and theatre. Instead, anxiety surrounding this amorphous relationship emerges throughout the discourse of the theatre controversy. The most striking element of the anxiety is that for both Boston's aspiring and incumbent leaders, the sanctioning of the theatre would entail the sanctioning of satiric representations of political leaders, a prospect that was threatening to leaders, both old and new. They viewed such representations as enflaming the rebelliousness of the citizenry and compromising the consolidation of power. Pantomime was seen as particularly threatening because it was accessible to all audiences and easily adapted to present political circumstances, thus making it a venue for political assassination through satire. Equating public ridicule to political death seems like overkill, yet, in the moment of Samuel Adams's silencing, the theatre's detractors witnessed what they feared the theatre would inspire: political unrest.

In the heady days of the early republic, opinions of theatre's legal status highlighted divisions between various factions, rousing the theatre's supporters as well as its detractors. Historians of the theatre and the early United States have contended that this period of national development was intimately tied to the status of theatre.[3] In a thorough history of the economics of the stage, Heather S. Nathans has demonstrated that the goals of the theatre's first investors were explicitly political because they aimed to "cement their cultural authority in the new nation" through their support of the theatre.[4] While the theatre inspired contributions from investors who made a bid for cultural authority, it also inspired average citizens who overcame political lethargy to become actors in the nation's creation. A new generation, too young to have led the American Revolution, began to assert its authority over questions of theatre regulation and norms of behavior, thus contesting the authority of a generation of American patriots. As generational differences heightened the conflict surrounding the theatre and its legality, the theatre debate became a lightning rod for individuals across the political spectrum.

The emblematic town meeting at which Sam Adams's authority was tested represented "a second attempt for a Theatre in this town—*that receptacle of the lewd and lazy*."[5] In an otherwise objective announcement for the town meeting, where issues such as the building of market stalls and the lighting of lamps would be discussed, The *Boston Gazette*'s contempt for the theatre demonstrates a clear anti-theatre stance, making its surprise at "a second attempt" rather predictable. The *Gazette*, like other opponents of the theatre, feared that theatre would corrupt the youth. Similar objections had been raised only a year prior when theatre managers Lewis Hallam and John Henry petitioned to end the ban. Hallam and Henry's petition was unsuccessful due to the continued animosity between the city's elder elites and the merchant class. Yet, despite the recently rejected petition, many Bostonians remained committed to legalizing and building a theatre, a task that was seen as the pet project of a new elite group who had profited from selling Loyalist properties after the revolution.[6] Members of this group had created a tontine, an investment strategy that is best described as reverse life insurance. When a member of the tontine dies, its members receive an annuity. Once the last living member collects the final annuity, the tontine is dissolved. Thus, the tontine is a bet on one's longevity, with the largest sum being awarded to the longest living person. The members of the Boston tontine wanted to protect their financial interests and to promote a more prosperous Boston. In her analysis of the Boston Tontine Association, Nathans has argued that "[the tontine's] interests had polarized tensions in the Commonwealth, tensions between old and new, urban and rural, and central and peripheral factions," "tensions" that heightened the divisiveness of the controversy surrounding the theatre ban.[7]

Members of the tontine, often participants but not leaders of the revolution, were perceived as using their new liberties for superficial ends, particularly in their desire to build a more cosmopolitan and playful Boston. This perception was founded upon their participation in tea assemblies, started in the 1780s.[8] Beginning in the 1780s, these assemblies gave Bostonians a space to dance and play cards while mingling in mixed company. Such pastimes, associated with sex and gambling, offended those who saw the assemblies as a sign of European corruption in the fragile and innocent republic. A closet drama, *Sans Souci, Alias Free and Easy: An Evening's Peep into a Polite Circle*, mocked the dissipation of the assemblies and the aspirations of their members. In a dialogue, Little Pert and Young Forward, two young and flirtatious Bostonians, hope that card players will make higher bets because higher bets signify sophistication, wealth, and an appetite for risk. As the characters aspire to urbanity, they disclose their embarrassment at their regional identity as Bostonians. Little Pert admits that she was ashamed to be recognized as a Bostonian while she lived among the British in New York City. For Little Pert, to be a Bostonian is to be on the periphery, removed from the metropolitan centers of New York and London. To rectify their regional alienation, the characters aim to alter the reputation of Boston; thereby, Young Forward advocates theatregoing and gambling: "We are often bemoaning the want of plays in this town; this will be a considerable introduction to this entertainment; we can with the greatest propriety ask permission for a theatre after we have been indulged with a card party; for of the two evils, plays must be considered the least;—so that we have nothing to do, but to resign for a season our card amusements until we can get a theatre erected, and after that we can return to our present entertainment by pleading *precedents*; for we must hold precedents as tenacious in the polite circle as we lawyers do *authorities* in our profession."[9] In the tenacious character of Young Forward, *Sans Souci* presents the legalization of the theatre as one piece of a plot to establish participation in tea assemblies as normative rather than subversive behavior. Such a change would require an alteration of social norms because the revolutionary generation viewed the assemblies as corrupt and their members as immoral. As Boston evolved into a city seeking formal incorporation, the anxieties over its planned incorporation surface during the theatre controversy because theatre was associated negatively with cities, an association that explains, in part, why the theatre initiative sparked concern. Conversely, for the commercial and cultural interests of the tontine, the theatre initiative was less a cause for anxiety than an inspiring symbol of Boston's evolution from rural periphery to metropolitan center. To become a metropole, Boston would need a theatre. The tontine's liberal motives share what T. A. Milford has interpreted as a preference for "growth before caution," a value that both Little Pert and Young Forward exemplify as they dream of the commercial and aesthetic maturation necessary to herald Boston as a cosmopolitan city.[10]

Gambling and theatregoing—the vices of cities—were debated not only in fiction but also in newspapers. Seeming to take its cue from *Sans Souci*, *The Herald of Freedom* objects to the sanctioning of lotteries by arguing that the theatre is a lesser evil than the lottery. The writer, using the pseudonym "Shakespear" [*sic*], accuses the town assembly of hypocrisy due to its firm stance on the moral corruption that attends theatregoing. Pointing out their inconsistency, Shakespear condemns the assembly because "[they] passed several acts sanctioning LOTTERIES, than which no law ever poisoned more effectually the minds, and depraved and corrupted the morals of the people; nothing more certainly encouraged idleness; prompted a passion for gaming; struck a more fatal blow to the root of industry."[11] After rejecting the lottery, the writer makes an argument about the nature of consumption; it is better to spend money at the theatre because a spectator may "draw" a moral worth more than the ticket value, whereas the gambler may leave the table with nothing. Furthermore, the writer worries about swearing because the gambler "rages, and curses, and swears, and blasts his luck" after losing.[12] *The Herald of Freedom*'s argument is an example of the long-standing association of gambling and theatregoing, two acts often deemed sinful.[13] In conclusion, the writer speaks to the local political foment: "Alas! I am but a drop of water in this ocean of politicos, and why should I fret, and swell and foam myself into a wave." The "politicos," as the writers I've discussed begin to demonstrate, made various arguments about the morality of the theatre to the public. By the 1790s, the theatre's supporters had become prolific waves in the ocean, to such a degree that the construction of a theatre began to feel inevitable.

The Silencing of Samuel Adams

When Adams stood up at the fateful town meeting, he was already in his sixties, viewed as an elder politician, and serving as acting lieutenant governor for Massachusetts. His disdain for the theatre was in line with his history as a patriot and leader of the revolution; he had supported the Continental Congress's ban on the theatre during the American War of Independence and, following the conclusion of the war, he continued to view the theatre as a vestige of British influence and oppression.[14] Given his personal history, his opposition to legalizing the theatre, in spite of its popularity, was well-known. The town meeting offered Adams another opportunity to reassert his opposition. To this end, he offered a history of the theatre from its inception in antiquity to its present state, a history that the participants in the town meeting found tedious. While nineteenth-century accounts of these events repeat the story of Adams's silencing as it was recorded in the *Argus*, twentieth- and twenty-first-century theatre histories moved away from local accounts, thus leaving the *Argus*'s account as the standard history of what was a contentious moment.[15]

The *Argus* does not provide the singular history of the meeting's events. There was disagreement among the newspapers as to what occurred at the meeting. First, it is unclear how much of a theatre history Adams was able to relate. This is because what occurred after Adams began speaking was subject to debate among the local newspapers. Competing narratives arose around Adams's supposed "silencing," contributing to a lack of clarity surrounding the event. Was Adams silenced, or wasn't he? The question hints at the anxiety surrounding the debate. Has theatre, even only in the discussion of its legality, already upended political hierarchies by allowing the people to protest an entrenched leader? These questions show what is at stake in what may appear, at first, as a minor squabble among newspapers. In returning the conflict to a broader historical context, it becomes clear that the story of Adams's silencing epitomizes fears surrounding the theatre's future in the new republic as well as the republic's future vis-à-vis Europe and the wider world. Would the republic flounder because it offered its citizens the freedom to challenge their leaders? Adams's silencing, because it embodies conflicts surrounding local and geopolitical power, takes on a greater significance in its ability to convey the stakes of determining an "American" identity that would forsake or accept the theatre. In the town meeting with Adams, the theatre had allowed exactly what its opponents feared, the opportunity for the people to challenge their leaders.

"Samuel Adams rose to speak in the midst of his fellow-citizens, and was silenced!": These are the words of Abraham Bishop, a Democratic-Republican with anti-theatre sentiments who devoted multiple columns of the *Argus* to the events that transpired at the town meeting. Although sympathetic to Adams's stance on the theatre, Bishop paints an unflattering portrait of both Boston's theatre supporters and its opponents, in the form of Adams: The theatre supporters appear vicious, while Adams appears superannuated. "Others, who were born but in season to enjoy the blessings" were listened to while Adams "could not even be heard." In other words, a cruel audience controlled a meeting that excluded those who fought for the "blessings" of American independence. Bishop's outrage becomes palpable as he thrice repeats the indignity that Adams suffered. In a more unlikely rhetorical move, Bishop writes Adams's suffering on his body, which appears as "at death." Segueing into an alternative blazon, which seems like an attempt to gain sympathy for the aging Adams, Bishop employs a series of rhetorical questions: "*Is his voice weak?*—That voice once made the proudest kingdom in Europe tremble to its Center. *Does his hand shake?*—That hand was once firm; strong were its sinews, and ably did it enforce the feelings of a firm heart.—*In whose cause has he grown grey? Was it difficult to hear him?* We would have listened with double attention." After characterizing Adams's voice, hand, and heart as strong, Bishop imagines that if these events had occurred in "enlightened Greece," the audience would have stopped the people who mocked Adams. And, among the unruly Bostonians, Bishop is happy to note that a few expressed, "some by looks, and some in words," their disapproval of the crowd's treatment of Adams. Bishop concludes by opposing partisan politics and explaining how laws should be passed: "Our measures are not to be carried by noise and cabal; not by silencing and drowning the voices of those, who oppose us."

Bishop's further expressions of national shame stem from his anger and disappointment at the audience's presumed failure to remember the role Adams played in their freedom to self-govern, including their ability to debate the legality of the theatre. Writing under the title "Tell It not in Gath," he frames the events of the town meeting as a public embarrassment, which should be hidden from outsiders but remembered by the local community. Bishop proposes, "Long may we remember, that he rose, to speak against a Theatre in Boston, and could not be heard!"[16] Bishop's call to memorialize what he perceives as a disgrace asks his readership to think about how they will treat their leaders. He wants young Bostonians to remember leaders whose "exertions have secured to you these blessings." By quoting an inscription on a monument at Beacon Hill, Bishop draws an analogy between the monument and Adams; Adams is a living monument who deserves reverence. But Adams has been ignored in what Bishop views as an act of hostility. For not addressing Adams with respect, Bishop scolds that we "have lost our senses."

Bishop's account, however, was not the only version of these events. In response to Bishop, the *Columbian Centinel*, a Federalist newspaper published by Benjamin Russell, printed an alternative account, claiming that Adams could be heard and expressing surprise that the *Argus* would print otherwise. Adams, according to the *Centinel*, may have aged, but he continued to be treated with deference by his fellow Bostonians. The *Centinel* argued that the crowd was not disrespecting Adams but rather asking for the conclusion of a long meeting. The writer claims that he, along with the "rest of my fellow citizens, heard that worthy patriot with the utmost attention, in a speech of near half an hour" and "when the town had heard all that could be said on the subject, they expressed anxiety for finishing the business." Even though the writer supports the proposal to establish a committee to examine the proposed repeal of the ban, the writer still shared "the same respect for our worthy Lieutenant-Governour [*sic*]." Adams received such respect, the writer explains, because the people understand "the infirmities of old age [are] sufficient without adding other troubles to them."[17]

The *Centinel* goes on to refer to Bishop, a native of New Haven and recent transplant to Boston after two years in Western Europe, as "a stranger sojourning in the town." Questioning Bishop's authority by attacking his regional identity demonstrates the significance of the role of who is speaking and who has the authority to speak in the controversy. Being called a "stranger" provoked Bishop, who swiftly responded with another string of rhetorical questions: "Has not a stranger eyes? Has not a stranger ears? Has not a stranger told the truth?"[18] These affirmative questions move the reader to agree with Bishop. To fortify the veracity of his original account, Bishop offered a second account of the events with greater description, including circumstantial particulars intended to produce a truth effect:

> Between 4 and 5 o'clock, Doct. Jarvis, was speaking in favor of a Theatre, all was attentive, as they ought to have been. . . . There was an interval of three or four minutes in Doctor Jarvis's speaking, when Mr. Adams rose to explain a fact in English History, which he had quoted; at that time, there was such coughing and

> moving, that Doct. Jarvis could hardly hear him. Several, who were standing nearly behind the board of Selectmen, did scrape their feet. But the time, to which I particularly refer, was, after the question had been put, and the vote carried, that the petition should not be withdrawn. Here the writer [the *Columbian Centinel*] does not deny; but attempts to apologize. . . . Mr. Adams rose and was silenced. If the people were tired, why did they not adjourn? Surely many opposed to a Theatre had not spoken . . . There was a hubbub and confusion, such as I never saw before in any town.

During Adams's first speech, Bishop remembers that the audience does not actively disagree with Adams but merely cough and move their feet. Their gestures, involuntary or not, hardly suggest a full-blown political confrontation; however, as the meeting continues, the tension escalates, and, in the end, there is a "hubbub" that indicates the disrespect, which offends Bishop.

What makes Adams's silencing a singular event is that it shows a longstanding leader being openly disrespected in a public forum, yet what is more important is how it also touches upon concerns raised by any discussion of the theatre. Such concerns speak to what Jonas Barish has described as "the protean nature of the antitheatrical prejudice, its indifference to consistency and its power to take on protective coloration from the times."[19] In this instance, the "antitheatrical prejudice" is colored by uneasiness over how the theatre would be used to create narratives about the powerful. Regardless of whether the educated and propertied men who led these debates supported or opposed the ban, they expressed concern over the proper regulation of the theatre. Questions of theatre regulation share similarities with questions related to proper regulation of the government and the role of the people in their own self-governance. In the account of Adams's silencing, the people have expressed exactly what elites feared, the theatre's ability to encourage the people to oppose a powerful leader. The theatre as catalyst for rebellion is threatening to those who have rebelled recently themselves, and to concede to the rebelliousness of the citizens at the town meeting is to concede that power is unstable. Shifts in political power, a characteristic of democracy, are not only reflected in the plays that appear on the stage but may be influenced by what appears there.

The Americanizing of the Stage

The debate over Adams's silencing began a year of intense discussion of the theatre in newspapers and pamphlets. The following pages will examine some of these documents, particularly as they address the perception of regional identity and power in relation to theatrical spaces and discourse. The anti-theatre campaign, as Odai Johnson has noted, demonstrates the "potency of theatre" in Boston's "cultural imagination," and the "Boston newspapers played a large role in publicly cementing" the association between deviance and the theatre.[20]

One concern that arose in the debate was a fear of "jests [being] represented as realities."[21] A correspondent for the *Independent Chronicle* ponders the problem of jests and realities, leading him to think about the nature of fiction and fact. The writer comes to the conclusion that, if this is the case, "exhibitions must be altogether fiction and deception: Those who form their manners, or regulate their conduct from what they observe on the Stage, are in danger of being bewildered in a labyrinth of error." However, theatre supporters imagined audiences with the ability to discern a "jest" from a fact, positing an intelligent audience with the capability to rule rather than a naive audience lacking the awareness required for self-governance. Another letter appearing in the *Independent Chronicle* and signed "Ramsey" offers objections to the theatre because, from the "Play-House," Americans will receive the moral instruction that they once received from "places of worship."[22] The writer, then, uses historical examples to claim that theatre always corrupts and to state that its greatest vice is the production of "merciless satire." Satire directed at leaders, like Adams, would foster disrespect and irreverence. Further, he objects to how the rhetoric of the theatre debate has been politicized, stating that the theatre ban "has no connection to *natural, unalienable rights* of the people."

By contrast, the *Columbian Centinel* published "Instructions to the Representatives of the Town of Boston," a document that summarized the committee's findings for the theatre and against the anti-theatrical statute.[23] The document is signed by the committee's chairman, Perez Morton, a member of the tontine and a theatre supporter. Morton had been mocked as a libertine in *Sans Souci*, and his political prestige had declined owing to his role in a family scandal. Undoubtingly, Morton's support of the theatre grew out of his political ambitions and economic interests. As a member of the tontine trying to establish what would become the Federal Street Theatre, Morton used the theatre controversy to reestablish himself in Boston life. For Morton, the committee was an opportunity to put aside his public reputation and use ameliorative rhetoric as a chairman writing and acting on behalf of a committee. With his personal reputation outside of the debate, Morton can sign a petition advocating "the right to relax from the toils of industry and the fatigue of business, by resort to any *rational and innocent amusement*, as constituting no inconsiderable part of the happiness of civil society, and one of the essential blessings confirmed to Men, by a free constitution of government."

So, how does Morton come to author arguments for a popular movement? As a local politician with conservative leanings and an appreciation for "amusement," Morton led a vocal battle among the citizenry, a battle in which he needed to champion the ideals that he had been derided for in the past. His personal choices may have reduced his opportunities to participate in local politics, but, as the rare conservative who supported the theatre, he was a good choice for the partisan politics of the debate. Rather than having a chairman who could convincingly argue the whole claim for the theatre, the committee needed a coalition. At the same time, many involved in the debate viewed the theatre's opening as a forgone conclusion. These circumstances arose because, as Milford has argued, "no one had an abiding interest in the ban, and principled objections could not carry the debate."[24] Given that support for the theatre was so strong, the debate was used primarily to negotiate other political and cultural issues, a factor that Morton's case makes plain. Members of the community, like Morton, were able to polish their reputations when debating a subject with such low stakes, because the theatre would be opened. Although Morton's reputation would not be rehabilitated to its former stature, he was able to reenter political life. These debates made other claims for Boston, for new individuals gaining political power, and for what Milford has described as "a telling moment, when a visible consensus emerged in the middle of polemical violence."

In their recommendations, Morton's committee uses the language that the *Independent Chronicle* objects to. For the committee, "the existence of that law, in its present unlimited form, operates as an undue restraint upon the liberty of the citizen, and as an infringement on his unalienable rights."[25] In addition to claiming the theatre as a right, they take aim at the perception of the corrupt theatre. Their theatre will encourage virtue as no play of "an immoral impression, may ever disgrace the American stage, and such only be presented to the view of the people, as shall be calculated to improve their taste, to mend their hearts; and to serve the great and beneficial purposes of public and private virtue." The "unlimited form" of the act is specified because the statute forbade all forms of theatrical entertainment, whereas the committee was willing to consider regulating only certain forms. Morton and the committee had a government censor in mind, advising that "the law of repeal may be so constructed, that no dramatic compositions shall be the subjects of theatrical exhibition, until they have first obtained a sanction from some authority to be appointed for that purpose."

Proposing an appointed censor was to suggest regulation like Britain's, and as a result, democratic newspapers viewed the recommendation as authoritarian. A writer at the *Independent Chronicle*, using the pseudonym "Bostonian," immediately disputed the idea by arguing that "should a body of censors pursuant to intrude themselves, they would, without much ceremony, exercise their 'unalienable rights' by exhibiting their *Honors* on the stage, in the garb of ridicule. This mode of reasoning must convince the gentleman, that their argument for the repeal of the act on the 'unalienable rights of man,' proved so much as effectually destroys their own proposition of censors."[26] Their suggestion of a censor would limit the newfound rights that the committee argued for when they supported the ban's repeal. The writer in the *Independent Chronicle* does not address how the business interests of the future theatre managers might result in "exhibiting their *Honors* on the stage," but it appears as a logical assumption. And, once again, it is implied that the stage could become the mouthpiece for a single political party because the owners of the stage could cast other parties in the "garb of ridicule."

A town meeting in January 1792 provided a forum to discuss the findings of Morton's committee. John Gardiner, a member of the committee and a proponent of the ban's repeal, gave the most discussed speech.[27] Although it called for an end to the ban, it was disliked by many who shared the same position. By the summer, when Gardiner's speech was published, several pamphlets attempted to amend Gardiner's arguments by addressing their reasons for asserting the ban's illegality. One such pamphlet, describing Gardiner's speech as "so much *burlesque* insinuation, so much *irony*, such an air of mockery," offered itself as the antidote to Gardiner's burlesque.[28]

The pamphlet *Effects of the stage on the manners of a people: And the propriety of encouraging and establishing a virtuous theatre* (1792) frames its support of the theatre as a rebuttal to Gardiner's facetious support. Written by "Bostonian," the pseudonym of William Haliburton, it presents a serious account of the ideal theatre. Such a theatre, far from the blight of ridicule, irony, or satire, would produce a polite society. Due to the pamphlet's limited scope and Haliburton's status as an amateur writer, the pamphlet has received scant attention; yet, it provides a daring and unusual vision of the theatre.[29] Haliburton, himself, was a unique voice in the Boston theatre debates; an American-born loyalist who resided in Nova Scotia, he happened to be visiting his children during the height of the theatre controversy. During his brief sojourn at his birthplace, he found himself caught up in Boston's post-Revolutionary identity crises. Through the debate, he explored his ambitions as a writer and philosopher, illuminating his concerns while attempting to establish, in a global landscape, a new "Bostonian" identity as an "American" from the Americas. In the Americas, he imagined that social engineering would create economic prosperity, a goal that many believed would be bolstered by the legalization of theatre.

Haliburton was attracted to what "[was] once more become the theme of general conversation" because the theatre had gained gravity as a subject and was recognized for the role it played in producing a virtuous citizenry.[30] In contrast to the degree of self-interest found in Morton and Gardiner's arguments, Haliburton's voice remained disinterested because he had little at stake in creating and maintaining a positive public image. Haliburton's pseudonym "Bostonian" obscured his identity and provided him with an adopted regional identity for the duration of the local controversy, making his arguments appear as benevolent and selfless as the paternalistic plans that he prescribed. Irrespective of Haliburton's limited personal ambitions, his goals for the theatre were far-reaching. He aimed to "suppress vice, promote virtue, and set on foot manufactures; and add likewise to the value of estates in town and country," aims that overlapped with the goals of pro- and anti-theatre writers alike.[31]

Effects of the Stage was modestly popular when it was published; George Washington, among others, eventually read, or at least owned, the pamphlet.[32] To encourage sales and introduce the pamphlet as part of the "general conversation," the *Massachusetts Mercury* ran a puff piece, signed by "C," that promoted Haliburton's pamphlet by emphasizing its lack of advertisements and recommending the author who, in supporting the theatre, "attempted more than the erection of a Temple to Pleasure": "He has contemplated the best interests of Virtue, opened new sources of affluence, found subsistence for the poor, given happiness to the rich, reserved equal felicity for the indigent, meditated essential service to the town, assigned a quantum of wealth to the country, laid the foundation of State manufactures, remembered the fatherless, and from the clerical widow, wiped away the tear of poverty."[33] Although the advertisement exaggerates the pamphlet's efficacy in curing social ills, it provides an accurate sketch of the ambitious nature of the work's content, which proposed extensive social engineering. The social engineering focused on the "fatherless," a concern for which Haliburton is applauded. The advertisement goes so far as to make Haliburton the benevolent father who can display his sensibility, not by crying but by "[wiping] away the tear of poverty."

As the advertisement suggests, a startling degree of sincerity characterizes Haliburton's moral theatre. Haliburton argues that the theatre will produce resources for the republic, opposing the common Republican argument that the republic's resources will be squandered on a luxurious theatre. Haliburton counters critics who describe the theatre as a luxury because such a view also labeled the theatre as a purveyor of European forms of vice. Like writers on both sides of the Atlantic, Haliburton used familial metaphors to recall America's colonial past and describe its new relationship to Europe. The new republic was "reared up by a nation, far gone in scenes of folly and dissipation; connected by habits of friendship and mutual intercourse with another, who hath made the greatest progress of any on earth in the refinements of luxury: Hath not America assumed the highest style of fashion."[34] Raised by Britain and befriended by France, American fashion has developed owing to the influence of these countries; however, America has assumed the "style" without the "dissipation." What, Haliburton asks, can be made of America's European inheritance? By describing a transit of ideas and fashion from Europe to America, he asserts Americans' freedom to adopt or dismiss European customs. For example, he is disappointed that "taste, high life, and musical glasses, have been transferred to America." Yet, he believes that theatre and music can correct a degraded taste because the state can intervene to exploit the beneficial effects of the arts. If done properly, "the Americans will have far excelled the celebrated Athenians."[35] In this regard, Haliburton, like the committee led by Morton, calls for the proper regulation of the theatre.

In continuing to think through the relationship between the United States and Europe, Haliburton moves beyond the familial metaphors and begins to employ aesthetic terms. Blending nationalistic discourse with his aesthetic arguments, Haliburton critiques the anti-theatre position by arguing that immoral entertainment is exclusively the product of Europe: "The portraits given by the English and French dramatists of the manners of those two kingdoms, represent gallantry, gaming, drinking and profanity, as the most prominent features of society in towns: Fox hunting, horse racing, bribery at elections, and rapes of women in the country: Dissimulation, over-reaching, intrigue, and sales of places at court: Dishonesty, hypocrisy, meanness, and poverty at church; they shew that the world is altogether a cheat, and that *they only* are fools and blockheads, who cannot act their parts therein with a good grace. And are such the manners to be introduced into America?"[36] The various forms of depravity that he ascribes to European plays demonstrate how he views the experience of theatregoing. The power of the theatre rests in verisimilitude; the theatre shows society to its audience, and the audience, already participating in what they see, copies the actions portrayed on the stage. How Haliburton defines spectatorship is limited and posits a naive audience; however, his views on spectatorship are like those popular at the end of the eighteenth century. Additionally, his assessment of European drama lends a sense of urgency to his call for American playwrights and actors. Acting, Haliburton says, "in America, would become a dignified distinction, and a desirable provision for life," an ideological shift in the respect granted to actors and a sign of the Americanization of the stage. Such changes would occur not only to the profession of acting but also to performance style:

"Banished forever, should be all unintelligible Italian airs, trills, affected squeaks and quavers; nothing but the deep-felt voice of nature, in harmonic sounds (vocal and instrumental united) can convey with fullest energy, the powers of music to an enraptured soul."[37]

American agency in the face of European hegemony can be asserted through the nation's approach to the theatre. To promote American interests, Haliburton discourages the use of foreign actors and writers, because "America is prolific in the production of genius; encouragement only is wanting to give her a high rank in the republic of letters."[38] Although Haliburton predicts that the republic will be corrupted by luxury, he uses this argument to affirm his belief in the proper regulation of the stage and in the state's role in running it. Haliburton envisions a close union between state and stage, proposing that the theatre include the offices of the State Senate. His plan unites two institutions that would alter the national culture, consolidating America's right to cultural self-definition.

Within his arguments about cultural self-definition, Haliburton shows how such self-definition depends upon economic success, which is not independent of the theatre's success. The success of the theatre forms the basis of Haliburton's restructuring of the local economy and the economic recovery that would ensue. For Haliburton, the theatre's virtue stems from its ability to employ, not entertain, the public. Haliburton makes plain that his plans will benefit both the rich and the poor, but he focuses almost exclusively on how the theatre will create new jobs in the linen industry. While he leaves the connection between the stage and the linen industry somewhat ambiguous (perhaps he imagines high returns on curtain material and costume production), he posits that the revenue from the theatre will be used to increase manufacturing and that manufacturing will, in turn, increase employment, in particular, "the hint of setting the poor females to work."[39] His argument genders the beneficiaries of the private and state subsidies that he believes the theatre will produce. In addition, Haliburton suggests that the theatre offer a benefit night to those employed in manufacturing.

Haliburton speculates that, as a result of his proposal, Boston will become a wealthy city. He dreams of making "Boston another Mexico; with rich and populous towns at the extremity of every bridge and causeway."[40] Haliburton looks to Mexico, not Europe, for a pleasing portrait of prosperity. By using Mexico as a benchmark for Boston's future success, Haliburton places his thinking squarely in the context of the Americas. The turn to Mexico is symptomatic of his discussion of the republic's recent past as a British colony and its development postindependence. While Haliburton presents the narrative in terms similar to a conjectural history with progress beginning in the so-called Old World and being realized in the New, it is neither a tale of the triumph of the

New World owing to its inheritance from the Old nor of the enduring superiority of the Old World. Rather, Haliburton argues that America took an inheritance from Europe but may develop like Mexico, allowing him to present all nations as equals and to narrate a tale of progress in the Americas.

The Politics of Pantomime

The British Licensing Act of 1737 created the role of the Lord Chamberlain to vet plays before they reached the licensed theatres and defined plays according to specific parameters that excluded some performances; restrictions like these were supported by Haliburton as well as Morton's committee. Haliburton proposed that Boston place restrictions on certain performances. These restrictions included a ban on pantomime because pantomime would undercut the spectator's ability to align their reason with their feelings, the sign of sensibility. To promote and sustain a theatre of sensibility, Haliburton suggests that after "the play ended, to preserve the good impression made, no further exhibitions should be suffered for that time. All farces, pantomimes, low-jesting, witticisms, buffoonery, rope-dancing, &c. (which serve only to waste the time and money of the people without any one benefit in return; and have moreover an evident tendency to deprave their taste and corrupt their morals) should be forever banished the Theatre, and all places of public resort, as infinitely beneath the dignity of a polite and sensible people."[41] For Haliburton, a polite piece of theatre would inspire a response that would unite the spectators' conscious reactions with their emotive ones. By contrast, an afterpiece would inspire only the physical and emotional response, inhibiting a rational one. Because of its tendency to produce only a sensory response in the audience, pantomime represented the wrong kind of theatre. As a result, Haliburton plans to eliminate afterpieces. To this end, he recites familiar arguments against them; afterpieces would "waste the time and money" of their audiences as well as ruin the audience's taste and morals. These conclusions, in part, condemn the audiences typically attracted to the afterpiece. Such audiences usually arrived later in the evening and paid for a half-price ticket, coming from their jobs (frequently in the manufacturing Haliburton promotes) or from an evening in the tavern.

Haliburton advocated opening theatres, yet he did so with reservations. One reservation involved the difficulty of regulating "ridicule"—the satirizing of individuals, particularly powerful ones. According to Haliburton, certain types of drama, specifically farce and pantomime, were more likely to incite ridicule. A fear of ridicule was the basis for many contemporary arguments against pantomime, which criticized the genre's ability to transform polite ideals and authoritative public figures into objects of ridicule. Due to this, Haliburton cautioned that "ridicule and satire against living characters, employed by so powerful an engine as the Stage, would be truly dangerous and pernicious; they are unfit to be used in that way before children, servants, and low, or, weak people, who having once learned such notes, are ever after insolent, refractory and ungovernable. . . . Living subjects now acting their parts upon the great Stage of the world, cannot with propriety be brought upon the Theatre of amusement; nor would it be useful."[42] Pantomime and ridicule presented a threat not only to aesthetic hierarchies but also to political ones.

Haliburton defines pantomime as "infinitely beneath the dignity of a polite and sensible people." Conflating politeness and sensibility was a hallmark of conservative sensibility, which supported polite discourse, whereas radical sensibility deemed polite discourse artificial.[43] On the issue of theatre, Haliburton espoused a view that only the "multitude of the chosen few" is fit to rule; the "people" were not to be trusted as judges of taste because they "may be persuaded to anything, and led any whither, provided you touch not their purse, and leave them at liberty to say they acted wholly of their own free will."[44]

There were theatre supporters with more radical views than Haliburton. Another theatre supporter, using the pseudonym Philo Dramatis, never advocated for censoring the theatre or banning pantomime. Anonymity continues to conceal the identity of Philo Dramatis, who wrote *The Rights of the Drama: Or, An Inquiry into the Origin, Principles, and Consequences of Theatrical Entertainments* (1792) and argued, like Haliburton, on behalf of opening theatres. Dramatis echoed Haliburton's sentiments on verisimilitude, writing that "the stage was employed to recall with mimic art from the oblivious silent tomb, the legislators, heroes, statesmen, philosophers, patriots and philanthropists of every age."[45] Unlike Haliburton, Dramatis remained receptive to different ideas of how to run the theatre and what plays to produce. For instance, Dramatis offered a generous account of the London stage, correcting the error that Rowe and Young were "banished" because "they were too chaste for an English audience."[46] During his seven months in London, Dramatis saw Rowe and Young perform to "crouded [*sic*] assemblies." Prior to his trip to Europe, he supported the theatre in his "private sentiments," but only after travelling to Europe and experiencing the theatre did he "publickly . . . address [his] countrymen."

Philo Dramatis advocated for pantomime, describing it as a pleasurable entertainment because "spectators are struck with a mixture of surprise and pleasure at the silent exhibition of a pantomime."[47] The audience's surprise and pleasure was the immediate consequence of a performance that strikes them and gives the "impression." Philo Dramatis had in mind one genre of "silent exhibition," the representation of history. He does not discuss comedy, romance, or other forms of pantomime. Instead, he addresses its ability to convey historical narratives and interrogates the effects of historical reenactments on spectators. Dramatis can only imagine the entertainment that may be provided when "seeing historical events re-acted, and pass in review before us," which Dramatis imagines would provide moral edification and improve the virtues of the audience: "[When they see] the Spanish Armada in the reign of Queen Elizabeth, or the defence of Gibraltar by Lord Heathfield, or the final preservation of a ship's crew in distress, by the fruitful expedients and resolution of a mere individual, incite us to detest the motives of cruel ambition, and lead us to cherish in our bosoms the sentiments of fortitude and humanity. [. . .] We profit of seeing the virtues of some, and the vices and ambition of others, properly pourtrayed [*sic*]. Our sensibility is excited, and we are compelled to weep over the miseries of life, and to drop a tear at the fate of the unfortunate."[48] Although Dramatis had several historic characters in mind, he showed a considerable interest in seafaring pantomime. One suspects that Dramatis had a front seat to a few aquadramas during his time in London. The aquadrama included cascading fountains and large pools that were used to stage naval battles and the rescue of young children by the wonder dog, an early Lassie. Such stage machinery would have been necessary for the naval battles and shipwrecks that Dramatis imagines. A "ship's crew in distress" could refer to any nation, but Dramatis refers only to events in European history and does not reference recent events in America that could have been staged through aquadrama, such as the Boston Tea Party or Washington Crossing the Delaware. Dramatis's selection of historical events highlights European events and an Anglo-American tradition as opposed to the nationalistic claims and calls for an "American theatre" that were employed in Haliburton's tract.

Despite their common argument in favor of the theatre, Haliburton and Dramatis demonstrate different political leanings relative to the imperial crisis and the development of the new republic. Dramatis approves of a diverse array of theatrical entertainments when discussing the didactic nature of the theatre. While audiences witness history on the stage, they see the "expedients and resolution of a mere individual." Through witnessing the actions of a "mere individual," the audience is asked to examine its own motives and to assess its actions in moral terms, an argument that evolves from Dramatis's knowledge of Adam Smith's *Theory of Moral Sentiments*. In accordance with Smith, Dramatis writes that "a moral sentiment is impressed most strongly from the stage, and sure the impression should be strong and forcible."[49] Through narratives of historic characters, spectators can see the "virtues of some, and the vices and ambition of others" and the subsequent "impressions" will activate a moral sense. To determine the success of a performance, Dramatis relies upon the audience's public display of tears; tears signify their sympathy, a moral response, has been activated. In this way, the stage can refine spectators' affective responses. Their display of sensibility transforms passive spectatorship into an active one.

Dramatis renders sensibility performative by making it a channel for moral behavior and making visible its performative nature. Concluding his meditation on history and pantomime, Dramatis claims that "the impressions we receive from readings, are not so lasting and pungent as those en graven by seeing and realizing."[50] His use of "impressions" and "en graven" points to the influence of associationism, a concept of learning first theorized by John Locke and then David Hume that posited the role of experience in creating thought. These ideas strengthen Dramatis's claims because they allow him to differentiate between reading a play and seeing a play. Creating a hierarchy of participatory activities, Dramatis argues that watching a performance makes a play more powerfully "en graven" than when it is read. He argues that neither silent reading nor reading aloud to an audience has the impact of watching a performance; reading does not produce as powerful sentiments, whereas "seeing and realizing"—the sensory and analytic experiences of the theatre—produce impressions that are more "lasting and pungent." With such a distinction in place, he makes an epistemological claim about how we experience the power of the stage and how the stage allows its audience to "know" and "feel" the performance. Dramatis's claims contradict the familiar counterclaim that reading produced too much sentiment in its audience, an argument that was leveled against readers of novels throughout the eighteenth century. With regards to the stage, however, Dramatis holds up the theatre as the best form of writing to "forcibly impress an idea on the mind" and "accelerate the progress of knowledge," an argument that, as we have seen, critics and supporters of the theatre used to different ends.[51]

The pamphlets written by Haliburton and Dramatis show how the theatre, and pantomime specifically, became a site for the debate over what the theatre meant and how it allowed its practitioners to define their experiences of performance and politics. Members of the Boston establishment may have questioned the value of pantomime as entertainment and instruction; however, in the debate over the repeal of the 1750 statute, the relevance of pantomime and its possible regulation moved to the heart of the debate and became newly significant once the Federal Street Theatre opened and staged an array of pantomime performances. Pantomime took its place on the stage, joining a host of other genres that would inform and excite Boston's theatregoers. In the acceptance of pantomime, the theatre's proponents offered a space for mockery and satire, allowing rather than foreclosing the possibility that the people can challenge leaders and assert self-rule.

Notes

1. *Argus*, November 1, 1791, 2. The *Argus* was a semi-weekly Democratic-Republican newspaper published in Boston from 1791 to 1793. Following Abraham Bishop's tenure as editor from 1791 to 1792, it was edited by Thomas Powars. The *Argus* published pieces, written by Bishop, in support of the French and Haitian Revolutions. For more on the *Argus*, see Seth Cotlar, *Tom Paine's America: The Rise and Fall of Transatlantic Radicalism in the Early Republic* (Charlottesville: University of Virginia Press, 2011) 21. Information on the politics of early American newspapers can be found in Donald H. Stewart, *The Opposition Press of the Federalist Period* (Albany: State University of New York Press, 1969); Bernard Bailyn and John B. Hench, ed., *The Press and the American Revolution* (Worcester, MA: American Antiquarian Society, 1980); Jeffrey L. Pasley, "*The Tyranny of Printers": Newspaper Politics in the Early American Republic* (Charlottesville: University of Virginia Press, 2001).
2. Peter A. Davis, "Puritan Mercantilism and the politics of anti-theatrical legislation in colonial America," in *The American Stage*, ed. Ron Engle and Tice L. Miller, 18–29 (Cambridge: Cambridge University Press, 1993). Heather S. Nathans, *Early American Theatre from the Revolution to Thomas Jefferson: Into the Hands of the People* (Cambridge: Cambridge University Press, 2003).
3. The past twenty-five years have witnessed several significant accounts of early American theatre: Jared Brown, *The Theatre in America during the Revolution* (Cambridge: Cambridge University Press, 1995); Don B. Wilmeth and Christopher Bigsby, eds., *The Cambridge History of American Theatre*, 3 vols. (Cambridge: Cambridge University Press, 1998–2000); S. E. Wilmer, *Theatre, Society, and Nation: Staging American Identities* (Cambridge: Cambridge University Press, 2002); Jeffrey H. Richards, *Drama, Theatre, and Identity in the American New Republic* (Cambridge: Cambridge University Press, 2005); Odai Johnson, *Absence and Memory in Colonial American Theatre: Fiorelli's Plaster* (New York: Palgrave Macmillan, 2006); Jason Shaffer, *Performing Patriotism: National Identity in the Colonial and Revolutionary American Theater* (Philadelphia: University of Pennsylvania Press, 2007); Tice L. Miller, *Entertaining the Nation: American Drama in the Eighteenth and Nineteenth Centuries* (Carbondale: Southern Illinois University Press, 2007); Peter Reed, *Rogue Performances Staging the Underclasses in Early American Theatre Culture* (New York: Palgrave Macmillan, 2009); and Sarah E. Chinn, *Spectacular Men: Race, Gender, and Nation on the Early American Stage* (New York: Oxford University Press, 2017).
4. Nathans, *Early American Theatre from the Revolution to Thomas Jefferson*, 2.
5. *Boston Gazette*, October 24, 1791, 3.
6. See Nathans as well as T. A. Milford, *The Gardiners of Massachusetts: Provincial Ambition and the British-American Career* (Durham: University of New Hampshire Press, 2005); and Bryan Waterman, "'Heaven Defend Us from Such Fathers': Perez Morton and the Poli-

tics of Seduction," in *Atlantic Worlds in the Long Eighteenth Century: Seduction and Sentiment*, ed. Toni Bowers and Tita Chico, 49–64 (New York: Palgrave Macmillan, 2012).

7. Nathans, *Early American Theatre from the Revolution to Thomas Jefferson*, 67.
8. For a history of the tea assemblies and an introduction to Perez Morton, one of Boston's theatre supporters, see Waterman, "'Heaven Defend Us.'" For more on Morton, see Milford, *The Gardiners of Massachusetts*, 158–59.
9. *Sans Souci, Alias, Free and Easy: An Evening's Peep into a Polite Circle* (Boston: Printed by Warden and Russell, 1785), 14. The authorship of the closet drama is disputed. Although it has been attributed to Mercy Otis Warren, it is unlikely that she wrote it.
10. Milford, *The Gardiners of Massachusetts*, 140.
11. *Herald for Freedom*, June 22, 1790, 115.
12. *Herald for Freedom*, June 22, 1790, 115.
13. Jonas A. Barish, *The Antitheatrical Prejudice* (Berkeley: University of California Press, 1981), 80–82.
14. Ira Stoll, *Samuel Adams: A Life* (New York: Free, 2008).
15. The *Argus*'s account is quoted in nineteenth-century histories, including in George O. Seilhammer, *A History of the American Theatre* (Philadelphia, Globe Printing House, 1891), 15. It is also quoted in biographies of Samuel Adams, including James K. Hosmer, *Samuel Adams Vol. 2* (Boston: Houghton, Mifflin, 1898), 362–63; and William V. Wells, *The Life and Public Services of Samuel Adams* (Freeport, NY: Books for Libraries, 1969).
16. "Tell It not in Gath," *Argus*, November 1, 1791, 2.
17. *Columbian Centinel*, November 2, 1791, 58.
18. *Argus*, November 4, 1791.
19. Barish, *The Antitheatrical Prejudice*, 298.
20. Odai Johnson, *London in a Box: Englishness and Theatre in Revolutionary America* (Iowa City: University of Iowa Press, 2017), 122–23.
21. *Independent Chronicle*, November 3, 1791, 2.
22. *Independent Chronicle*, November 24, 1791, 2.
23. Perez Morton, "Instructions to the Representatives of the Town of Boston," *Columbian Centinel*, November 12, 1791, 71.
24. Milford, *The Gardiners of Massachusetts*, 159.
25. Perez Morton, "Instructions to the Representatives of the Town of Boston," *Columbian Centinel*, November 12, 1791, 71.
26. "The Theatre: To the Inhabitants of Boston," *Independent Chronicle*, November 18, 1791, 2.
27. For more about John Gardiner and the scope of the theatre controversy, see Milford's *The Gardiners of Massachusetts*, 139–60.
28. Bostonian [William Haliburton], *Effects of the Stage on the Manner of the People* (Boston: Young & Ethridge, 1792), 16.
29. Haliburton is briefly mentioned in Milford's account of the controversy. One mention of Haliburton in an early theatre history calls him in "advance of his times." William Warland, *A Record of the Boston Stage* (Boston: Munroe, 1853), 18.
30. Bostonian, *Effects of the Stage on the Manner of the People*, 4.
31. Bostonian, *Effects of the Stage on the Manner of the People*, 5.
32. A copy of the tract, found in Washington's library, is bound with *Lionel and Clarissa: A Comic Opera*.

33. *Massachusetts Mercury*, January 5, 1793, 2. The *Massachusetts Mercury* was a short-lived tri-weekly publication from Alexander Young and Samuel Ethridge.
34. *Massachusetts Mercury*, January 5, 1793, 7.
35. *Massachusetts Mercury*, January 5, 1793, 28.
36. *Massachusetts Mercury*, January 5, 1793, 20.
37. *Massachusetts Mercury*, January 5, 1793, 22, 11.
38. *Massachusetts Mercury*, January 5, 1793, 40.
39. Bostonian, *Effects of the Stage on the Manner of the People*, 25.
40. Bostonian, *Effects of the Stage on the Manner of the People*, 43.
41. Bostonian, *Effects of the Stage on the Manner of the People*, 43.
42. Bostonian, *Effects of the Stage on the Manner of the People*, 12.
43. On differences in conservative and radical sensibility, see Chris Jones, *Radical Sensibility: Literature and Ideas in the 1790s* (New York: Routledge, 1993).
44. Bostonian, *Effects of the Stage on the Manner of the People*, 13.
45. Philo Dramatis, *The Rights of the Drama: Or, An Inquiry into the Origin, Principles, and Consequences of Theatrical Entertainments* (Boston: Printed for the author, 1792), 33.
46. Dramatis, *Rights of the Drama*, 33.
47. Dramatis, *Rights of the Drama*, 39–40.
48. Dramatis, *Rights of the Drama*, 40.
49. Dramatis, *Rights of the Drama*, 26.
50. Dramatis, *Rights of the Drama*, 40.
51. Dramatis, *Rights of the Drama*, 16.

From Moscow to Simferopol

How the Russian Cubo-Futurists Accessed the Provinces

—RYAN TVEDT

With their famous 1912 manifesto, "A Slap in the Face of Public Taste," the Russian cubo-futurists challenged what they derisively called the "common sense" and "good taste" of their audience. No more would they politely defer to the classics; even names such as Pushkin and Tolstoy felt suffocating, and the time had come to throw these writers "overboard" from what they called the "ship of modernity."[1] The following year, two signatories to this document made an ad hoc journey into the provinces, advocating for the principles laid out in their manifesto, in what became known as the futurist tour. For the next three months, leading artists of the cubo-futurist movement traveled provincial cities espousing their radically anti-bourgeois avant-garde aesthetic to audiences far removed from the cosmopolitan urban centers that had helped incubate their philosophical program. Their rejection of Russia's most distinguished artists and writers, often through insult and mockery, ensured that the group would meet with resistance.

Already accustomed to provoking backlash from audiences and city authorities alike in Moscow, the futurists would also antagonize provincial authorities and audiences in Imperial Russia who, at times, refused the group access to performance venues or reacted negatively to their provocations.[2] In spite of this, Vladimir Mayakovsky and his cubo-futurist colleagues, representing changes in art and industry taking place in the cities of Moscow and Saint Petersburg, managed to overcome both wary local authorities and audience resistance to the avant-garde, gaining access to theatres and lecture halls, generating extensive press coverage, and engaging closely with audiences all along their 1913–1914 tour.[3] The extent of the newspaper coverage conferred on the futurists a sense of legitimacy, while their close, if tense, relationship with local police and city officials amounted to tacit sanction of their project.

The cubo-futurist tour succeeded, against long odds, in gaining access to Russian provincial cities and their performance spaces even as its members carried out an avant-garde program of artistic rebellion that targeted the cultural tastes of the middlebrow public. Their association with the art and literary movements taking place in Moscow and Saint Petersburg, two cities that have traditionally dominated Russian cultural life, helped them overcome the negative consequences of their provocative and shocking tour. Audiences in the provinces associated Moscow and Saint Petersburg with the fascinating but as yet still poorly understood trend of futurity. Industrialization, mechanization, and cultural experimentation percolated in the two cultural capitals, and its artists and poets who traveled into the provinces came to personify the intriguing effects of these changes. The move from center to periphery, then, brought with it expectations of representing the latest technological and artistic developments in these two cities and enabled the futurists to overcome the disadvantages implicit in their challenge to the artistic standards established by their predecessors in the realms of literature, painting, and performance.

The traveling group that set off from Moscow in 1913 included the poet and playwright Vladimir Mayakovsky, tour organizer and painter David Burliuk, and Vasily Kamensky, one of Russia's first professional pilots. While still a boy, Mayakovsky moved to Moscow with his family after the premature death of his father. He spent a year or two on the streets handing out socialist leaflets before enrolling in the Moscow School of Painting, Sculpture and Architecture.[4] His political leanings occasionally landed him in prison, where he nevertheless continued to write poetry. Mayakovsky joined the art group Hylaea in time for the group's release of the aforementioned manifesto "A Slap in the Face of Public Taste." David Burliuk, a poet and painter often credited with organizing the tour, was born in Kharkov and grew up on a large estate his father managed in southern Ukraine. The early futurist movement benefited from his ability to identify and bring people together from different spheres, including painting, poetry, and theatre. He and his brothers, Vladimir and Nikolai, at least initially, comprised the main part of Hylaea, which morphed into cubo-futurism. Kamensky, the third main member of the tour, had worked as a railroad clerk, spent time as a Marxist agitator, and toured the provinces in seasonal theatre troupes before turning his attention to aviation.[5] Igor Severyanin, another poet, occasionally joined the group early in the tour.

Influenced and inspired by urban developments in industrialization and mechanization sweeping across Russia from Western Europe, including airplanes, elevators, express trains, and telephones, and by artistic ferment taking place in cities like Paris and Milan, the futurists' artistic rebellion and avant-garde aesthetic drew upon both recent technological innovations and their feelings of disgust at stagnant trends in literature, poetry, and theatre. In 1903, engineers completed the last track connecting Moscow and Saint Petersburg to Vladivostok in the Far East.[6] The extension of rail across the country along with inventions such as the internal combustion engine helped the futurists break free from physical limits that had otherwise confined them to Moscow. Instead, they embraced movement as a way both to spread their ideas and to test out new literary theories that depended on the dislocation that continual travel and touring provided.

During their tour, Mayakovsky, Burliuk, and Kamensky used the felt effects of speed to shape an emerging aesthetic. The repetition in their daily travel schedule along with the extended duration of the tour influenced Mayakovsky's artistic outlook. From train travel, he learned "how many miles it takes to shave, and how many miles there are in a soup."[7] In this, Mayakovsky suggests reworking his understanding of everyday activities in light of the rhythm and meter of movement. The sensations of machine-era travel served a nascent cubo-futurist project to disrupt conventional aesthetics. The futurists saw that Russian writers and poets venerated the classics, including Tolstoy, Pushkin, and Dostoevsky, who, more than anything else, simply took up too much space in the Russian literary tradition. This made it difficult, the futurists felt, to be responsive in their literary work to the present moment. The futurists sought, after all, to redefine what words themselves could do, focusing less on meaning, more on rhythm, and even on the visual aspect of the word itself, the presentation of the text.[8] For example, the futurists tried to disrupt the everyday act of reading, "to liberate words and letters," using "fragmentation, distortion, disrupting and shift of traditional verb units, associations and sounds."[9] Movement, speed, and travel allowed the futurists to enter actively into the center of their new aesthetic universe, to intuit personally its felt effects, and instead of replicating the reverence of the traditional spectator, to enter into the artistic or literary object and actively shape its form.

The futurists saw, more keenly and quickly than their contemporaries, how the airplane, the automobile, and particularly, the train, could radically alter the landscape and shake up the perceptions of travelers. They would have agreed with the poet and traveler Blaise Cendrars, who called the railroad a "new geometry."[10] The initial futurist struggle against static realism and the ossified con ventions of painting and theatre predisposed them to see travel as a means of escape and liberation. They believed that movement could bring about "enlightenment and progress," just as they pushed back against "isolation and disconnection."[11] Automobiles, planes, and trains transported the futurists beyond the reach of Moscow authorities and a too familiar artistic milieu. They believed these conveyances could influence their artistic practice by enabling a new kind of physical exploration of the Russian landscape. In the futurists' train tour, travel spurred artistic discovery by reorganizing the individual's relationship to the surrounding environment, consonant with what Jeffrey Schnapp has referred to as speed's ability to enlarge the sense of self and to transport it into new states of being.[12] This process refashioned travel from mere drudgery to a liberating activity that, while arduous, could benefit artists.

The Russian cubo-futurist touring group performed in sixteen cities in roughly three and a half months. Using today's political map, the group traveled through six countries, albeit then all part of the Russian Empire. Although tour cities varied in size, from the relatively tiny city of Kerch to the major metropolitan centers of Kharkov, Kiev, and Kazan, most at least qualified as regional or trade centers, transportation hubs, or strategic ports. They lay along a path located mostly to the south of Moscow (Kazan, an exception, lay straight east) in cities that reached to the shores of the Black Sea in the southwest and to the Caspian Sea farther east and concentrated to a great degree in present-day Ukraine. While Burliuk had grown up in southern Ukraine and Kamensky had previously toured in the provinces while working as an actor, Mayakovsky, after leaving his native Georgia as a young child, had never visited or toured the provinces.[13]

The group first performed in Kharkov, after which they swept through several other cities in Ukraine, including Poltava, Simferopol, Sevastopol, Kerch, and Odessa. The group then detoured into Moldova, stopping in the city of Kishinev. From there, they stopped in Nikolaev while on their way to Kiev in northern Ukraine. Continuing north, the futurists stopped in Minsk, went back to Moscow to protest the visit of their Italian rival Filippo Tommaso Marinetti, and then traveled east before reaching Kazan. Then, moving south, they stopped in Penza, Samara, and Rostov-on-Don. The group then turned its attention to Georgia, visiting Tbilisi in late March 1914, followed by the last stop on the tour, Baku, Azerbaijan.[14]

Although distinctive in its mobility and direct appeal to the public, the aesthetic of the cubo-futurist tour also owed something to the artistic experimentation already roiling the cities of Moscow and Saint Petersburg. Specifically, the cubo-futurist performances revealed the influence of a new type of performance expression, cabaret, which provided a forum for experimentation, a new performance space not overly subject to tradition, and a creative process too nimble and ephemeral for the censor. Cabaret proliferated in Russia's two major cities before the First World War, with as many as 125 cabarets and miniature theatres.[15] The form and ideology of cabaret fit the times well, with its ability to bring artists together under informal circumstances, prepared to satirize the mores of what they saw as an irredeemably base and petty society.[16] Cabaret dispensed with the wide gap between the performers and the audience, bringing them into close, and sometimes deliberately uncomfortable, quarters. The influence of cabaret upon cubo-futurist performance could be seen in the way the group adapted their shows to local conditions, adding or removing material as they deemed appropriate and necessary. Its influence could also be seen in the willingness of the cubo-futurist performers to engage with audiences both onstage and outside the theatre or performance hall.

Another influence on the cubo-futurists, *estrada*, sometimes called theatre of miniatures or small forms, included a broad range of performance. The estrada of prerevolutionary Russia originated in part on nightclub stages and in part in folk festivals. It represented a wider swath of Russian society than traditional theatre, and it could include pagan elements, puppetry, and song. Performers in this style employed a broad repertoire, minus certain standard theatrical elements, that held appeal for both popular and upper-class audiences. For example, Richard Stites notes that folk dramas lacked a working script, leaving them changeable and open to improvisation.[17] This left open the possibility of combining the "elitist and anti-elitist points of view," allowing the stages of the era, for example, to include lectures by specialists, and artists impersonating those same kinds of specialists.[18] The range of styles in estrada increased the acceptable range of performance material and loosened restrictions on mixing classes and sensibilities. This feature could be seen in the tendency of the cubo-futurists both to lecture on special topics and to satirize pedantry and dry, colorless scholarship. This aesthetic played well in the hands of Mayakovsky and Burliuk, who wanted to experiment with new artistic forms but also to both challenge and engage with the latest intellectual trends.

Cubo-futurist performances combined disparate elements into a mélange meant to consistently provoke audiences. To set the mood, the group often began their shows seated at a table drinking tea. The futurists created tension and sought to unsettle the audience by suspending a piano above the stage or by hanging a green ball in the place of an absent colleague.[19] Critics of the futurists claimed that they deliberately provoked the audience to attract attention. Mayakovsky, at a performance in Saratov, acknowledged that some audience members had shown up to witness a scandal: "You heard that we are brawlers, hooligans, vandals," he said, "who came to destroy."[20] By February 1914, the Moscow School of Painting, Sculpture and Architecture had kicked Burliuk and Mayakovsky out, and provincial and Moscow newspapers ran with accounts of their dismissal as well as notes on the futurists' insults against Pushkin and the painter Ilya Repin.[21] Despite their protests to the contrary, the futurists could not escape the tint of scandal and outrage that swirled around their tour.

The more formal, and slightly more conventional, part of the show usually began with speeches by each of the three performers, sometimes including the poet Igor Severyanin or other guests. The format of the talks fell somewhere between lecture and demonstration. For example, Burliuk often spoke about the history of painting, taking care to decry "provincial aesthetes" who depicted "pretty women in church-gold frames."[22] Mayakovsky extolled scientific thinking as well as his belief that the entire world was turning into a gigantic city.[23] Kamensky's lecture, "Laughter Is Our Answer," a riposte against futurism's critics, whose attacks followed the group from city to city, also discussed three elements of futurist creativity: the intuitive beginning, personal freedom, and abstraction.[24] These more formal elements of the shows, the lectures and poetry readings, often gave way once again to noisy discussions and arguments with the audience.

Not content to toy only with literary traditions, the cubo-futurists experimented with their appearance as well, using costumes and face paint to add to the provocative aspect of their personas. No less than the content of their lectures and poetry readings, their appearance helped them unsettle both audiences and critics. In Simferopol, Burliuk sported red eyebrows and the image of a sea monster on his forehead, while Kamensky appeared in colorful and unusual costumes that reminded one reviewer of a circus clown.[25] Mayakovsky, already a formidable public speaker and stage presence, heightened the effect of his persona by painting his face and wearing a bright red or yellow coat, a sartorial detail that annoyed both the police and his colleague, Severyanin. In fact, the latter joined the tour on the condition that the group stop appearing in unusual costumes. When a sold-out audience in Simferopol grew indignant when the performers appeared onstage without their well-known costumes and painted faces, Mayakovsky appeased the audience by including a line about lying in a "soft bed of real manure," a turn of phrase intended to placate an audience led to expect a certain amount of scandal.[26] The effect of the cubo-futurists' fashion experiments extended beyond the stage, as they also used these costumes to attract attention outside the theatre before their performances.

The futurists combined their penchant for unusual costumes and makeup with unorthodox publicity. Their self-promotion began the moment they jumped down off the train in a new city and included nearly everything they did in public. As their train rumbled into a new city, the trio disembarked and sauntered noisily through the streets. The futurists began the first stop of the tour in Kharkov by walking downtown wearing yellow jackets with radishes stuck in the lapels of their coats. Eventually, they stopped to hang show posters and attracted a small band of followers, who trailed them to breakfast at a nearby restaurant.[27] In Odessa, the futurists got the woman working as a ticket cashier at the theatre to paint her face with ancient religious figures and her lips and nose in gold.[28] The night before their scheduled show in Kerch, Mayakovsky and Burliuk attended a performance at the Winter Theatre of Edmond Rostand's romantic drama *The Princess Far-Away* to arouse the curiosity of locals and build suspense leading up to their own show. The two futurists caused a stir as they entered the theatre and settled into their box seats. At intermission, a group of spectators gathered on the main floor of the theatre and gawked up at the avant-gardists, using binoculars and lorgnettes to examine their strange costumes and the elaborate images painted on Burliuk's face. Meanwhile, Mayakovsky wore an unusual collarless, open shirt, which failed to meet normal standards of decorum for the occasion.[29] Although transgressive of social norms, these publicity stunts helped the futurists to gain a following in each new city they visited.

Audiences' responses to futurist stunts ranged from open hostility to unabashed excitement. The reception the futurists received from particular audiences depended on the ever-changing format and content of their program, local customs, and the kind of press coverage they received in newspapers leading up to the show. The enthusiastic and energetic curiosity of Kharkovites toward the futurists in their first tour stop was not repeated in every city. The audience in Odessa distrusted the futurists from the beginning of their program and responded tepidly to the visiting artists.[30] Similarly, much of the audience in Sevastopol, according to the local newspaper, *Southern Bulletin*, chose to go home early, even as they had filled up the local assembly hall.[31] During the tour, the futurists enjoyed many successes, but their program did not play well in every locale. The advantage of the tour in these situations was that they could simply move on to the next city.

The cubo-futurists' visit to Odessa, as much as any other city on the tour, can be viewed as typical of their efforts to engage with a sometimes uncomprehending and even hostile audience. The local critic Peter Pilsky, produced by the futurists as evidence that not all reviewers opposed their program, introduced the traveling artists, calling them the "spokesmen of the soul of the city."[32] Kamensky, always conscious of the group's image, tried to assure a packed theatre that their main interest lay in experimenting with poetry rather than in creating scandal.[33] Mayakovsky, as usual, directly challenged the audience, dismissing the Russian poet Konstantin Balmont and drawing applause when he told the audience he preferred the whistles of factories and locomotives to anything associated with a symbolist. Mayakovsky also read some of his own poetry, including "From Street to Street" and "And You Could?," before also reciting poems by Khlebnikov and even Severyanin, with whom he had recently feuded. Despite the best efforts of the touring group in Odessa, however, the majority of the audience ridiculed their reports.[34] The cubo-futurists' experience in Odessa showed them willing to present their artistic program despite a lukewarm or even hostile audience.

Underneath antics clearly designed to shock, create outrage, and therefore attract publicity lay the serious purpose of the cubo-futurists: the desire to set themselves apart as artists from the classical and realist masters. In their performances, the cubo-futurists attacked the classics to free themselves and their contemporaries from artistic dogma. In Kharkov, Kamensky called the artistic climate "stagnant" and a "putrid swamp covered with a thick layer of mold." This kind of language helped the futurists as they sought to tear down the image of the old masters, whose work still had a strong hold on their audience. Burliuk proclaimed that artists must exercise their will and "live only for today in the name of the future."[35] The cubo-futurists repeatedly discussed the homogeneity and lack of innovation in artistic practice in the hopes of creating a more permissive climate for artistic and literary experimentation.

Despite their relative lack of advance organization and planning, their incendiary rhetoric and visuals, and close monitoring by the police and city political leaders, the futurists gained an extraordinary level of access in the provincial cities and capitals they visited. Their association with artistic developments in Moscow and Saint Petersburg, Kamensky's distinction as a former pilot, and Mayakovsky's crowd-pleasing performances helped establish a reputation that fascinated audiences in the provinces. They gained access to prominent performance spaces, extensive (if not always positive) coverage from local newspapers, and tacit acceptance from police and city officials. Local authorities' willingness to allow the group to perform in prominent theatres and public halls conferred a level of status on the cubo-futurists. It helped attract audiences used to looking for entertainment at these venues, and it made performance conditions more predictable and reliable. Newspaper coverage helped generate publicity, and quite often a sense of scandal, around their shows. The fact that police usually chose to merely harass rather than obstruct the futurists meant they could spend their time publicizing and then performing, rather than on making endless appointments with local officials to press them for permission to perform.

In spite of the individual cubo-futurists' generally humble origins, provincial audiences could not help but identify the group with Russia's two cultural, economic, and political centers. As the hubs of Russian life, Moscow and Saint Petersburg conferred an elevated social status on those who lived there. The three main touring members began their artistic careers in Moscow, part of a larger futurist crowd that at one time included Benedict Livshits, Velimir Khlebnikov, Aleksei Kruchenykh, and Elena Guro.[36] The group's origins in Moscow, and to some extent in Saint Petersburg, allowed them to draw upon the urban environment for artistic inspiration, as evidenced by their repeated mentions of its effect on their aesthetic. The group members felt that the age of machines, the widespread use of electricity, and the advent of high-speed transportation, elements most prevalent in the modern city, required new means of expression. Mayakovsky, a leading proponent of this idea, linked the poetry of futurism to the city, with its urban experiences and impressions unknown to previous generations of poets.[37] Burliuk, in one of his talks, mentioned urban culture and its new machines, electricity, and global reach.[38] The futurists repeatedly invoked contemporary developments in the city and in technology more broadly, contending that art and literature had failed to capture their disruptive potential. Local authorities on the tour, while often suspicious of the group's ability to stir up audiences and flout convention, tended to give the group from Moscow and Saint Petersburg the permits they needed to perform.

Despite their ad hoc planning and lack of detailed preparation, the futurists secured permission to perform in well-established and notable performance spaces throughout their tour. Prior to embarking on the first leg of the tour, they sent letters to random addresses in cities situated across Russia and received several invitations sight unseen to give lectures about futurism. They often performed in well-known, centrally located public spaces and performance venues such as Minsk's Merchants Assembly Hall, Sevastopol's Public Meeting Hall, Kishinev's Hall of the Noble Assembly, and Kharkov's Public Library.[39] The futurists' ability to represent urban artistic trends helped them overcome audience discomfort with the criticism they leveled at well-known Russian literary figures. The cubo-futurists also gained access to proper theatres in several cities on the tour. In Odessa, Kamensky's visit with the governor helped secure permission to perform in the Russian Drama Theatre.[40] Other performances at established theatres took place at the Winter Theatre in Kerch and Kiev's Second City Theatre.[41] The group's ability to gain access to such spaces revealed that these cities' cultural and political elites tacitly accepted the presence of the futurists. Despite the unconventional, sometimes shocking futurist program, their access to well-known and respected local venues indicates they nevertheless maintained a close, if tense, relationship with city officials and cultural leaders.

The futurists' ability to establish mostly amicable relationships with provincial police officials also helped them gain access to performance spaces. More than that, the futurists' tour of the urban hinterlands of the Russian Empire in 1913, intent on provoking and shocking audiences at each stop, brought them into direct contact with the police, the gatekeepers of access and social order in the Russian provinces. Even their initial walk through the streets of a new city, much less their scheduled performances, required some form of police permission. The police did monitor their performances, imposed limitations upon the cubo-futurists' activity in their cities, and on occasion intervened in the middle of a performance. Police intervention occasionally hindered futurist efforts to connect with locals, but such official actions did not occur regularly. The futurists appeared to take close police scrutiny in stride.

The Russian national police monitored a range of theatrical performances and concerts as part of their responsibility for maintaining public order.[42] In the two largest cities of the empire, the imperial theatres reserved seats each night for the secret police. This allowed them to observe performances, check adherence to censorship protocols, maintain order in the auditorium, and protect visiting dignitaries, including heads of state. Tsarist agents known collectively as the Okhrana kept more than ten seats on permanent reserve for its officers at Saint Petersburg's Mariinsky and Alexandrinsky Theatres.[43] Observation and control of theatrical and performance events by Russian law officers meant that theatre and popular performance artists needed to negotiate the terms of the permissible and to contend with the possibility of adverse reaction to their performances. However, incidents like the riot at the Mariinsky Theatre in Saint Petersburg in October 1905 and the assassination of Premier Petr Stolypin at the Kiev Municipal Theatre in September 1911 had provided the authorities with evidence of theatre's disruptive potential.[44] As relatively recent security events taking place in established, institutional theatre spaces, these incidents gave police cause to keep a watchful and attentive eye on theatrical activity.

Maintaining a presence at most futurist performances and outdoor impromptus, the police held in reserve the ability to step in should the touring group's provocations threaten local standards of decorum. In both Odessa and in Kiev, the police, not bothering to wait for futurist provocations, sent an unusually large number of officers to monitor the performances.[45] Sometimes, the routine civic duty of monitoring visiting futurist provocateurs turned into a more serious and calculated attempt to intimidate. Kamensky interpreted the Poltava police chief's presence in the front row of the theatre as an "evil sign," an effect compounded by the phalanx of deputies strategically situated behind him.[46] The prominent position of the police in the theatres sent a message to the futurists about the potential costs they could incur for overstepping boundaries.

When local police intervened to either stop a show or to comment on a specific element of a performance, they often did so at times when the audience responded strongly to the futurists. In other words, direct police intervention appeared timed not only to prevent what must have felt like chaotic scenes within the theatres but also to prevent the futurists from engaging too closely with local audiences. In Nikolaev, the police, responding to press speculation about scandal involving the visiting touring group, forbade them access to the streets for their normal publicity stroll and asked them to submit a detailed outline of their upcoming performance.[47] Police went backstage during a performance in front of a raucous Kharkov crowd and told Burliuk they would stop the show unless Mayakovsky, who they knew as the man in the yellow jacket, took his hat off.[48] In Kazan, the police intervened a total of six times, trying to calm a boisterous crowd of students whose frenzied reaction to the futurists' entrance set the tone for the evening.[49] Officials' intervention took a sharper turn in Poltava when the chief of police stepped up onto the edge of the stage in the middle of a show and yelled "It's over. Drop the curtain."[50] The futurists tried to walk a fine line that allowed them to provoke local audiences and authorities alike without in fact encountering any lasting resistance that would prevent them from continuing their tour. Most of the time they succeeded.

Just as the police usually allowed the cubo-futurists enough freedom to complete the bulk of their shows as planned, local administration officials and governors more often than not granted the group permission to perform in their cities. Similar to their relationship with local newspaper reporters and editors, whose sometimes negative coverage of futurist activity made up a familiar part of the background of the tour, the futurists understood that city officials and governors viewed them with suspicion. For that reason, they made a concerted attempt to request meetings so that they could explain their program to local officials in person. Much was at stake in these conversations. In their first tour stop, Kharkov, the governor, after a visit from Kamensky, granted them permission to perform in the Public Library Hall.[51] Kamensky also played up futurism's connection to aviation, a topic much less controversial than criticism of Pushkin. When asked to explain the tour, he offered that it gave them an opportunity to praise the achievements of aviation.[52] Odessa's governor, in formulating his decision to allow the group to perform there, told Kamensky he was not surprised that pilots engage in "eccentric" activity. After all, he reasoned, any pilot must also be a futurist. Although the futurists cancelled a planned show in Ekaterinoslav after local administration officials refused to grant them the necessary permits, the cubo-futurists, on the whole, enjoyed access to prominent theatres and public meeting places in the majority of their tour stops.[53]

Despite the imposing spectacle of secret police maintaining theatre reservations and monitoring performances, the members of the cubo-futurist tour managed to continue their work even under the watchful gaze of both the police and city political officials. After 1905, tsarist censors relaxed restrictions on theatre across the Russian Empire, as the country moved, momentarily at least, toward greater permissiveness of theatre and performance.[54] In a practical sense, as Paul du Quenoy has pointed out, the Russian police during this time simply lacked the necessary manpower to monitor all of the performances running at any one time.[55] Performers could improvise from theatrical and performance texts in ways not visible to the censor, evade police supervision, and, via popular acclaim, appeal to the good sense of officials loathe to oppose the people. The futurists complicated the job of the censor and of the police since they did not fit the profile of an ordinary classic ballet, opera, or theatre company. While this group of young male artists pledging to overturn the established canon often drew extra scrutiny from police and city officials, there are no indications their work went through the censor's formal approval process.

Meanwhile, as the futurists, for the most part, adroitly navigated their relationship with the police and local political officials, they also managed to attract critical attention from the press. Local journalists, while not always kind or even welcoming of the group, nevertheless covered the tour extensively and on several occasions interviewed cubo-futurist tour members. Local newspapers also ran advertisements for upcoming performances. Kamensky, for example, on January 5, 1914, visited newspaper editors in Odessa at publications like *Southern Thought* and *Odessa News*, placed advertisements, and gave interviews in which he tried to explain the cubo-futurists' aesthetic. Mayakovsky, similarly, visited several editorial offices in Minsk to place advertisements for futurist shows there.[56] The futurists understood the value of newspaper coverage and criticism, which helps explain why they paid a lot of attention to critical newspaper commentary.

Newspaper reviewers alternately praised and criticized futurist stage shows. Of the latter sort, they accused the cubo-futurists of offences ranging from bad manners to tedium, obscurity, and unnecessary provocation. They also criticized the futurists when they failed to ignite scandal, as in Nikolaev, where the group neglected to live up to expectations and sufficiently antagonize the audience. Critics in Sevastopol called them "a group of sick people" trying to have fun at the expense of the locals. Kishinev newspaper reviewers noted both the small crowd and the failure of the group to generate excitement among the audience.[57] However, not all reacted negatively. A reviewer in Kharkov praised Mayakovsky's personal appeal and charisma.[58] Critics in Odessa also noted how the crowd responded to Mayakovsky. In Nikolaev, a reviewer wrote that it had been a long time since he had enjoyed anything as much as this cubo-futurist performance.[59] On the whole, newspapers awarded futurist readings and performances with mixed reviews. However, newspaper advertisements, interviews, and reviews gave the futurists much-needed publicity. That critics did not universally accept them mattered less than that they generated significant public discussion of their tour.

The cubo-futurists' ability to very quickly adapt emerging technologies for use in service of their literary and artistic innovations stands as one of their most significant legacies. Through continued movement, and specifically, via the sensation of speed, cubo-futurist artists proactively adapted urban developments in industrialization and mechanization to work in their favor. During their provincial tour of 1913–1914, Russian futurists came to be associated with frenetic movement and far-flung travel. This achievement was all the more remarkable since Imperial Russia often tried to prevent the movement of its own citizens, in part through the use of an internal passport system. By 1935, five years after Mayakovsky's death, when Soviet leader Joseph Stalin memorialized the poet by renaming a central Moscow square, it had been more than twenty years since the end of the first futurist tour. Even then, however, Stalin showed little interest in creating a space representing the futurists' link with movement and travel. However, the addition of the Mayakovsky Metro station adjacent to the square in 1938 immediately transformed the space into a transport hub capable of representing aspects of cubo-futurist movement and travel. Their fascination with speed and movement and what it could do to alter their perceptions of words, letters, and images helped motivate three key members of the group to embark on their tour in 1913.[60]

Today, a tall statue, although immobile, stands at the fulcrum of an area with several tangible connections to the kind of movement and travel espoused by Mayakovsky and his colleagues. Mayakovsky's statue, which finally appeared in 1958, sits in the middle of the square, as one might expect, facing Tverskaia, one of three avenues that spike outward from the Kremlin (figure 1). The statue, now juxtaposed against fast food and sushi restaurants as well as the historic

Figure 1. The statue of Vladimir Mayakovsky finally appeared in Mayakovsky (Triumph) Square, Moscow, in 1958. Photo by Ryan Tvedt.

Peking Hotel, stands silent witness to a modern city full of energy and motion. East of the square, the major Moscow roadway, the Garden Ring (Sadovoe Koltso), runs under Tverskaia Street and into the distance toward the Kudrinskaia Square building, one of Stalin's "Seven Sisters."[61] The confluence of Mayakovsky Square and the Garden Ring invites an outward-facing perspective, one that at first glance seems to promise escape from central Moscow and its congestion and traffic into the vast landscape of Russia. This sense, however, is illusory. Instead, and more in keeping with traditional limits on travel in Russia, the Garden Ring encircles an urban core composed of the Kremlin and the city's most influential government buildings, reconstructed churches, and memorial spaces. It offers a chance at movement, but not the opportunity to escape, as the cubo-futurists once did, the confines of the city.

The metro station adjacent to the square also reminds its passengers of the futurists' fascination with movement. With vivid shapes and colors, the avant-garde art on the walls of the entrance to the Mayakovskaya Metro station projects utopian optimism to passengers who enter the station from Mayakovsky

Square. Remodeled in 2005, the station's elaborate design, making liberal use of avant-garde elements, syncs with the ambitious aesthetic project once undertaken by Mayakovsky and the futurists.[62] Underground, off the platform, a series of false cupolas with mosaics by Aleksandr Deineka showcases emblems of the Soviet aerial age, including military parachutists and bomber squadrons flying in formation.[63] These images of aviators as war heroes not only underscore the station's connection with the futurists and their fascination with motion and travel but also remind us that the revolution in speed and movement eventually affected nearly all spheres of life.

Even the designer of the Mayakovsky metro station possesses a biography that helpfully connects movement-oriented projects across the Eurasian landmass, fulfilling a vision of transportation futurity envisioned by the futurists. Aleksey Dushkin helped develop travel hubs across the former Soviet Union, many in cities visited by the futurists in their 1913–1914 tour, including the Kropotkinskaia and Novoslobodskaia metro stations in Moscow and railway stations in Simferopol and Dnepropetrovsk.[64] Dushkin devised three Moscow Metro stations and also had a hand in designing train stations in areas outside the traditional centers of Moscow and Saint Petersburg. Dushkin's involvement in these geographically distant metro and rail projects, besides Mayakovsky Square, connects Mayakovsky's memorial space with movement generally, a pillar of the early cubo-futurist aesthetic, and with the kind of train touring the cubo-futurists undertook in 1913–1914. The futurists' affinity for the new machines of the great transportation age, or what one contemporary observer called "the age of express trains, zeppelins, and dreadnaughts," increased their visibility, gave the group added cachet, and helped it capture the imagination of the public.[65] The cubo-futurists' use of the train to tour outside of Moscow and Saint Petersburg energized their movement and allowed them to speak to people directly. It enabled the futurists to focus their relentless energy and striving; a sometimes-shocking assault on the classics acquired purpose via the railroad lines that drew them forth from Moscow's artistic and political cauldron and into the unknown sphere of the provinces. Mayakovsky Square provides an enduring link to a critical aspect of early futurist activity: touring and travel. Its permanence, on the other hand, serves as a counterpoint to the ephemeral nature of the cubo-futurist tour and performance generally.

The cubo-futurists' revolt against what they saw as a bourgeois, often philistine adherence to classic form and the slavish praise of established writers, poets, and theatre figures might have been expected to close off access not only to the provincial cities in their tour but also subsequently to performance spaces and official press coverage. However, despite their rebellion, the relationship of Russia's two major cities to the provinces in late Imperial Russia worked in their favor, granting them cachet and a favorable kind of notoriety, as provincial audiences identified the cubo-futurists with the comparatively cosmopolitan cities of Moscow and Saint Petersburg. To provincial audiences, the cubo-futurists represented new trends and technologies then transforming large and well-connected urban areas, offering them a glimpse of the futurist vision of big city artistic life. Among the first to not only adopt these new technologies but to incorporate them into their artistic work, the futurists, upon leaving Moscow and Saint Petersburg, tried to sustain the raucous evenings they had staged there, arguing with audiences, insulting critics, and lambasting bourgeois art. Their tour attracted a lot of attention, but police and city officials stood back and out of their way, giving them relative freedom to engage with audiences and advocate for their movement.

Despite their campaign against realism and conventional representation in Russia in 1913, despite numerous run-ins with police in Moscow even prior to their tour, and despite brash, often provocative performance strategies, cubo-futurism enjoyed significant structural advantages during its provincial tour. These advantages suggest that the futurists overcame relative obscurity outside of Moscow and Saint Petersburg by capitalizing on the public's interest in their scandal-tinged image, provocative performative elements, and unconventional style. This allowed them, as putative members of the artistic elite struggling to expand artistic boundaries, to rail at restrictions placed upon artists and writers.

First, the group secured permission, in the majority of cases, to perform at established theatres and performance spaces, thereby enjoying the implied status conferred on any group performing in these venues. Second, the futurists attracted significant publicity from local newspapers and critics. Although press coverage included a fair amount of negative commentary, the fact that reviewers chose to cover them at all again conferred on the touring group a sense of legitimacy it otherwise lacked. Finally, and perhaps most important, the cubo-futurists enjoyed the tacit sanction of local officials and police. Again, the caveat applies that the futurists did not always successfully make their case to perform in every city and that certain police chiefs proved more accommodating than others. Some, as noted, even forbade them to walk the streets or to perform. Overall, however, while police kept a close and watchful eye over futurist activity, their presence at futurist stage shows functioned not only as a tacit warning but also as a kind of approval and sanction, suggesting that city authorities recognized the significance, if not the meaning, of their artistic program.

The lack of such scrutiny in the Russian Empire at this time, indeed, would have been unusual, since authorities watched and monitored public space, restricted movement, and kept public spectacles in check. The presence of police at futurist stage shows, while sometimes nettlesome to specific futurist performance goals, fell within the range of normal law enforcement activity, even as it served to place some limits on their performances.

Dedicated first of all to destruction of literary and painterly traditions, the futurists found in their tour's continual movement and speed the means by which to experience reality in a new way. They hoped to go beyond chaos and scandal in order to supersede the entrenched positions of the classics of Russian art and literature. The futurists used the opportunities presented to them by the urban age, in which movement and speed allowed them to elide official Russian control and overpower the past, to explore movement, to reorganize their own spatial geography, and, as Mayakovsky declared in his poem "A Vy Mogli By? ("And You Could?"), to "smear the map of everyday life."[66] The futurists' desire to move beyond the realistic depiction of reality reinforced their reliance on an emerging urbanist vision, one that offered new opportunities to transcend the aesthetic and personal experience of everyday Russia. By forcing encounters and collisions befitting a new urban era, they sought out experiences that would test their belief in the ability of continual movement to reshape their artistic worldview.

Notes

1. D. Burlyuk, Alexander Kruchenykh, V. Mayakovsky, and Victor Khlebnikov, "A Slap in the Face of Public Taste," in *The Ardis Anthology of Russian Futurism*, ed. Ellendea Proffer and Carl R. Proffer (Ann Harbor, MI: Ardis, 1980), 179.
2. During the tour, the group referred to themselves mostly as "futurists." This article refers to the group as both "futurists" and "cubo-futurists" to distinguish them from other groups that also laid claim to the futurist label. For example, another literary group active during this time, led by Igor Severyanin, came to be known as "ego-futurists." The cubo-futurists grew out of the group initially called "Hylaea," after the region near the Black Sea in the Crimea, but came to be associated with Moscow-based poets and artists. The ego-futurists, meanwhile, were more active in Saint Petersburg.
3. Transliterations of Russian names, places, and text follow the Modified Library of Congress System. I have retained some common spellings, including those of well-known figures such as Mayakovsky and Kamensky, within the text of the essay. The use of diacritical marks is limited to the notes. All translations, unless otherwise noted, are my own.
4. Victor Shklovskii, *O Maiakovskom* (Moskva: Sovetskii Pisatel′, 1949), 14.
5. N. L. Stepanov, "Vasilii Kamenskii," in *Vasilii Kamenskii: Stixotvorenia i Poety*, ed. N. L. Stepanov (Moscow: Sovetskii Pisatel′, 1966), 6–7.

6. Stephen Kotkin, "Introduction: Rediscovering Russia in Asia," in *Rediscovering Russia in Asia: Siberia and the Russian Far East*, ed. Stephen Kotkin and David Wolff (Armonk, NY: M. E. Sharpe, 1995), 5.
7. Viktor Shklovskii, *Mayakovsky and His Circle*, trans. and ed. Lily Feiler (New York: Dodd, 1972), 186.
8. "Introduction," in *Russian Futurism through Its Manifestoes, 1912–1918*, trans. and ed. Anna Lawton (Ithaca, NY: Cornell University Press, 1988), 13–14.
9. Juliette Stapanian-Apkarian, "Modernist Vision in the Poems of Mayakovsky," in *Voices of Revolution: Collected Essays*, ed. Patricia Railing (Cambridge, MA: MIT Press, 2000), 72–129.
10. Blaise Cendrars, "*Prose du Transsiberien et de la petite Jeanne de France* (Prose of the Transsiberian and of Little Jean of France)," in *Selected Writings of Blaise Cendrars*, ed. Walter Albert (New York: New Directions, 1966), 66–99.
11. Wolfgang Schivelbusch, *The Railway Journey: The Industrialization of Time and Space in the 19th Century* (Berkeley: University of California Press, 1986), 197.
12. Jeffrey Schnapp, "Crash (Speed as Engine of Individuation)," *Modernism/Modernity*, 6, no. 1 (1999): 19.
13. V. V. Kamenskii, *Zhizn' s Maiakovskim* (Munich: Fink Verlag, 1974), 61.
14. The futurist touring group gave two performances in Kiev and Odessa. In all the other cities, they gave one.
15. Liudmila Tikhvinskaia, *Kabare i Teatry Miniatiur v Rossii, 1908–1977* (Moscow: Gvardia, 2005), 219.
16. Harold B. Segel, *Turn-of-the-Century Cabaret* (New York: Columbia University Press, 1987), xiv.
17. Richard Stites, *Russian Popular Culture: Entertainment and Society since 1900*, Cambridge Soviet Paperbacks (New York: Cambridge University Press, 1992), 17.
18. Spencer Golub, "The Silver Age, 1905–1917," in *A History of Russian Theatre*, ed. Robert Leach and Victor Borovsky (Cambridge, UK: Cambridge University Press, 1999), 278–301.
19. A. B. Krusanov, *Russkii Avangard: 1907–1932* (Saint Petersburg: Novoe Literaturnoe Obozrenie, 1996), 209, 215.
20. V. Katanin, *Maiakovskii: Literaturnaia Khronika*, Izdanie Chetvertoe Dopolnennoe (Moscow: Gosudarstvennoe Izdatel'stvo Khudozhestvennoi Literatury, 1961), 60–61.
21. "Gonenie na Futuristov," *Russkoe Slovo*, Starosti.ru, March 8, 1914, accessed June 3, 2018: http://starosti.ru/article.php?id=40737.
22. Kamenskii, *Zhizn' s Maiakovskim*, 69.
23. Katanin, *Maiakovskii*, 56.
24. Savvatii Mikhailovich Gints, *Vasilii Kamenskii*, ed. N. Gasheva (Perm': Knizhnoe Izdatel'stvo, 1984), 93.
25. Krusanov, *Russkii Avangard*, 205, 215.
26. Krusanov, *Russkii Avangard*, 201.
27. Krusanov, *Russkii Avangard*, 196; Kamenskii, *Zhizn' s Maiakovskim*, 64.
28. "Vecher Futuristov," *Odesskii Listok*, Starosti.ru, January 29, 1914, accessed June 3, 2018: http:starosti.ru/article.php?id=40231.
29. Krusanov, *Russkii Avangard*, 205.
30. "Vecher Futuristov," *Odesskii Listok*, Starosti.ru, January 30, 1914, accessed June 3, 2018: http:starosti.ru/article.php?id=40247.

31. "V Nochlezhom Priiute," *Iuzhnye Vedomosti*, Starosti.ru, January 25, 1914, accessed June 3, 2018: http:starosti.ru/article.php?id=40167.
32. "Vecher Futuristov," *Odesskii Listok*, Starosti.ru, January 30, 1914.
33. "Vecher Futuristov," *Odesskii Listok*, Starosti.ru, January 29, 1914.
34. N. Xardzhiev, "Turne Kubo-Futuristov: 1913–1914" in *Maiakovskii: Materialy i Issledovaniia*, ed. V. O. Pertsova and M. I. Serebrianskogo (Moscow: Gosudarstvennoe Izdatel'stvo "Khudozhestvennaia Literatura," 1940), 401–27.
35. Kamenskii, *Zhizn' s Maiakovskim*, 66, 69.
36. Vladimir Markov, *Russian Futurism: A History* (Berkeley: University of California Press, 1968), 31–32.
37. Katanin, *Maiakovskii*, 56.
38. Kamenskii, *Zhizn' s Maiakovskim*, 67.
39. Krusanov, *Russkii Avangard*, 216, 202; Katanin, *Maiakovskii*, 55–56.
40. Kamenskii, *Zhizn' s Maiakovskim*, 82.
41. Krusanov, *Russkii Avangard*, 204, 215.
42. George Kennan, "The Russian Police," *Century* 37 (November 1888–April 1889): 891–92.
43. Murray Frame, *The St. Petersburg Imperial Theatre: Stage and State in Revolutionary Russia, 1900–1920* (Jefferson, NC: McFarland, 2000), 123.
44. Abraham Ascher, *P.A. Stolypin: The Search for Stability in Late Imperial Russia* (Stanford: Stanford University Press, 2001), 371–72; Paul du Quenoy, *Stage Fright: Politics and the Performing Artist in Late Imperial Russia* (University Park: Pennsylvania State University Press, 2009), 51.
45. Krusanov, *Russkii Avangard*, 209, 215.
46. Kamenskii, *Zhizn' s Maiakovskim*, 79.
47. Krusanov, *Russkii Avangard*, 213.
48. Kamenskii, *Zhizn' s Maiakovskim*, 72.
49. Xardzhiev, "*Turne Kubo-Futuristov,*" 423.
50. Kamenskii, *Zhizn' s Maiakovskim*, 80.
51. Kamenskii, *Zhizn' s Maiakovskim*, 61–63.
52. Vasilii Kamenskii, "Iunost' Maiakovskovo," in *Vladimir Maiakovskii: Pro et Contra*, ed. D. K. Burlaka, 85 (Sankt Peterburg: Russkii Xristianskoy Gymanitarnoe Akademii, 2006), 85.
53. Gintz, 96. Yekaterinoslav later became known as Dnipropetrovsk. In 2016, the name of this city was changed to Dnipro.
54. Louise McReynolds, *Russia at Play: Leisure Activities at the End of the Tsarist Era* (Ithaca, NY: Cornell University Press, 2003), 70.
55. du Quenoy, *Stage Fright*, 50.
56. Krusanov, *Russkii Avangard*, 208, 216.
57. Krusanov, *Russkii Avangard*, 204, 212–13.
58. Kamenskii, *Zhizn' s Maiakovskim*, 74–75.
59. Krusanov, *Russkii Avangard*, 210, 213.
60. After Stalin's death in 1953, Soviet citizens with memories of the original futurist aesthetic began to gather in the square, taking advantage of Stalin's absence to help reconnect the space to the artistic principles that had animated Mayakovsky as a young artist. Vladimir Bukovsky, *To Build a Castle: My Life as a Dissenter*, trans. Michael Scammell (New York: Viking, 1978), 143. The official name was changed back to Triumfalnaia (Triumph) Square after the dissolution of the Soviet Union.

61. The Seven Sisters are a series of distinctive buildings constructed in Moscow at Stalin's behest between 1947 and 1953.
62. John Freedman, "Vladimir Mayakovsky Bust, Moscow Metro," *Russian Culture in Landmarks*, accessed August 21, 2017: https://russianlandmarks.wordpress.com/2014/12/04/vladimir-mayakovsky-bust-moscow-metro.
63. Alexei Tarkhanov and Sergei Kavtaradze, *Architecture of the Stalin Era*, comp. Mikhail Anikst, trans. Robin and Julie Whitby and James Paver (New York: Rizzoli, 1992), 79.
64. Dushkin worked with the architect Lichtenberg on the Kropotkinskaia Metro station and with Strelkov on the Novoslobodskaia Metro. Tarkhanov and Kavtaradze, *Architecture*, 185.
65. Krusanov, *Russkii Avangard*, 205.
66. Vladimir Vladimirovich Maiakovskii, "*A Vy Mogli By?*" In *Sobranie Sochinenii v Vos'mi Tomakh*, Tom 1, ed. L. V. Maiakovskoi, V. V. Vorontsov, and A. I. Koloskov (Moscow: Pravda, 1968), 18.

So Long Ago I Can't Remember

GAle GAtes et al. and the 1990s Immersive Theatre

—DANIELLA VINITSKI MOONEY

Predating the immersive theatre upsurge of the early twenty-first century, GAle GAtes et al. was a major site-specific company that operated internationally, throughout the Manhattan Financial District, and later out of their 40,000-square-foot warehouse home in DUMBO (Down Under the Manhattan Bridge Overpass), Brooklyn, from approximately 1995 to 2003. GAle GAtes was named after artistic director Michael Counts's grandmother, a painter who served as Count's lifelong inspiration. Known for its scale and spectacle, the company's content took autobiographical elements as inspiration, blending them with classic literature and historical moments, like *The Divine Comedy* and the burning of Rome. Although the company established itself through notable reviews and funding from the National Endowment for the Arts, its immediate audience was largely limited to the New York downtown circles of the late 1990s as a response to the remote geography of company work. *Field of Mars*, *Tilly Losch*, *1839*, and *So Long Ago I Can't Remember* constitute GAle GAtes's most significant works before its closing.

According to scholar Marvin Carlson, a retrospective glance at the late-twentieth-century theatre posits GAle GAtes as an important forerunner to the contemporary immersive theatre movement. "I think the emphasis in a good deal of contemporary performance has shifted from the 'total work of art' to the 'total experience of art,'" he writes, "for which the currently popular term (unknown in the GAle GAtes era) is 'immersive' theatre." He continues by crediting GAle GAtes (together with iconic director Reza Abdoh) as "the true modern innovator of this approach."[1] While contemporary theatre companies such as Third Rail and Punchdrunk have largely taken on this aesthetic through their own signature voices, GAle GAtes's work stands as an important artifact and model of the immersive theatre framework.

GAle GAtes's site-based mission included creating work specific to its unique playing space and adapting to idiosyncratic architectural and geographical details through the framework of interdisciplinary collaboration. The company was also, however, rooted in a rich theatre history lineage, from promenade medieval pageants to the American avant-garde. GAle GAtes's commitment to the dreamlike image, the unification of the arts, the re-creation of space, and immersive mise-en-scène, for example, are visible in the works and writings of precursors such as the surrealists, the writings of Richard Wagner, and the theories of Antonin Artaud. Director Robert Wilson, whose celebrated Theatre of Images navigates a labyrinth of images and music collectively working to favor spectacle over story, best embodies GAle GAtes's major inspiration. The pyrotechnic spectacle of the Wilsonian theatre utilizes musicality, collage, dimension, the visual and the kinetic, as well as the unique exploration of time, as some of its major facets. Perhaps it is no coincidence that GAle GAtes core member Kate Moran, now an established French film and experimental theatre actress, later performed in the role originated by Lucinda Childs in the 2013 remount of *Einstein on the Beach*. GAle GAtes founder Counts himself held an awareness and appreciation of this larger history, which informed the spirit of his own work: "Robert Wilson is a hero. Reza Abdoh. Richard Foreman. Joseph Cornell. Cage/Cunningham. . . . Antonin Artaud, Gertrude Stein. . . . I felt I understood what they meant, intuitively, and it helped me along my path."[2]

The following article will trace the company's founding and early work briefly and elaborate Counts's gravitational pull toward a more permanent indoor site-specific playing space, specifically 1990s DUMBO, with a honed description of the formerly remote area and the idiosyncrasies of the warehouse theatre itself. The argument will explore the inverse relationship of site-bound performance to its immediate geographic landscape, one in which the immersive experience arguably begins far before the performance itself. Finally, this article details two case studies that include GAle GAtes's later productions, *1839* and *So Long Ago I Can't Remember*, with a focus on descriptive narrative, dramaturgical construct, and the championing of audience autonomy, leading to the question of site-specific work and sustainability in an ever-increasing, gentrified urban locale.

Founders Michael Counts, Michelle Stern, and John Ogolvee met in New York and Prague in the early 1990s. Stern and Ogolvee had initially formed the Teleotheater Company near the end of their Tisch studies at NYU, together with former GAle GAtes lighting designer Jason Boyd, and had traveled to Prague for the summer to perform in various festivals. Ogolvee returned to Prague the following year and by happenstance met Counts, who was then creating large-scale site-specific productions around the city and among its historic castles with his first company, C. & Hammermill. Instant chemistry led Ogolvee to suggest that Counts meet Stern on their return to New York. After successfully connecting in New York in 1995 and creating a site-specific piece based on Gertrude Stein's *Listen To Me* on the steps of the Metropolitan Museum of Art, the three became inspired to join as a company, forming GAle GAtes. They grew their membership and continued to make site-specific work around the Manhattan financial district and throughout Asia, in thanks to major grants from the Lower Manhattan Cultural Council and the Asian Cultural Council, among others, including a short venture at the Bangkok-Bali-Berlin festival and a significant residency at Min Tanaka Body Weather Farm in Japan.[3]

Among GAle GAtes's early New York productions, a generous Lower Manhattan Cultural Council grant allowed GAle GAtes to use the entire fiftieth floor of a high-rise in the heart of New York's financial district to create an installation-performance. Through this grant the company produced *90 Degrees from the Equinox? Where Are We? And Where Are We Going?* (1995), a twelve-hour performance that took place over the course of six days in a 65,000-square-foot office floor. "I was able to get this huge, cavernous, empty, gutted office building floor to do a show, which was really the first GAle GAtes production," says Counts. "It was our field of grass piece."[4]

In this work, GAle GAtes transformed the business office into an immersive marsh landscape, with paths carved throughout. Tall phragmite grass was manually cut down from the Jamaica Bay wildlife refuge, and two trailer trucks of Styrofoam sheets were donated to the company, allowing them to cover the whole area and replant the marsh grass. The piece itself consisted of seven performers, many with "home bases," while a more free-moving female character was able to travel throughout the space to a hybrid text of original and found works. The primary inspiration for the work came from an image of a field of grass, as well as a John Cage text that shares a deep connection to nature and a walk through the woods; the performance involved highly trained physical theatre performers from New York University's Experimental Theatre Wing and Ann Bogart's SITI Company.

Over time, Counts sought to find a more permanent indoor playing space that could also speak to the company's site-specific mission. During the course of his search, a friend eventually connected Counts to the Walentases, the mega-successful father-son development team of Two Trees Management. At the time, the Walentases had ownership of an underdeveloped area in DUMBO, Brooklyn, that they were seeking to cultivate. According to Counts, "no one knew what DUMBO was yet. And I drove out there and I met with a Walentas representative and said, 'This is who we are and what we do, and we are looking for a space to plant our flag somewhere and be a cultural institution.'"[5] The first meeting ultimately led to Counts meeting Jed Walentas himself. "I made a few pieces of art just for him, just for Jed," shared Counts. "To understand who we were. And he said, 'I can't tell you why but something about [. . .] who you guys are and what that space looked like I find compelling."[6] Afterward, the Walentases gave the company reign over the 40,000-square-foot DUMBO warehouse space with the understanding that GAle GAtes would help transform the area into a cultural beacon.[7]

At the time, the DUMBO area was relatively unpopulated and dangerous. When asked to describe the region, Counts describes it as "lawless and weird," akin to the Wild West or like the film *After Hours* about Soho in the early 1980s. "Our publicist used to tell the press, if you get there at night, run from the subway to GAle GAtes. There was lots of crime."[8] GAle GAtes actress Beth Kurkjian recalls often leaving early because she lived in the separate direction of other company members, and felt unsafe on the subway and the walk home alone. "I was fearful but at the same time I came from being inspired by Bogart coming to life, by the Wooster Group. I felt ownership of the company."[9] Over the duration of their stay, the company fulfilled their promise toward the artistic/cultural growth and development of DUMBO, including securing a feature in the *New York Times*.

The warehouse given by the Walentases was a waterfront building, with approximately one-third of a city block to play within. Natural and mechanical power still surrounds the site; a large power station sits directly across from the space and side windows look out onto the water. In total, the company space made up four areas on three sublevels. The first room consisted of a main lobby twenty-three feet high, which overlooked the river. On the far end of that room was a balcony, which could allow one to look up into the mezzanine, which was 120 by 80 feet. Stairs led up to the mezzanine or down toward the office and studios. The offices and restrooms were located on the mezzanine level, which served as a production and exhibition space.

The space had several idiosyncratic qualities, such as a ramp, arches, a freight door, and three feet of reinforced concrete columns built every sixteen feet in the center. Counts recalls, "I used those columns in every way you possibly could."[10] The company often shifted the entrance and exit per production. "It was about meeting and defying expectations," Counts says. "Part of it was changing the orientation of the space. I loved that."[11] According to technical director Jeff Suggs, "There's no way you would have experienced a show and said, 'Oh. That's what the floor plan of the space was.' Maybe if you were an architect and completely sober. But 99 percent of the audience was neither of those things."[12] The enormity of space was significant. "Before the digital age I used to take cubistic photographs. To try to explain the space. It was very hard to understand how much space it was and how the space looked," says former resident artist Michael Anderson. "If you took only one picture you wouldn't be able to get the scale. We could ride our bikes through it."[13]

The productions themselves, supported by a company of talented artists and performers and largely led by Counts's vision, were dramaturgically based in visually inspired and immersive installation experience rather than traditional narrative story.[14] The unusual physical playing space of the DUMBO warehouse was reinvented for each production, often allowing for promenade through a surreal and thematically assembled multifocal installation environment. For those productions borrowing the proscenium and seated audience structure, the company played with the spatial dynamics of the warehouse itself through the use of multiple false walls, turntables, and wheeled sets, which were in turn animated by resident composer Joseph Diebes's ambient sound score and Counts's imagery. The effect was a lyrical and immersive landscape theatre experience, described by Diebes as a "360 Sensorium," in which visceral modes took front seat to conventional narrative-based proscenium drama.[15] Here, the spectator took on special agency, experiencing a sonically/visually driven world in which sensory experience informed the stage world at large.

In all these works and future productions, the experience of the production did not sit safely within the confines of the actual theatre but physically encompassed audience entry and exit. As Carlson notes in his *Places of Performance: The Semiotics of Theatre Architecture*, "the entire theatre, its audience arrangements, its other public spaces, its physical appearance, even its location within a city, are all important elements of the process by which an audience makes meaning in its experience."[16] This concept of urban/rural placement and the significance of theatre architecture and immediate surroundings are intrinsic to all GAle GAtes's audience experience.

GAle GAtes's later works in its DUMBO warehouse, for example, involved the audience experience in a physical journey that began far earlier than the entrance through its doors: Audience experience presumably bridged the journey from bustling metropolis via subway or car, through the dark unlit streets of the then-nonresidential and dim DUMBO, to the company warehouse and the otherworldly experience of a GAle GAtes production. In this way, the company space served as a literal safe house for invention and exploration. In all productions, it was, however, not only the physical environment of the GAle GAtes residencies that promoted a sense of otherworldliness but also the physical construction of its theatrical sets.

In *1839* (1999), GAle GAtes's third major production within the DUMBO space, Counts merged classical imagery and text with radical space reconfiguration. This piece borrowed the proscenium structure while integrating large-scale machinery and fluid sets, which played with the perspective of the enormous space in various reveals and dramatic spatial cuts. The title *1839* was derived from the year of the invention of the camera and borrowed from the Oedipus tale in the representation of a fractured family, with a primary lens on a young man in the roles of both Oedipus and a character named Henry. According to the company press release, the play is described as a dream by the inventor of the camera, J. M. Daguerre, "in which a child, in the guise of Oedipus, wanders through a landscape peopled by narcissists in love with their own photographed images."

1839 has a loose narrative structure, borrowing elements from the Greek tale. The maternal bond, the inherited sins of the (absent) father, and taboo are thematically visited. The set, braced by two enormous classical-inspired white pillars, and the simple costuming suggest a theatrical world outside of human history but reflective of an antiquated age. This is further supported by the text, which largely borrows from Sophocles's play. Dialogue is rarely (if ever) exchanged between characters in a naturalistic exchange. Text, however, saturates the performance through endless speeches, both contemplative and expositional, and is often delivered both fast and clipped, or as in the case of Jacinta/Henry's mother (D. D. Duvalier), melodious and song-like, so that the sense of the words themselves is subverted for the sound.

Certain phrases thematically resound throughout the play: "It's so pretty, Henry," and "That's the book of the dead" are often heard. "Are we leaving this ruin now?" asks the figure of Henry/Oedipus's mother in a seeming key moment, "are we all blind now?" As she speaks, she gazes at her naked self before a mirror. In this moment, she seems to refer not only to Thebes but also to the relationship of self to image: Consumed by one's self, one becomes blind to one's surroundings and its subsequent disintegration. In another instance, the characters stand on the stage against a whirlwind of moving lights and beeps, suggesting an exterior world artificial, if not apocalyptic, in design. Moran, performing the role of an ingenue, stands in a demure pose, then cocks her head, stamps a foot, and revolves away, each movement deliberate and poised. The fragmentation of her movement within this world suggested a hybridity of the organic and fragmented, accentuated by the set itself.

Figure 1. GAle GAtes et al. *1839*. Archival photo courtesy of Manju Shandler.

The setting for *1839* seems to take place in the cavern of a palace, continuously shifting through sliding floors and turntables, pits within pits, walls that emerge from nowhere, and a high distant perch from which Jacinta sits and looks out a window. Her dialogue reveals that this is a universe with no stars and an eternally full moon: It is unclear whether there is ever daylight, aside from slits of light that randomly fall from above during some scenes. Time does shift over the course of the play, as suggested through the cycled image of a young man (Henry/Oedipus) with his arms outstretched toward his mother. In the first instance, the young boy, dressed in a navy sailor suit, is in fact a statue seemingly made to represent the malleability of youth. His outstretched posture is later recreated by an adult actor dressed in the same costume, suggesting Henry's maturation. The image of red autumn leaves, placed downstage right, is also recurrent and shows the passage of seasons, time, and place.

Joseph Diebes's musical composition for *1839* is described, by critic Michael Rush, as maintaining "an eerie tension through a layering of indecipherable voices."[17] Diebes heightened tension through dissonance, specifically, by layering natural sound, such as wind chimes, rustling grass, and water, against a disruptive electronic score. In discussing his process, Diebes says, "The idea of sonic weather makes sense to me. The idea of sound as energy makes sense to me. Duration of time, not materiality; sound can somehow embody this. These very essential things—water, birdsongs, the sound of fire. And then the indiscernible. I would have voices in other languages percolating through this thing. They were kind of escaping you."[18] Language was also often written in non sequiturs, and as Living Theatre actor and *1839* performer Tom Walker recalls, Counts directed speaking to be "80 miles an hour in an act of loquacity." At the same time, the natural world of the play was populated by aberrant and peculiar beings, which culminated in a climactic moment: the reveal of an exposed naked female body within the armadillo.[19]

The large armadillo played a central role, despite its few appearances. The oversize puppet, otherwise re-created in the likeness of the animal, would in select moments move slowly across the stage. In a key instance, Walker's character was given a "long, beautiful and meditative speech" as the armadillo slowly plodded toward a hole. The piece was an excerpt from Holocaust survivor Elie Wiesel's memoirs: "I thought about it with apprehension day and night: the duty to testify, to offer depositions for history, to serve memory. What would man be without his capacity to remember? What does it mean to remember? It is to live in more than one world, to prevent the past from fading and to call upon the future to illuminate it. It is to revive fragments of existence, to rescue lost beings, to cast harsh light on faces and events, to drive back the sands that cover the surface of things, to combat oblivion and to reject death."[20]

Moran played the pivotal role of the armadillo, as well as that of a hermaphroditic child/ingenue who shifts genders over the course of the play. *1839* was Moran's first production with the company, and she was cast while an undergraduate at the Experimental Theatre Wing at New York University. The connection was made through Counts's friendship with dancer/choreographer Annie-B Parson. Counts recalls:

> Annie said, I think you're looking for Kate, and I think Kate's looking for you. She came and auditioned. I just pushed and pushed on her audition and to see the limits of where she would go. She would go anywhere. She had such poise. She was wise beyond her years. Even then: very mature, very sophisticated. A great performer. Riveting. I've had Kate do nothing, nothing on stage and you're on the edge of your seat.
>
> The armadillo, with this beautiful naked girl inside. Some of it is obvious. That to me was a little bit about who it was. It was Kate. It was a little bit about beauty protected by layers and layers and layers of defense. It was about that feeling that

> I had at the [Metropolitan Museum] sometimes. Both feeling like I'm an outsider that I'm looking at the world through four inches of plate glass and it's all on the other side. And feeling those things that I want that aren't accessible. That there's this itch that will never be scratched. Existential. But to me its beauty. What makes me weep at the Met sometimes is seeing a beautiful piece of art or a beautiful piece of anything: you want to commune with it; you want to fall through it and never come back.[21]

The armadillo is remarkable in the loss it evokes in performance: This seems to be quite literal as the image of the wandering armadillo is echoed throughout the piece. It is never threatening but plods through the set with a slow grace, seemingly in lost discord with the harsh world of *1839* itself. In certain moments the armadillo is seen resting and traveling within a dark pit whose presence beneath the stage seems to evoke the image of the grave: Does the armadillo then represent an aspect of human nature near extinction?

It is not only death and art that Counts referred to through imagery but also erotics. In one instance, two masked characters with elongated noses engage in a hot and juvenile dialogue of swirling hips and graphic language. The figure of the naked sacrificial virgin visits throughout. In a particularly moving image, the figure of an adolescent (Moran) sits by an enormous sleeping cat, which is revealed in a video that plays above them to be dreaming about nature and a run through the woods. When asked to elaborate on the figure of the cat, Counts explains that the composition was derived from a classical still life painting. Counts, initially trained as an artist and whose frequent visits to the Metropolitan Museum of Art were keystones of his theatre productions, referenced both his own work and various other artists and paintings throughout his works. For Counts, many such scenes sought to resonate with elements of the classical, beautiful, and dead.[22]

Perhaps the most nightmarish character is that played by Anika Barkan, a trained dancer. The character first appears when the name "Apollo" is cried out; it is unclear whether the figure has been summoned or manifests of its own accord. Grotesque and macabre, it appears to haunt the scene: Its presence is never acknowledged by other characters, and it is accompanied by strange music and, in one instance, the armadillo. The figure is costumed in only an enormous fat-suit and an Elizabethan collar. In at least one instance, it communicates directly with the audience, speaking in a prerecorded male voice. Barkan seamlessly executes movement, communicating through a restrained, difficult dance and gesture. In another instance, the character turns its attention to the sleeping figure of Jacinta and ominously runs toward her, only to be cut off at the last moment by a wall that appears out of nowhere.[23]

In many ways, *1839* represents the culmination of the company's technical experimentation. Lighting designer Jason Boyd worked on the company's first piece in the space, *Field of Mars*, and went on tour with musician Natalie Merchant as part of the international Lilith Fair soon after. According to Boyd, the tour taught him to master moving lights in extravagant ways, which informed his work in *1839*. Intricate specialized lighting known as cyberlights were essential to this production, as they were to earlier works, and in the original blocking, the first scene alone had 157 cues; by final count, the entire work had approximately 750.

During the production, former Reza Abdoh producer Diane White was also in dialogue with the company over the prospect of funding a tour of *1839*. To this end, many of the complex set designs were created to support this possibility. Designer Jim Findlay was recruited to help with the designs, such as the collaborative engineering "of a huge wall that had to spin down on a single pivot point and become the floor. It was something like 18 feet tall and 35 feet wide and it just had to, boom, lay down really fast, but in a controlled way."[24] Critical reviews described the set as a "fascinating living creature" that "spins, slides and hides" seemingly of its own accord.[25] There was also a rotating turntable built on wheels; in one particularly evocative example, as Jacinta was positioned on a chaise she tracks off into the distance and disappears one hundred feet away.

With effects that range from the startling to the hypnotic that scholar Michael Rush describes as a "cinematic dreamscape of gods, beasts, nudes, forests, temples, and velvet divans," *1839* was celebrated as stunning and dreamlike. "In *1839*, extraordinarily precise lighting and gesture cues isolate moments of genuine beauty," Rush writes. "The crowning moment in this visual feast is when Oedipus/Henry's mother, in a naked re-enactment of Manet's *Olympia*, lies on her illuminated bed and drifts away on it, deep into the vast upstage playing area."[26] In her *Village Voice* review in 1999, Alexis Soloski writes, "*1839* is unabashedly, ineluctably lovely." She also describes designer Jason Boyd's lighting design as hypnotic and "heartbreakingly" beautiful. Archival pictures reveal a nuanced blend of cerulean, indigo, and other blues, bathed in whites and shadows. For Rush, *1839* is a pre–American Revolution landscape dense with images of fertility, the macabre, and decadence. He writes, "It is an Oedipal conflict in revolutionary era America, which leads to a pregnant mother's death by arrows as participants in a life drawing class and over-sized escapees from a bestiary do a *dans macabre* [*sic*] in the falling house of Atreus. Clear? Not to worry, with Counts's work the play is not the thing," and he concludes by hailing the director as having emerged with "his own brand of [exquisite] theatre of images"[27] (figure 2).

During our interview, actor Walker, who performed alongside Josh Stark

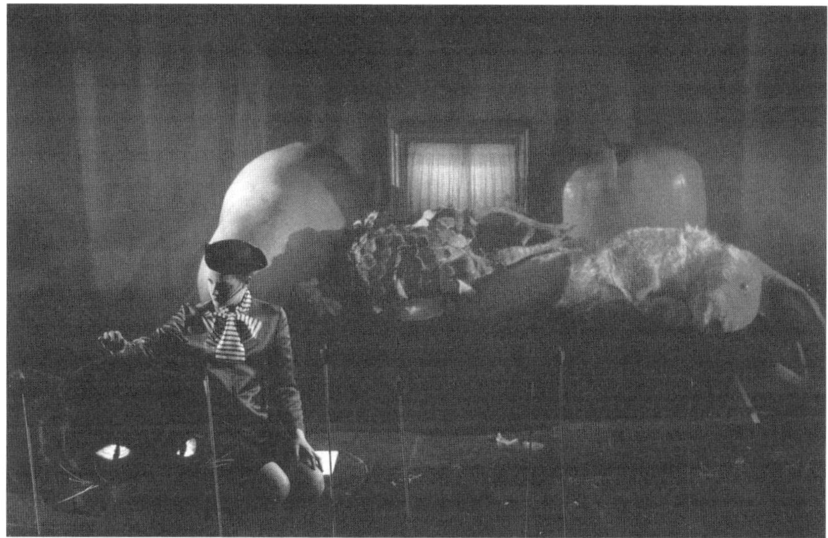

Figure 2. GAle GAtes et al. *1839*. Kate Moran (featured). Photo courtesy of Manju Shandler.

in a duo that blended elements of commedia dell'arte and *A Clockwork Orange*, describes the production as "this magnificent, incredible, atmospheric, mysterious thing":

> And there happened to be a little acting going on as well. There were the two gladiators with the Pinocchio noses [Stark and Walker]. There was Kate Moran, who was at times a young boy, at times a young girl. She was hermaphroditic. She was the armadillo, which appeared once, maybe twice. There was a pair of classical lovers [performed by D. D. Devalier and Peter Jacobs]. And then there was this girl, and she was in some sort of a strange costume. It was a horrible endurance test. There was a statue of a little boy. So those were the characters. There were oversized heads in this play. They may have floated through space. There was this contrast of beauty and ugliness that Michael was toying with. I can tell you it was very much like a dream. I felt that Michael was creating a world where it was hard to find clarity, and it was heartbreakingly tender and beautiful.

In Walker's view, "there was a great sadness to the play—it was trying to make sense of a world that could not entirely be made sense of."[28] For the actor, the production invoked a feeling of dislocation, which was accentuated by the enormity of the playing space and furthered his character's sense of loneliness. Walker describes the production as fueled by an "impossible effort to break through." He says, "I felt disembodied. There was a disconnectedness. They could have had a plate of glass and we could have been given sledgehammers to try get through it, and that would have represented the sorrow and the pity."

1839 most evoked the dream state through its utilization of imagery, which was both decadent and alienating. According to Counts, *1839*'s Oedipal structure allowed him to explore the inner conflict of "both a terror and gratitude for life" as well as his own fears over the prospect of parenthood and the nihilistic impulse, "at times even the wish to never have been born."[29] *1839* also explores childhood, its moments of isolation, and the passions of a transitioning young man. Says Counts, "*1839* had a lot to do with Oedipus and my mother and maybe even thoughts of being a parent one day. Love of passion and lust and infatuation." In this way, *1839* represented a deeply personal investigation into the existential, a revisiting of those youthful sentiments relating to love, and the tension between fact and poetic memory. It was the only production created for the possibility of tour, though it was simultaneously crafted within and for the unique spatial nuances of the warehouse, and whose surreality lay in its unique dialogue with the cavernous and remote space.

For many critics and artists, however, *So Long Ago*, the final major GAle GAtes production to be produced in DUMBO, was the crowning achievement of Counts and company. In this production, Counts pivoted the warehouse's spatial configuration so that the audience entered through the back of the space and exited through what was previously the foyer. A utopic view of Manhattan and the water thus became the audience's final image. The production consisted of a fifteen-installation walking tour of the space, based on Dante's *The Divine Comedy* and including the nine circles of hell, purgatory, and paradise. "It was like a maze, but where everything was revealed one after another," says actor Brian Bickerstaff.[30] According to a company publicity statement, the structure of the piece did not so much employ Dante's text as emphasize the imagined changes in the landscape of hell, purgatory, and paradise since his death seven hundred years ago.

While the performance established no clear narration or protagonist, the role of Dante and Virgil were woven through the structure, performed respectively by Bickerstaff and Moran. Among the performance's many images were "a Las Vegas dance number created by Reza Abdoh choreographer Ken Roht, a purgatorial autumn forest animated by a quartet of female singers, a boat traveling the river Styx, and a one-hundred-foot steel bridge ascending over a bed of fog as the character of Dante's Beatrice (Adrienne Campbell-Holt) performed an aerial dance."[31] The production referenced literal epochs in human history, such as the rise of the Nazi Empire and the Spanish Inquisition, and also incorporated abstraction and spectacle, as in a performance moment inspired by

Buster Keaton, a Fred Astaire and Ginger Rogers tap duet (featuring Bickerstaff and Stern), an eighty-foot falling wall with accompanying blast of cold wind, and a rock-inspired tour guide dressed all in black (Moran), all to the backdrop of Diebes's industrial score. For this production, Counts approached playwright Kevin Oakes, whose work was associated with establishments such as the Ontological-Hysteric Theater and Soho Rep., and the two worked in careful collaboration. "Working with Kevin [Oakes,] I realized I was not a writer," shared Counts in a 2001 *TheatreForum* interview. "I have in the past compiled text from various sources. . . . I did not however hear [the dialogue]."[32] Counts had been composing ideas for the piece for six months before meeting Oakes; after their meeting, Counts temporarily relocated to Avignon, France, where he completed storyboards for the structure of the piece. The two artists worked with Dante's text as well as contemporary and Renaissance art as sources of inspiration. Oakes's writing seemed to subvert language more consciously than previous productions through its mix of nonlinear dialogue, multilingual text, and use of echoes and acoustics. A prerecorded text was filtered through the space to which performers recited alongside their prerecorded selves.

So Long Ago began after the audience entered through the backspace of the warehouse, at which point they were introduced to an image of the river Styx and a boat immersed in fog that transitioned to a café scene adapted from Dante's "dark woods." The café was populated with various deviant characters—as Oaks describes it, "a watering hole for those in spiritual jeopardy"—placed seated along a twenty-foot wall. "They were people that you might [imagine] encountering on your way to hell, and the text supported that," Bickerstaff says.[33] These characters don't dialogue with each other as much as voice concerns and dark memories:

WOMAN ONE: He thinks scrubbing my face and shouting,
"You look like a dirty whore" is sex. . . . He makes me sit on the toilet with my pants pulled down then he removes all my make up.[34]

Another character says, "my favorite books are no longer a comfort to me. They're belittling me. I hate it when this happens."[35] Yet another tries to seduce a young woman, telling her, "I saw the way you smiled when I said the word 'machine,'" to which she responds, "'You didn't say the word 'machine.'"[36] Often lines are punctuated by other languages, promoting an atmosphere of disjoint. Oakes says, "I often allow the characters' subconscious desires to bubble up and permeate the spoken language, so that their dialogue becomes an interesting mix of what they might actually say in a given situation, and their private obsessions. . . . As it turns out, this is a good strategy for writing lines for the damned. Many of the characters in *So Long Ago* are afflicted with a sort of confessional Tourette Syndrome."[37]

As the scene progressed, Bickerstaff emerged in the role of Dante and stood on a platform silently observing the audience. The music became louder and more incoherent, at which point Moran appeared (the only character to perform with a live mike) and authoritatively dictated a list of things the audience could not do, such as touching the performers and going beyond delineated spaces. "As that went on the music grew louder and louder and all the tables and chairs were pulled offstage by a rope," recalls Bickerstaff. "The air was moving with the sound, the music crescendoed and it just went out."[38]

The supports on the wall then clicked out, and the wall fell toward the audience, revealing Bickerstaff in a tuxedo and top hat and a slick blood-red floor. A cold gust of wind resulted from the falling wall, which was heightened by fans hidden backstage. "People's hats would fly off. It was pretty intense," Bickerstaff says. The moment itself recalled a significant moment in cinema history: In Buster Keaton's piece *Steamboat Bill, Jr.*, Keaton is standing in front of a facade of a house, which falls down around him in a storm. Two dance numbers followed, choreographed by Ken Roht. In another key moment later in the production, titled "Gargoyles (Things the Devil Might Say)," four gargoyles discuss the nature of the devil. "What sort of thing am I?" asks one. "The thing I am doesn't even have a name anymore." Another tells the audience: "This is a death time story. . . . What am I? A human idea. A very bad human idea."[39]

The audience was then led to purgatory, which was produced as an opera that took place on a raked forest stage where the audience was seated. "It was an eerie, in-between world," says Bickerstaff. "You see certain characters from the inferno wandering around, as if they made their way through and are trying to find their way on their journey. There were wounded soldiers who may have died during the Civil War and who were part of a war they didn't ask for, who had killed people and found their way in purgatorio." From purgatory, the audience was led to the finale, which took place over a steel serpentine bridge hung over a lake of mist. Stern was visible ascending a staircase in the distance, while the recurring character of Dante's Beatrice (Adrianne Campbell-Holt) performed a slow aerial dance. The audience then exited the warehouse to an immediate view of the waterfront and Manhattan skyline. Neil Genzlinger of the *New York Times* described the conclusion of the piece as "leaving a vision of hell . . . [and entering] a sort of urban heaven on earth."[40]

For various designers, the image of the finale, specifically, the one-hundred-foot steel bridge constructed for *So Long Ago I Can't Remember*, is a seminal memory. Resident artist Tom Fruin remembers the creation of the bridge and lake as being a "gargantuan effort . . . [and] through the human spirit of volunteering and longer hours—while inhaling welding fumes,"[41] these things were made. Indeed, the final installation of *So Long Ago* required tremendous experimentation and effort. The serpentine bridge was created in a different portion of the warehouse and brought in after the final performance space was sealed with pond liner. However, havoc followed the initial attempt to create the "paradise" installation. Suggs recalls:

> Basically, we wanted to fill this gallery with water. So, we block off the edges and put in the pond liner for the purpose of the very last installation. We build the serpentine pieces of the steel structure somewhere. We built the legs. We put down the pond liner. Seal that. And then we bring the seal in to put the bridge on. Make sure the legs aren't puncturing the rubber or anything like that. We have welded the legs. So now we're welding over this rubber pond line. This isn't so . . . smart. But we're being diligent. We're using the blankets for cover—but we're just never going to win those battles, right? So, it's 4 in the morning when we finally finish and decide to fill up the pond because that was the only time we could get to the fire hydrant. Because that's how much water you need for an 80 by 80 foot pool. So, we fill it up. Great. Dye it blue.
>
> Everything's cool.
>
> The next day . . . two days later . . . we start noticing that the water levels are going down. So thus, the debate ensues: No, it's just evaporation, there's a lot of surface area. No, that's a half an inch dropping water leave, that's not evaporation. That is water leaking. So, we drain it. The floor was destroyed. How that problem was solved was we ended up filling it up with dry ice, cold fog, and it was gorgeous. It really was. The water was weird because it is very hard to light. The smoke looked fantastic. And it was done.

The falling wall in the beginning of the piece was also a technological challenge for the company. Its dimensions were sixteen feet tall by sixty feet long, and it had to fall each night, after which two characters (played by Michelle Stern and Brian Bickerstaff) would perform a Fred Astaire and Ginger Rogers–inspired tap dance number on the fallen construction. "It couldn't be a light, flat wall. And then it had to do that for every night for four months or so," says Sugg. "It was all totally manual."[42] For Counts:

> So much effort was put into creating an experience for the audience at the end that was my rendering of paradise. And the progression through the piece had been that this girl in a red dress was introduced and reintroduced and reintroduced throughout inferno and purgatory, then reappeared in paradise. We took this enormous front room of GAle GAtes and painted the entire thing black.

> Created this steel bridge that the entire audience would assemble on. We filled it with smoke, and the idea was it was to be in this depthless, vast open space. You couldn't see the stairs themselves, but you could see people walking up them. This couple, from earlier in the production [would ascend]—you could watch them ascend for essentially forever. Then the woman in the red dress appears in a red bathing suit, essentially on a ledge. In slow motion she dives over the audience into the water and as she approaches the water or smoke there is a blackout, and that's the end of the piece.
>
> And what does a woman diving into the ether and disappearing into the water or smoke mean about paradise? I'm not sure but I have a feeling, it always struck me as so evocative, in ways that were both referencing things that you may have seen before but just as a stand-alone image, this idea of this youth, beauty, sexuality and innocence that his actress really depicted so well. And the idea of diving into the unknown—a moment of release and a moment of abandon represents so many things on so many different levels that are about these peak moments of our human experience.[43]

While *1839* retained a static audience seating structure, it immersed its audience in a visceral cascade of images both nightmarish and elegant, evocative of both the classical and the meta-form. *So Long Ago* also centered on the dangers of hedonism at the intersection of classical and contemporary life; it both exercised the elements of a cautionary tale and avoided the pedantic through large-scale abstraction and spectacle. The promenade aesthetic served to both viscerally and philosophically engage the audience, whose sense of physical discovery may have been echoed in internal leaps and metaphysical connections.

In general, company work required an artistic sensibility on the viewer's part, in that language and story were not provided in a cohesive narrative. Rather than providing an overarching chronological story that would unfold over the course of production, GAle GAtes's work explored content imagistically and thematically and would allow for multiple audience perspectives to emerge, not unlike the experience of the museumgoer or gallerygoer. Audience subjectivity and their active participation in the unfolding of the piece were thus integral. However, company work was not entirely abstract; it utilized elements of rhythm and repetition, thereby allowing for thematic associations to emerge. In this way, GAle GAtes's theatre could also be considered ruminations on a theme (such as the destructive quality of political power), dreamscapes, or embodied metaphors for innate human preoccupations (such as love, masochism, or warfare).

However, for Counts, even within the darkest and most cerebral of his work, art remained "a celebration; the idea of putting your hand out [to an audience]" in the act of showing "something beautiful and challenging."[44] This artistic impulse and trust within the theatregoer's imagination reflects the "poetic, associative narrative" that scholar W. B. Worthen describes in his elegant review of the much-lauded *Sleep No More*.[45] The result of championing both mystery and audience autonomy becomes, as scholar Jacques Rancière writes, independence. The immersive and total theatre contributes to an evolved society of "active interpreters" able to "render their own translations and appropriate the story for themselves," thereby creating an "emancipated community of storytellers and translators."[46]

In our phone interview, Dr. Gautam Dasgupta, Counts's longtime mentor and cofounder of *PAJ: A Journal of Performance and Art* with scholar Bonnie Marranca, described Counts's theatrical work in such a fashion: "The [GAle GAtes] experience was democratic because each [spectator] took what he or she wanted to take from the functions of the narrative or the display. There wasn't closure or the sense that there was only one single way of seeing the work and the artist wasn't going to constrict you in a prescribed manner."[47] Counts said, "I think it is a service to the audience to meet their expectations, to go to them where they are, and then to undermine them, to take them somewhere different. Issues I have with some avant-garde theatre are that there's this, 'we're going to do what we want. And if you don't get it you're not in our club.' And to me that's so elitist and so unnecessary and I've never liked that kind of approach. I've done very, very abstract work, but it's always been done with a hand out to the audience."[48]

In conclusion, GAle GAtes represented an avant-garde ideal: In an obscure and site-specific locale, the company drew a specialized and elite public. Its mission of hybridity and its site-specific dimension contributed to an identity innately allied to the avant-garde, as the work could not be reproduced or commodified. But the company was neither opposed to the mainstream nor working from an ideological vantage point; rather it was led by the fire of artistic intuition and an overwhelming impulse to create, often out of the deeply personalized vision of artistic director Michael Counts, which in turn was informed by not only his visual arts background but also the insight of fellow company members. To this end, the company was largely unique in its company model, sensibility, and aesthetic: that being a hybrid of site-specific and immersive performance/installation/opera with a mission toward the sublime. GAle GAtes both flew and collapsed under the epic weight of its site-specific vision and genius, and it remains an important artifact of the twentieth-century experimental theatre landscape.

Notes

1. Marvin Carlson, email to author, February 2, 2013.
2. Michael Counts, personal interview, September 19, 2012.
3. For more intensive detail on the company's experience overseas, see my chapter "Butoh, Landscape Theatre, and the Physical Dramaturgy of GAle GAtes," in *Physical Dramaturgy: Perspectives from the Field*, ed. Rachel Bowditch, Jeff Casazza, and Annette Thornton.
4. Mooney, "Butoh, Landscape Theatre, and the Physical Dramaturgy of GAle GAtes."
5. Mooney, "Butoh, Landscape Theatre, and the Physical Dramaturgy of GAle GAtes."
6. Mooney, "Butoh, Landscape Theatre, and the Physical Dramaturgy of GAle GAtes."
7. While the initial contract proposed only one year of support through free space, the company was responsible for heat and electricity. To maintain stability and fulfill its role as a beacon of the arts, the company hosted nonstop parties, performances, exhibits, and miscellaneous events around the clock.
8. Mooney, "Butoh, Landscape Theatre, and the Physical Dramaturgy of GAle GAtes."
9. Beth Kurkjian, phone interview, January 29, 2013.
10. Beth Kurkjian, phone interview, January 29, 2013.
11. Beth Kurkjian, phone interview, January 29, 2013.
12. Jeff Sugg, personal interview, September 19, 2012.
13. Michael Anderson, personal interview, March 1, 2012.
14. Gertrude Stein composed a 1935 lecture on the theatre titled "Plays" in which she called for a new form of spectacle-driven drama, which she terms "landscape drama." In calling her plays landscapes, Stein draws a parallel to the fine arts, specifically that of the landscape painting. In this way, Stein generated a theatre paradigm that subverted traditional expectations of the literary in favor of the visual and immersive. According to scholar Hans Lehmann, critical aspects of Stein's theory are a delocalization of all parts, the abstraction of time, and the privileging of atmosphere. Character is a result not so much of the Stanislavsky circumstance but of physical environment. To best appreciate Stein's concept of landscape theatre, one may attempt to imagine the panoramic view. For scholar Una Chaudhuri, landscape theatre indicates a new and important frame for understanding theatre of the twenty-first century, which she addresses in her anthology *Land/Scape/Theater* (2002). GAle GAtes's works can largely be seen and experienced through the lens of Stein's concept of "landscape" theatre.
15. Joseph Diebes, personal interview, March 1, 2012.
16. Marvin Carlson, *Places of Performance* (New York: Cornell University Press, 1989), 2.
17. Michael Rush, "Italicized Monsters and Beached Whales," Review of *1839*. *PAJ: A Journal of Performance and Art* 22, no. 1 (2000): 93.
18. Joseph Diebes, personal interview, March 1, 2012.
19. According to a statement from puppet designer Manju Shandler, "my main recollection working with Counts was that of pushing the boundaries of perception and scale. The puppet was an absurd and poetic piece of the action that changed audience impressions depending on if it was viewed at a distance—taking advantage of the 40-foot depth of the stage, up close, or as a reveal to show the vulnerable naked individual beneath the hard and prickly exterior."

20. Heather Lehr Wagner, *Elie Wiesel: Messenger for Peace* (New York: Chelsea House, 2007), 44.
21. Michael Counts, personal interview, September 19, 2012.
22. Michael Counts, personal interview, February 6, 2013.
23. Mooney, "Butoh, Landscape Theatre, and the Physical Dramaturgy of GAle GAtes," 205.
24. Jim Finley, email to author, January 4, 2013.
25. Alexis Soloski, "Truth or Daguerre," Review of *1839*, *The Village Voice Online*, Village Voice, LLC, November 23, 1999. Web. October 2011.
26. Rush, "Italicized Monsters and Beached Whales," 93.
27. Rush, "Italicized Monsters and Beached Whales," 92–93.
28. Tom Walker, personal interview, September 18, 2013.
29. Michael Counts, personal interview, September 19, 2012.
30. Brian Bickerstaff, phone interview, March 22, 2013.
31. Mooney, "Butoh, Landscape Theatre, and the Physical Dramaturgy of GAle GAtes," 208.
32. "Dreaming the Same Dream: Kevin Oakes and Michael Counts Discuss Making *So Long Ago I Can't Remember*," *TheatreForum* 21 (1999): 16.
33. Brian Bickerstaff, phone interview, March 22, 2013.
34. "Dreaming the Same Dream," 21.
35. "Dreaming the Same Dream."
36. "Dreaming the Same Dream," 23.
37. "Dreaming the Same Dream," 17.
38. Brian Bickerstaff, phone interview, March 22, 2013.
39. "Dreaming the Same Dream," 34.
40. Neil Genzlinger, "It's Strange and Unsettling; Adrift Amid Hellish Images," Review of *So Long Ago*, *New York Times Online*, New York Times Company, April 20, 2001, Web. March 15, 2012.
41. Tom Fruin, personal interview, February 27, 2012.
42. Jeff Sugg, personal interview, September 19, 2012.
43. Michael Counts, personal interview, September 19, 2012.
44. Michael Counts, personal interview, September 19, 2012.
45. W. B. Worthen, "'The Written Troubles of the Brain:' *Sleep No More* and the Space of Character," *Theatre Journal* 64, no. 1 (2012): 82.
46. Jacques Rancière, "The Emancipated Spectator," *ArtForum* 45, no. 7 (2007): 271–80.
47. Gautam Dasgupta, phone interview, October 22, 2012.
48. Michael Counts, personal interview, September 19, 2012.

Part II

THE SITE-BASED THEATRE AUDIENCE EXPERIENCE: DRAMATURGY AND ETHICS

—EDITED BY PENELOPE COLE AND RAND HARMON

Site-Based Theatre

The Beginning

—PENELOPE COLE

Editors Penelope Cole and Rand Harmon co-organized and led a working group titled *Site-Based Theatre as a Trans-Contextual Experience* at the American Society of Theatre Research (ASTR) conference in Minneapolis in November 2016. Mike Pearson and Michael Shanks, speaking about site-specific performance in their book *Theatre/Archaeology*, contend that "performance recontextualises such sites: is the latest occupation of a location where other occupations—their material traces and histories—are still apparent: site is not just an interesting, and disinterested, backdrop." Further, they suggest that "interpenetrating narratives jostle to create meanings."[1] Inspired by the insights of Pearson and Shanks and the idea of the multiple occupations, or contexts, present in sites, the goal of our working group was to explore the very specific moment in the performative event when these multiple contexts intersect. We hoped through close analysis to unpack how performers and viewer/participants navigate between and among the disparate, and often competing, contexts of the theatrical event. The strength and breadth of the ideas exhibited in the papers by the participants in this working group, as well as the discoveries engendered through spirited, impassioned dialogue, inspired this collection of articles and conversations for *Theatre History Studies*. Some of the articles in this special section were first presented as part of the working group and have been revised and refined. Other articles represent the ongoing scholarly work in site-based theatre of working group members. Still others are written by scholars new to the field who bring a welcome fresh voice to our collective scholarship.

Our explorations of the interactive moment in site-based work emphasized how contexts collide, shift, blur, merge, and are reimagined, revealing the power embedded in the moment of performance. Our discussions also exposed how ripe these moments of interaction are for transgressive social behavior or the promotion of exclusivity, or both simultaneously. We aimed to articulate the unique dramaturgies of site-based theatre as defined by those moments of interaction through this work. By centering our discussions on the affective responses generated in the negotiation of multiple contexts by the performer and the spectator/participant in interaction, we gained compelling analytical perspectives on site-based theatrical events. Potent ideas about how creators of site-based work can engage with and capitalize on moments of interaction emerged. Finally, these exchanges led us to questions surrounding ethics and site-based theatre.

As the ideas for this special section developed, we became most interested in grappling with *how* the visceral/affective impact on the spectator/participant of a site-based event is created as well as *how* the spectator/participant may come to embody characters, the narrative itself, and/or the themes and ideas of the event. Additionally, raising and addressing concerns regarding potential societal and behavioral transgressions created by the unconventional spectator/performer relationships and interactions found in site-based events was another area of extreme interest. To these ends we sought, as articulated in our call for papers, "case studies that explore the unique dramaturgies of site-based performances or engage the ethical implications of disruptive audience conventions." We also welcomed "submissions analyzing spectator embodiment and engagement or exploring aesthetic innovations or ethical challenges experienced by audiences in site-based productions."

The articles found within this section speak to these questions in a multitude of ways. The first three papers are case studies of three widely different site-based performances personally experienced by the authors, and the next article examines how the creators of site-based work utilize various dramaturgies and techniques in the conception of site-based events. The final portion of this special collection is a curated conversation between four scholars/directors revolving around distinctive ethical concerns raised by their personal experiences with either attending or creating site-based work.

Terminology and Definitions

A large body of work attempts to define the multiplicity of terms used to signify theatrical work performed outside the boundaries of more conventional theatre spaces.[2] The editors of this special collection have deliberately chosen the generic umbrella term "site-based" to encompass the ever-growing variety of these types of outside-the-auditorium events. The term "site" or "sited" in this instance is used to signal that the performances under consideration are taking place outside of an established theatrical venue (admittedly a formal theatre is a site in and of itself) as well as outside of the customary conventions of behavior and interaction found within those established venues. Additionally, in sited performance, the performer/viewer relationship is not fixed and often ever-changing. The term "based," in conjunction with site, embraces the multitude of ways in which a "site" is employed in the creation and experiencing of the performance. Shared characteristics of site-based performances include an unconventional audience/performer proxemic relationship, the utilization of non-theatrically identified spaces as performance places, and the potential for direct audience participation in the performance itself. We feel that to explain why we chose the term "site-based," a closer examination of the terminology that has been applied to various types of sited productions is in order.

Perhaps the two most pervasive terms in use are "site-specific" and "immersive," the meanings of which as applied to a wide variety of theatrical events seem fluid. Indeed, the meanings have shifted over the decades as more theatre artists have begun working in these forms. To explicate some of the nuances of these labels, we offer a brief examination of the history and development of the practice of sited, participatory theatrical events. The term "site-specific," Bertie Ferdman asserts in her book *Off Sites: Contemporary Performance Beyond Site-Specific*, "originates in the visual arts and is grounded in the minimalist art practices of the 1960s." She notes, "In practice, 'site-specificity' initially referred to artwork creatively tailored for a specific location—the architecture or geography of the space." "Site" in this instance refers to "an actual, physical, geographic location, a tangible reality" that established the boundaries for the work. She continues, "Critical debates regarding minimalist art centered on the importance of the *encounter* [of the body] with the art object."[3] Analogous to the experiments in audience configuration in theatre, these artists privileged the body and its interaction with the work of art, thus challenging the perception of the artwork itself.

In *Theatre and Audience*, Helen Freshwater notes, "The desire to reconfigure the relationship between theatre and its audiences was a recurring theme in experimental theatre practice during the twentieth century and continues to preoccupy many practitioners."[4] Exploring the potential found in disrupting the conventional performer/audience relationship was a key element in the twentieth-century theatrical experiments of many practitioners, including Jerzy Grotowski, Peter Brook, Julian Beck and Judith Malina, and Richard Schechner, among others. Schechner's "environmental theatre," namely, theatre that erases the divide between performers and viewers; Beck and Malina's shattering of the fourth wall by inviting audiences to join the action; and Brook's articulation of four qualities of theatre performance, Dead, Rough, Holy, and Immediate, as well as his subsequent theatrical experiments such as *The Mahabharata* can be identified as some of the foundational ideas and practices fueling more recent site-based theatre practices. As in the minimalist art movement, these unorthodox audience and performer relationships placed the body of the spectator in a much closer, physical relationship to the work of art, often within the theatrical action itself, thereby also privileging the experience of the body in these interactions.

In the early experiments in site-specificity in the visual arts, dance, and theatre, the phrase referred to a discrete, physical location that inspired, inflected, and housed a specific artistic work or performance event. Victoria Hunter, writing about dance and site-specific choreography, maintains, "There is a specific interdependence between the site and the performance. Move the performance from the location and its significance will be either lost completely or weakened dramatically."[5] In *One Place After Another: Notes on Site-Specificity*, Miwon Kwon states, "Site-specific work in its earliest formation, [. . .] focused on establishing an inextricable, indivisible relationship between the work and its site and demanded the physical presence of the viewer for the work's completion."[6] Site-specific theatre is similarly defined by Fiona Wilke in her 2002 article, "Mapping the Terrain: A Survey of Site-Specific Performance in Britain," as "performance specifically generated from/for one specific site."[7] Mike Pearson of Brith Gof identifies site-specific work as performance that is "inseparable from its site."[8]

However, as more artists began to experiment with site as an element of art, the relationship between the site and the artwork began to shift, as did the understanding of the term "site." Scholars and artists alike strove to more accurately describe the differences between various sited performance events. In *Being and Circumstance: Notes Toward a Conditional Art*, published in 1985, Robert Irwin suggested terms such as "site-adjusted," "site-dominant," and "site-conditioned/determined."[9] Wilke proposed a continuum to illustrate the varying levels of specificity found in sited theatre. Placing conventional theatre on one end and site-specific at the other, she identified "Outside the Theatre," defined as performances that take place outside a theatre building (such as Shakespeare festivals), and "Site-sympathetic," defined as an "existing performance text physicalized in a selected site," as falling between the two poles.[10] Ten years later, Gareth White would define site-sympathetic work as work created "for the site where it is to be performed but without responding directly to the site's history or context."[11]

The mobility of the audience, whether to and from the event, or within the performance, or both, began to be a focal point in both the creation and the interrogation of site-based work. In 2008, Wilke wrote, "A shift in form can be noted from performance that *inhabits* a place to performance that *moves through* spaces: from a concern with the political and cultural meanings of particular locations to a focus on broader questions of what *site* might mean."[12] Site then becomes less grounded in, less connected to, a discrete, physical locale that informs the work than to a location to which artists can apply dramaturgical questions that frame their creative choices and reinform the site itself. This, in turn, opens a space wherein the multiple contexts contained within the site, the work of art, and the composition of the audience can collide, perhaps even contradict one another, enhancing and deepening the thematic possibilities of the work.

"Site-specific" is generally acknowledged as a label that has become so nonspecific that it is no longer a useful description. There is no doubt that it is an overused and misapplied categorization, often employed by theatre marketing departments to promote their more experimental, outside-of-the-auditorium performances, regardless of site or specificity. "Immersive theatre" is another such term. Josephine Machon, who has written extensively on immersive theatre, notes that "the term is now used freely (sometimes excessively) to describe contemporary performance practice involving a visceral and participatory audience experience with an all-encompassing sensual style of production aesthetic." However, she contends there are some defining features of the immersive event, including the establishment of "an 'in-its-own world-ness' where space, scenography, sound and duration are palpable forces that comprise this world." Furthermore, "some kind of 'contract for participation' is shared early on between the spectator and artist, inviting and enabling varying modes of agency and participation." With the emphasis on the experiential, she maintains that the "spectators can become submerged in a medium that is different to the known environment and can become deeply involved in the activity within that medium, all their senses engaged and manipulated. Bodies are prioritized in these worlds."[13]

The prominence of the spectators' bodies in immersive work, with all senses engaged in generating a visceral experience, can be considered a direct descendent of the prioritization of the viewers' bodies in the experimental theatre of the twentieth century discussed earlier. So, too, Machon's argument that immersive theatre is a "radical repositioning of the performance/spectator relationship" that "destroys the binaries of the auditorium/stage and spectator/performance" is a reflection and heightening of the disruption of the conventional audience/performer relationship explored by Schechner, Beck and Malina, Kantor, and others. Immersive audiences are not just placed in the playing space near the performers but are now "fundamentally complicit within the form and content, a living part of the aesthetic and a crucial element of any structural, narrative or thematic composition."[14]

Scholarship regarding site-based work has increasingly sought to tease out the unique and distinct characteristics of such work in an effort to grasp not only what defines each form but also *how* the dynamic relationships shaped through the spatial dislocation and relocation of the viewer are created. The variance in the taxonomy of site-based work, including the identification of form as well as the terms used to identify audience members, is considerable, exposing the instability of the terms "site," "specific," and "immersive," and some of their problematic implications. Kwon lists several invented terms used by artists to describe their work, including "site-oriented, site-referenced, site-conscious" and "context-specific, debate-specific, audience-specific."[15] Viewer, participant, spectator, interactor, spectator/participant, and audience/participant are some of the more common appellations applied to the theatregoer. Inevitably, there is a hybridization of the vocabulary surrounding the categorization of site-based work and the characterization of its audiences.

Andrew Filmer observes that "contemporary immersive theatre constitutes an extension and intensification of techniques of 'site-sympathetic' and 'promenade' performance and that overlaps between 'immersive' and 'site-specific' work are significant." In his well-argued essay "*Coriolan/us* and the Limits of 'Immersive,'" Filmer observes that "the real and meaningful differences between works that are variously labelled as 'immersive' or 'site-specific' exist in the nature of their critical and conceptual address to their location, to existing models of practice and to dramaturgical logics." Suggesting that the addition of terminology surrounding site-based work is unhelpful and unnecessary, he instead urges scholars to take a more "interrogative and inductive approach" involving "examining the experiential textures of performances in detail, elucidating their dramaturgic and aesthetic logics, particularly in the ways in which they situate and orient spectators, and the nature of the participation they invite, require or coerce." Most importantly he contends that this type of analysis must be "based on a researcher or critic's personal experience of a work."[16]

Each of the articles in this special section features a researcher and critic's personal experience of the work under analysis. The four essays and the curated discussion that concludes the section fall firmly in the realm of Spectator-

Participation-as-Research (SPaR), where the authors apply their own experiences as audience members or spectator/participants or makers of theatre in conjunction with theoretical considerations to critically engage with specific performances. Francis Babbage maintains that "over the last 20 years or so, practice as inquiry has become firmly established as a productive, valid, wide-spread and diverse mode of critical inquiry." Speaking of her own research, she states, "I seek out, consult and draw knowledge from live performances . . . in recognition that experiential engagement produces discoveries that cannot be reached by other means." As a researcher/participant, Babbage reports that she "pay[s] attention not (only) to the show as something that exists outside of/separate from [herself], but (also) the particular quality of each encounter: the bodily sensations, the minute-by-minute thoughts and emotions . . . simultaneously immersed . . . and critically noting what occurs within as well as in front of and around [her]."[17] The authors of the case studies here describe their personal experiences of the performances they participated in, noting times of fear, joy, fatigue, wonder, and confusion among other responses, and through the application of a wide variety of theoretical work concerning site-based work and audience experience, they share their unique discoveries about the work and themes embedded therein.

The editors' and individual authors' approach to the collection is in sympathy with Filmer's call to interrogate, from a basis of personal experience, "the dramaturgical and aesthetic logics" of the performances under consideration, and, in particular, to examine the viewer/performer relationship, both in terms of proximity and orientation and how participation is encouraged and created. While we are interested in refining a vocabulary with which to discuss site-based theatre, we are not proposing new terminology but rather attempting to deepen our understanding of the dynamics of the relationships created between viewers and performers in the shifting landscape of site-based performances.

The Articles

The first four articles in the special section are case studies of a variety of site-based works considered from the viewpoint of either the viewer/participant or the creator of the work. A curated discussion of ethical considerations unique to site-based performance rounds out the collection.

Mike Pearson and Mike Brookes's 2012 production of *Coriolan/us* is the subject of Penelope Cole's article "Becoming the Mob: Mike Brookes and Mike Pearson's *Coriolan/us*." This ambitious and highly successful production has been analyzed by both Andrew Filmer and Peter Primavesi, who focus variously on the immersive qualities of the performance or the political nature of the text in performance. In this article, Cole relates her experience of attending two performances, examining in depth how Brookes and Pearson integrated a variety of production elements, including the site (a disused RAF aircraft hangar), scenic installations, moving vehicles, multimedia, complex choreography, and text to invite the audience to reimagine themselves as the citizenry of Rome.

Similarly, Sean Bartley analyzes his experience of David Levine's *Private Moment* in "A Walk in the Park: David Levine's *Private Moment* and Ethical Participation in Site-Based Performance." All of New York City's Central Park was the site for this performance, which re-created iconic moments from eight different films shot in the park. Reenacted live in the original locations, these short scenes played in a continuous loop as audience members journeyed through Central Park in search of the individual vignettes. Negotiating his role as an audience member was a large part of this experience where the bulk of the time invested was in searching out the various scenes rather than watching them.

In "'I Want You to Feel Uncomfortable': Adapting Participation in *A 24-Decade History of Popular Music* at San Francisco's Curran Theatre," author David Bisaha investigates how Taylor Mac and his collaborators transferred a production originally conceived for and staged in a wide-open warehouse space to the confines of a conventional proscenium theatre. Bisaha relates how Mac utilized the hierarchal, segregated spaces of the Curran Theatre—that is, the orchestra, mezzanine, and balcony, as well as the lobby and stage, and the distance between them—to underscore many of the thematic elements of social construction and American history present in the performance.

"Navigating Neverland and Wonderland: Audience as Spect-Character" is the final case study of the collection. Director Colleen Rua details her approach to the creation of two site-based works, one based on J. M. Barrie's novel *Peter Pan* and the other on Lewis Carroll's *Alice in Wonderland*. Inspired by the work of Boal and Brecht as well as of contemporary site-based creators, she proposes the term "spect-character" to describe the multiple roles that audience members play, by design, in her productions: as a spectator and as invested characters invited through the structure of their encounters with the actors and the stories.

From a proscenium auditorium to a disused aircraft hangar, from Central Park to Plimoth Plantation, the sites employed by the makers of the productions under consideration are quite disparate. The content of the productions, ranging from a classic Shakespearean text to iconic cinematic moments, from devised experiences based on well-known novels to American popular music, is also widely divergent. However, the collection, when examined through the lens of the audience experience, reveals many common threads of discussion. Ideas of identity, journeying, movement, distance, complicit behavior, and a diversity of experience are some of the concepts found running throughout the case studies. Among the most potent connections explored are the creation of a sense of identity among audience members that articulates their role in the narrative; the manipulation of distance, including of the proxemic relationships between the performers and viewers, the viewers themselves, and the distances imposed by the site, required to traverse the geography of the performance space; and an examination of how site-based work enhances a diversity of experience among the participants.

In line with the editors' interest in *how* the viewer/participant may come to embody the characters, the narrative, and/or the themes of the production, the notion of identity is discussed frequently. As Bisaha notes as a participant in Taylor Mac's *A 24-Decade History of Popular Music*, he and the others in the audience were "encouraged to identify ourselves, or even experiment with different versions of self" through participative opportunities structured into Mac's performance. The use of the Curran Theatre, a fixed, iconic, conventional performance space replete with behavioral expectations, as the site for this performance complicated the challenge Mac issued to the participants to be active, to make choices, and to identify or reidentify yourself in the space, in multiple communities, and in American history. Bartley describes his trajectory as an audience member walking upward of seven miles through New York's Central Park as he searched out and watched the various cinematic moments of David Levine's *Private Moment*. Each encounter with one of the eight staged scenes served to add more information on how to be an audience member until he "felt implicitly that part of my role as audience member was to help the actors blend into their surroundings." To this end, he embraced anonymity, blending into the crowds of strangers across the wide expanse of Central Park by keeping his sunglasses on, wearing headphones (that weren't plugged in), and tucking his program into his back pocket before approaching the scene. In this way, he took up the challenge articulated in the program to "infiltrate . . . the private scenes themselves instead of simply operating as a spectator."

Rua and Cole each discuss the intentional casting of the audience in specific roles throughout a performance. Rua relates a moment in *An Awfully Big Adventure*, based on *Peter Pan*, where an individual audience member was invited to play catch with one of the boys. While engaged in playing, the actor delivered a monologue about fathers. One participant (or spect-character in Rua's terminology) told her afterward in an interview that "he called me 'Dad' at the very end and I realized who I was supposed to be and I felt like I wanted to go back and give him a hug, so I did." Being singled out to play catch with a boy who spoke in general about fathers and then being verbally identified as that boy's father created a potent moment of connection, realization, and identification for the spect-character. Cole notes that Brookes and Pearson intended from the first to employ the audience as the "the populace of Rome, the body politic, citizens, soldiers, rioters, to occupy, inhabit and define the public spaces within and upon which the action takes place." Traversing the immense space of the site following the performers and the action, as well as the use of live-streamed video on two large screens in the space, continually reinforced the perception of the viewer/participants as a mass of people, a unit rather than individuals. In each of these instances, a sense of identity was created through movement and specific types of engagement or nonengagement with the actors, which the site reinforced.

Distance and the need to negotiate distance is also examined with some frequency. The large scale of the sites encountered in the first three case studies (the Curran Theatre, Central Park, and an aircraft hangar) prescribed a certain kind of movement and required a physical journey to traverse the site. In each article, the authors suggest how the use of physical distance and the need to navigate this distance deepens the viewer/participant experience, further unlocking the themes of the work. The hierarchical distance between the orchestra, mezzanine, and balconies of the Curran Theatre, Bisaha maintains, "turned into an analogy for the difficulties of communication, progress, or movement in history." By inviting audience members to move through this space, at times displacing one another, the inequities in American society were underscored. Viewers moved as groups and as individuals, breaking away from one group to coalesce with another, depending on the time period and the communities Mac was focused on in the moment. In contrast, Bartley's hike in Central Park engaged him as an individual in a highly personal and solo trek. He notes that along the path to finding the scenes of the production, he also found himself detouring when he saw a familiar location that was used for a film not on the program, thereby creating his own text and discovering thematic connections along the way. Unlike the distinct, assigned characters such as Dad, a Roman citizen, or a political prisoner, as illustrated in the other case studies, Bartley was free to decide what his role would be as he continued his journey, trying on various roles and ways of interacting along the way.

Distance is also explored as the interplay of near and far or proxemic intimacy versus proxemic remoteness, which is examined in depth in Cole's article. She describes the opening moments of the production when the viewer/participants are forced into close physical proximity, entering the aircraft hangar cheek by jowl, only to find themselves adrift in the vast space of the hangar. The constant shifts in spatial relationships, to the performers, to each other, and to the site, demanded a physical response from the viewer/participants, creating a dynamic trajectory through the story and the site that continued unabated throughout the performance. Each spatial adjustment brought the viewer/participants into a new relationship that challenged their sense of self, their identity within the narrative, and their connection to the other viewer/participants through which new perspectives were unlocked.

It is commonly accepted that each audience member brings with them a set of beliefs, experiences, preconceptions, and expectations that inflect their experience of a performance, whether they're seated in an auditorium or walking through Central Park. Additionally, the audience member in the front row will be engaged in a different way than the spectator in the balcony in a conventional Western purpose-built theatre building. However, the spatial relationships to each other as spectators and to the stage in these venues rarely change over the course of the performance, which imbues the experience with a continuity that is not present in site-based work. Nor do the spatial relationships of the performers to the audience change once the conventions of movement and place for the production have been established, again engendering a continuity that then allows a viewer to claim their space/place and sit back to watch and listen as a story unfolds. Theatre performances that are housed in conventional theatre auditoriums are created to play to the whole house, to ensure sight lines are adhered to so that no one in the audience has a blocked view, and to create the illusion that each member of the audience has an equal experience.

Conversely, site-based theatre, whether it is conscious of embracing a diversity of experience for the audience/participants or not, does just that. Some companies and creators purposefully create divergent paths for their audience, such as This Is Not A Theatre Company's *Versailles*, where viewers had to choose a predetermined track through the apartment that housed the performance, or *Leaving Planet Earth* by Grid Iron, where audience members checked in at one of three kiosks and received a colored wrist band that determined the order in which the scenes were experienced. However, for other performances, the very act of requiring the audience to move, shift, or transverse a site disrupts the proxemic relationship between performer and viewer in a way that proscenium theatre does not and that in turn forces a diversity of experience among the viewers. If you are two feet away from a scene/performer, you will experience the moment differently than someone who is twenty feet away. Moreover, this distance does not remain stable, so your own experience shifts as you find yourself far from one scene of the performance and in another having the interaction happen almost in your lap.

The case studies in the special section range from performances that provide very little in the way of direction for the viewer/participant to those that provide a great deal. In the arguably most solo of viewing experiences described in the collection, Bartley notes that "*Private Moment* offers a map, but no prescribed paths or trajectories for the individual audience member to take." He contends that this allows each audience member to explore "their agency in the theatrical event by moving and by noting the experiential effects of the trip." On the other hand, Rua describes the multiple tracks designed for her audiences in both of the productions she created. Audience members for *An Awfully Big Adventure* "began by following a Lost Boy but were then handed off to various characters as they traveled throughout Neverland and London. *Alice in Wonderland* was completely guided, with one actor-guide assigned to each track." Rua suggests that the connection between the audience members and the individual guides "resulted in the spect-characters' investment in both the character they followed and their own storylines," becoming "collaborators in the process as they made active choices, engaged in dialogue and crossed borders to move in and out of multilayered roles." In each of these models of audience participative guidance, however, the divergence of audience experience is encouraged and, indeed, a valued part of the dramaturgy of the piece.

The concluding offering of the collection is a curated discussion of various ethical considerations that creators of site-based work must consider and grapple with when devising, imagining, and presenting performances outside the boundaries of more conventional theatre venues. Site-based work creators and scholars Guillermo Aviles-Rodriguez, of California State University, Northridge, and Erin B. Mee, of This Is Not A Theatre Company, joined the editors, Penelope Cole and Rand Harmon, to consider a variety of ethical questions. The topics discussed included ideas of postcolonial intrusions and appropriations, the extent of the responsibility of the creators of site-based work to provide a parity of experience for differently abled audience members, and trust and consent in the interactions between the performer and the participant, how to build trust, and what happens when that line is crossed. Drawing on their combined vast experience of site-based work, as both creators and audience members, many ideas and solutions are proposed, and further questions identified.

The editors of this special section are very grateful to the contributors whose insightful and exciting work have allowed the conversation around site-based theatre to flourish. It is clear from the variety of the performances and productions discussed in the case studies and in the curated discussion and from the multiple theoretical frameworks employed throughout the articles that site-based work continues to challenge our understanding of theatre, performance, and audience. Our hope is that these articles and conversations will provide a basis for continued analysis and thoughtful, informed theatremaking.

Notes

1. Mike Pearson and Michael Shanks, *Theatre/Archaeology* (London: Routledge, 2001), 23.
2. See Adam Alston, *Beyond Immersive Theatre* (London: Palgrave Macmillan, 2016); Anna Birch and Joanne Tompkins, *Performing Site-Specific Theatre* (London: Palgrave Macmillan, 2012); Josephine Machon, *Immersive Theatre, Intimacy and Immediacy in Contemporary Performance* (London: Palgrave Macmillan, 2013); Mike Pearson, *Site-Specific Performance* (London: Palgrave Macmillan, 2010); Gareth White, *Audience Participation in Theatre: Aesthetics of the Invitation* (London: Palgrave Macmillan, 2013). Fiona Wilke, "Mapping the Terrain: A Survey of Site-Specific Theatre in Britain," in *New Theatre Quarterly* 18, no. 2 (May 2002).
3. Bertie Ferdman, *Off Sites: Contemporary Performance Beyond Site-Specific* (Carbondale: Southern Illinois University Press, 2018), 10–11.
4. Helen Freshwater, *Theatre & Audience* (London: Palgrave Macmillan, 2009), 2.
5. Victoria Hunter, "Experiencing Space: The Implications for Site-Specific Dance Performance," in *Contemporary Choreography: A Critical Reader*, eds. Jo Butterworth and Liesbeth Wildschut (London: Routledge, 2009), 399.
6. Miwon Kwon, "One Place after Another: Notes on Site-Specificity," in *October* 80 (Spring 1997) 86, accessed September 30, 2018: http://links.jstor.org/sici?sici=0162-2870%28199721%2980%3C85%3AOPAANO%3E2.0.CO%3B2-I.
7. Wilke, "Mapping the Terrain," 150.
8. Pearson, *Site-Specific Performance*, 5.
9. Robert Irwin, *Being and Circumstance: Notes Toward a Conditional Art* (Larkspur Landing, CA: Lapis, 1985). Quoted in Ferdman, *Off Sites*, 11.
10. Wilke, "Mapping the Terrain," 150.
11. Gareth White, "On Immersive Theatre," in *Theatre Research International* 37, no. 1 (September 2012): 223.
12. Fiona Wilke, "The Production of 'Site': Site-Based Theatre," in *Contemporary British and Irish Drama*, eds. N. Holdsworth and M. Luckhurt, 100–101 (Oxford: Blackwell, 2008), quoted in Ferdman, *Off Sites*.
13. Josephine Machon, "Watching, Attending, *Sense*-Making: Spectatorship in Immersive Theatres," *Journal of Contemporary Drama in English* 4, no. 1 (2016): 35–36.
14. Machon, "Watching, Attending, *Sense*-Making," 36–37.
15. Miwon Kwon, *One Place after Another: Site-Specific Art and Locational Identity* (Cambridge, MA: MIT Press, 2004), 1–2, quoted in Andrew Filmer, "*Coriolan/us* and the Limits of 'Immersive'" in *Reframing Immersive Theatre: The Politics and Pragmatics of Participatory Performance*, ed. James Frieze (London: Palgrave Macmillan, 2016) 289–302.
16. Filmer, "*Coriolan/us* and the Limits of 'Immersive'" in *Reframing Immersive Theatre*, 296–97.
17. Francis Babbage, "Active Audiences: Spectatorship as Research Practice," in *Studies in Theatre and Performance* 36, no. 1 (2016): 48–51.

Becoming the Mob

Mike Brookes and Mike Pearson's *Coriolan/us*

—PENELOPE COLE

People milling about, chatting. Drizzly rain. The bang of port-o-potty doors. The rustle of paper. Smells of beer, wet earth, water. Huge blue doors. More people. Headphones? Laughter. Excitement. Disquiet. Wonder. Brrrr. And then, pushing from behind, WHAT? A horn honking, WHERE? Swiveling our heads to see . . . a Van?! driving through the assembled masses? OUT OF THE WAY! Blue doors sliding open, visions of a throng of people on movie screens football fields away. That's US! And then we're in. The "play" has begun.

Hangar 858, RAF St. Athan, in the Vale of Glamorgan, Wales, was the site of Mike Brookes and Mike Pearson's 2012 production *Coriolan/us*, produced by the National Theatre Wales in association with the Royal Shakespeare Company, commissioned for the World Shakespeare Festival. A conflation of Shakespeare's *Coriolanus* and Brecht's adaptation titled *Coriolan*, the action of the play (both dramatic and physical) is located predominantly in public spaces replete with crowds of supporters and/or detractors. From the beginning, the principle concept driving the production was the mobs embedded in the architecture of the two texts, which informed the scale and scope of the site and, in turn, determined the use of multimedia within the production. In this article, I explore how the aircraft hangar and installed scenic elements as well as the collective movement through the space by the audience/viewers and the performers, combined with projected images and sound piped through headphones, invited us to reimagine our (the audience/viewers') place and identity in Pearson and Brookes's world of *Coriolan/us*.[1]

The crowds of people prominent in both Shakespeare's original text, appearing in twenty-five out of twenty-nine scenes, and Brecht's adaptation, wherein "the people" are the focus of the action, spurred Brookes and Pearson's interest in the plays. In the *Coriolan/us* program, Mike Brookes explains how this central image of the masses influenced the production. "In our imaginings, from the inception of this work, *Coriolan/us* was always going to unfold amongst a crowd, as it moved and flowed around the open public space of this event."[2] Mike Pearson, in his article "National Theatre of Wales's *Coriolan/us*: A 'Live Film,'" noted how crowded the world of Shakespeare's *Coriolanus* is and remarked on the multiplicity of generalized public locations (battlefields, streets, marketplaces, and the like) required by the text.[3] Based on these and other features found in the texts of the plays, Pearson recounts that the "decision was made . . . to regard the audience from time to time and unwittingly perhaps, as citizens, army, bystanders, film extras, etc., and to achieve the production . . . with only two Citizens and two Tribunes . . . No massed supernumeraries, no rioters, no foot soldiers to hinder the momentum of the events."[4] Thus, the audience/viewers were, from the first, cast in the role of the populace of Rome, the body politic, citizens, soldiers, and rioters, to occupy, inhabit, and define the public spaces within and upon which the action takes place.

Additionally, the movement of these multitudes figured in the imagining of the production. In the program notes, Brookes articulates a dynamic movement flowing through an open space, "act following act, one then leading another, the rolling consequences of our choices and reactions accumulating as they ripple on through the body and structure of a social forum **constituted by all those present**" (emphasis mine).[5] This social forum, the various peoples of ancient Rome, was to be created, in theory and in practice, in large part by the choices in movement the audience/viewers made as they negotiated the site, physically, mentally, and emotionally, in response to the production choices, the complex choreography of the performers, and the architecture of the aircraft hangar.

To accommodate the flowing movement of the imagined crowds of Rome as well as the scope of the action of the play, Brookes and Pearson sought a large, wide-open space that could be easily traversed. Brookes states, "It was always going to happen to scale. A large open place where that crowd was free to gather and move as it needed to. Where scenes and incidents could be placed, constructed, and walked to—finding themselves within a 'field' of activity where ideas and individuals might meet and locate themselves in actuality."[6]

In May 2012, the National Theatre Wales announced that the location of *Coriolan/us* would be a disused, decommissioned World War II aircraft hangar in St. Athan, about sixteen miles west of Cardiff, a choice that Patrick Primavesi contends is "the most important decision made by Pearson and Brookes"[7] in regard to this production. Brookes declared, "Walking into Hangar 858 for the first time . . . it was immediately clear that here was a building that all these intentions and aspirations might actually be possible."[8] Indeed, the specific architecture and location of this hangar greatly influenced the realization of the imaginings of Brookes, Pearson, and their creative team in the creation of *Coriolan/us*. Pearson writes, "In developing the production's dramaturgy and scenography . . . we worked from both the text and the site, towards the creation of a theatre machine."[9] Brookes asserts that this "vast open space . . . provided us with both a place to realize this work, and also a **context** within which we can locate it. And **all the formal and structural details of *Coriolan/us* have developed and taken shape specifically within that context**" (emphasis mine).[10]

For these theatremakers, the vastness, and emptiness, of the aircraft hangar inspired their responses to the texts and the ideas contained within, affecting the artistic choices they made in the conceptualization and realization of *Coriolan/us*. Furthermore, the selection of Hanger 858 and the given physical, cultural, and social contexts contained within fostered their conceptualization by locating the narrative within a specific and unique site, shaping both the pragmatic and aesthetic choices that were ultimately made.

Practically, the sheer size of the physical space, ninety meters by fifty meters, ensured there was more than enough room for the 350 people who attended each performance to move about, coalesce, and disperse as the situation, action, and their own reactions warranted. The open, smooth surfaces, created to withstand the weight of aircraft, allowed the team to use various vehicles, such as vans and cars, as the performers moved from locale to locale, creating an even greater sense of distance within the hangar that contained the forums and villas of Rome, the battlefield between Rome and Antium, and Antium itself. The use of the vehicles, which drove at a good clip through the space around and through the crowds, heightened the sense of movement that Brookes envisioned and complicated the choices the viewers made. The ten-second echo of the hangar, created by the magnitude of the space and the preponderance of concrete surfaces, necessitated the use of headphones to ensure the viewers heard the actors and allowed for a focus on the language of the play. The hard, unforgiving concrete floor led to the decision to provide 150 chairs for those who might need a place to sit, which, in turn, led to some viewers choosing to sit and watch the action unfold on the screens from a distance. These practical decisions solved challenges posed by the site and, also, had very real aesthetic consequences.

I was fortunate to attend two different performances of *Coriolan/us*, experiencing the production with a different set of contexts and expectations each evening. Some responses remained constant, while others radically shifted, primarily because of my personal choices regarding when, where, and how to engage with the actors, action, site, and fellow viewers, choices that were influenced in part by my previous experiences with site-based work as well as by my first encounter with this production. Our entrance into the hangar was a startling moment for me both evenings. Upon entering the interior of the hangar as an audience member, my initial impressions were of an unending expanse of curved ceiling that emphasized our insignificance and aloneness. The rapid shift from jovial crowd of theatregoers socializing under the open sky, each in our socially comfortable bubbles, to the unexpected, and a bit frightening, crush of the mob as the van's movement compressed us together through a narrow opening, and then to our expulsion into this dark, immense, shadowed, cold, forbidding, foreign, virtually empty space was breathtaking and disorienting. Separated from those we came with, we had to make instant decisions; where to go, where to look, what to listen to, how fast to move, and when to stop. The massive movie screens at the far end of the hangar visually dominated the expansive space that was horizontally bisected by a corridor constructed of two walls of concrete blocks with an opening in the middle. Three caravans in opposing corners of the hangar, a collection of orange, plastic, institutional chairs, and vertical, fluorescent floor lights completed the few scenic installations we could immediately identify. The hangar itself was an indomitable presence: ominous, cold, sparsely occupied, full of shadows, hard edges, and rough textures, and devoid of color.

In these opening moments of transition from outside to inside, theatregoer to viewer, observer to participant, contexts altered quickly. The visceral nature of our entrance into the hangar and the immediacy of the images on the screens fused with the voices of the performers coming through our headphones and propelled us with great urgency into this new world. The rapid shifting and layering of contexts contributed to this sense of urgency and immediacy as we were forced to process a lot of information literally on our feet, in motion. The relentless, quickly changing rhythm of the production was established in these very first moments, as we, as theatregoers, were shocked into movement, shifted into a state of tension, and placed on high alert as we sought to make sense of what was expected of us, locate who was talking, and try to catch our breath.

Our immersion into this unfamiliar and shadowed world was achieved through multiple means, not the least of which was the need to move our bodies. Rose Biggins writes of "immersion as a cognitive phenomenon defined by high engagement, emotional investment, rapt attention, sensory stimulation, emotion, empathy or make-believe."[11] The activity of needing to move to get out of the way of moving vehicles and other theatregoers, monitoring the livestreamed multimedia, and negotiating a foreign site created this engagement and attention, stimulating our senses, emotions, and sense of make-believe. As lost and overwhelmed as we might have been in the vastness of the hangar and the sea of contexts, production elements such as the voices of the performers in our headphones, the tactile, aural, and olfactory reality of the van, the interplay of shadow and light, the images on the screens and, finally, our fellow audience/viewers framed and focused our experience. Each of these facets served as an access point through which we organized ourselves, discovered where to stand, and began to understand ourselves to be part of the citizenry of this world. Biggins suggests, "A more specific phrase for make-believe is *conceptual blending*, a theory concerned with the way an audience member is able to hold multiple truths or images in her mind."[12] Quoting Bruce MacConachie, she continues, "'Spectators also engage in conceptual integration,'[13] blending an actor's performance with their own concepts, which might include the space, their relationship to the actor or memories . . . of earlier theatrical experiences."[14] Our jarring, physical entrance into the world of *Coriolan/us* found us juggling a variety of ideas and images, sorting through each while in motion, bringing our expectations and previous experiences together with the information we gathered upon entering, and blending these concepts to find our focal point: the opening dialogue of the play spoken by First Citizen and Second Citizen.

In the opening scene, the two rabble-rousing citizens jump out of the van they have just driven through the throngs to address the crowd pointedly, pacing through the assembling audience/viewers and throwing their arms around individual members of the mob. Their movement around the van, as well as through the middle of the throng, created a shared public space within which we all were invited to perform. They behaved as though we had always been there, part of this city: citizens suffering the effects of famine and bad government right alongside them. Assuming our sympathy with them in this struggle, these two rumpled, earnest, forthright citizens encourage us to follow them into action.

In these opening moments of *Coriolan/us*, we, the audience/viewers, immediately became a mob, in this instance, the lower-class inhabitants and citizens of Rome. The imminent threat of being run over jostled us out of our pre-show anticipation and socializing into necessary action. Our new collective identity was created through the shared experience of moving as a mob to successfully enter the hangar, headphones that ensured each viewer heard the performers in a uniform sonic mix, and the assumption by the characters, through word and interaction, that we were peers complicit in the action of the play. Furthermore, all the action was captured by live-feed video cameras, both handheld and aerial, that projected our image as a crowd of concerned faces and moving bodies as we entered the hangar. Seeing ourselves as a moving mass immediately projected us into the role(s) we were to assume as the evening unfolded. Continuing to see ourselves as an assembled crowd side by side with the individual actors for the entirety of the event constantly reminded us of our role(s) and the performative nature of our actions. And finally, the massive scale of the site, Hangar 858, allowed the audience/viewers the space to perform "the replication of the performative phenomena of the city: ceremonial entries, victory parades, street demonstrations and riots,"[15] as needed, as the events of the play unfolded.

It was not only the site and the sparse scenic installations but also the human-embodied activity engaged in within the space that defined the play's locations—namely, Rome, Antium, battlefield, or forum—and opened a space within which we performed as a mob. Human activity assumes, assigns, and creates meaning. Therefore, "site . . . becomes part of a 'cultural landscape' that accounts for human interaction in, through and around geographical space."[16] Negotiating the geographical space of the hangar, following the performers, moving from shadows to areas of light, scattering in front of the moving vehicles, crowding together to peer into the caravans, and so on built our knowledge of the space and the specific locales assigned to the space (i.e., Rome was the front half of the hangar and Antium was on the other side of the concrete block corridor), thereby creating a new and unique cultural landscape informing us of who and what we were performing and why. Patrick Primavesi asserts, "*Coriolanus* is a play about politics as performance, about the public itself as a scene and a theatre, moving through the city of Rome. This movement includes the experience of performing and of becoming a spectacle, but also of becoming a spectator, a witness, and a possible participant."[17]

At moments throughout the performance, we, the audience/viewers, were all these things—spectators, witnesses, and participants—our roles determined largely by our responses to the words and actions of the performers, our comfort level within the physical space of the hangar, and the choices we made in terms of proximity, visual engagement, and movement.

As we came to understand our position and to assemble around the citizen's van for the opening scene, each vying for an acceptable and comfortable view, our attention was then free to begin to make more sense out of the site in which we found ourselves and to juggle the multiplicity of contexts with which we were confronted within that site. Mike Pearson contends in his article "Haunted House: Staging *The Persians* with the British Army" that site is not ahistorical. The copresence of the historical significance and current use (or disuse) of site and the interpenetration of the production serve "to render both palpable."[18]

Related to the previously discussed idea of conceptual blending, copresence requires audience members to integrate their disparate knowledge of site and spatial organization to come to a new understanding of the experience. The aircraft hangar, in its overwhelming, unforgiving presence, was both a concrete object and an almost neutral site whereupon the conflicts and political upheavals of Rome were enacted.

Moreover, as in *The Persians*, wherein Brookes and Pearson neither directly acknowledged nor disavowed the historicity of the site, Hangar 858 was not specifically referenced; no direct allusion to the former use of the site existed in any way. In the Rome and Antium of *Coriolan/us*, the former use as well as the current disuse of the aircraft hangar existed, informed our experience, but was not pointed to. Nor was the site conceptually forced into an allegorical role analogous to a specific event or political conflict. The hangar was essentially emptied of those material things that had formerly identified it and therefore was rendered purposeless, yet the hangar carried echoes of the past, a life at/of war, and armed conflict. The current disuse could suggest either the futility or success of those martial activities; impermanence and the fleeting nature of human activity; or contest legacy, a challenge to Coriolanus's authority and the authority of the Roman politicians. These are a few of the thematic elements revealed through the dynamic interaction of the text and the movement of the audience/viewers and performers throughout the hangar. Additionally, the interpenetration of the production, including the scenic and multimedia elements, the text, the performers and technicians, and the audience/viewers remade and reused the site as a frame for a specific narrative. These multiple contexts, or copresences (former use, disuse, reuse), forced us to engage on many different levels with the site: at a distance, hearing the echoes of soldiers past; in the present, where the disused state of the site enhanced and exposed the themes of the production; and in the moment, as we negotiated the intricate choreography of the space while allowing the soundtrack of composed music and performers' voices to invite us into this embodied story.

The tension between distance and immediacy informed this entire production. In the opening moments, we were compelled into a physical intimacy with our fellow theatregoers to safely enter the hangar and then expelled into the immensity of the hangar and the world of the play, putting us at a greater distance from each other, a distance we needed to negotiate as the opening spoken scene of the play began. This sequence of intimacy and distancing was played out over and over throughout the performance. Just as we would establish ourselves in an acceptable relationship to one another and the performers, a vehicle would drive up to, through, or away from us, the actors would run straight at

Figure 1. Coriolanus (Richard Lynch, on tires) First and Second Citizens (John Rowley and Gerald Tyler). Photo: Mark Douet/National Theatre Wales.

us, or the lights would go dark, thus splintering our newfound order and again spurring us into physical action, into making choices, in an attempt to reestablish and redefine ourselves in relation to the performers, the site, the story, and each other. The rapidly shifting contexts that marked the opening sequence of the production continued unabated with each scene change.

Even within scenes, we were often challenged to move and interact. In act 2, scene 3, in which Coriolanus asks for the support of the people as their consul, the citizen's van is again the loci of the action, as the scene opens with First Citizen and Second Citizen setting up for Coriolanus's appearance before the citizens of Rome. As the citizens discuss how to question Coriolanus and how to involve the assembling people, Menenius and Coriolanus are situated in the midst of the crowd discussing how Coriolanus should address the citizens of Rome. We find ourselves eavesdropping on a private interchange at the same time as we are part of the masses waiting for the reluctant would-be politician to appear. The physical presence of Menenius and Coriolanus in the milling mob engages those nearby their exchange in the interaction, and as they move to the waiting speaking place, all of us have to move to get out of their way, sending ripples of movement through the crowd.

The two parts of this scene are also intertwined through the live-feed video on the screens. Depending on where each viewer is located, their experience of this scene involves differing contexts. Those nearer to the Citizens are urged to come close, to physically define a space within which a public speech will be given and received. Those near to Menenius and Coriolanus are privy to Coriolanus's contempt for the masses of Rome (us), his pride, and his great reluctance to ask anything of these people he is petitioning and whom he deems lesser than himself. We all can see both sides of these interchanges on the screens, and we, the mob, figure prominently in both views. Again, the media is reinforcing our identity as a unit, the citizens of Rome. Additionally, our relative proximity to the live action and our view of the close-ups and long shots of the live-feed video reinforce the effect of distance versus immediacy, keeping us moving between the *experience* of the scene and the *analysis* of the scene.

Moreover, a tension is exposed between anonymity and public recognition, a prominent theme in this scene and in Coriolanus's life. Regardless of our physical proximity and visual access to the scene, the words spoken by all the performers are uniformly experienced by the viewers through our headphones, creating a very interesting paradox of closeness versus distance. The intimacy of the voices speaking directly into our ears in contrast to where we are physically in the space links us to each character and grounds us in the action of the play. In addition, the public nature of the play's action is emphasized, as we can hear, very intimately, private interactions that as a crowd we are not supposed to hear. This eavesdropping affects our choices in the scene, inflecting our movement when we are urged to directly interact with (close in on and/or walk by and touch) the blindfolded Coriolanus while he is on the speaking platform—in this case a pile of tires (figure 1).

The use of moving vehicles and the immobile caravans, which imply movement and impermanence, as well as the burned-out cars we have discovered in the concrete block corridor, reinforce the importance of movement to the production. Highlighting the public nature of the action of the play, the moving vehicles create a context of open spaces, boundless and distant. The few private scenes involving Coriolanus and his family are played out in the caravans, which ultimately are not private, as we can see all the interactions either on the video screens or through the windows and door of the caravan, emphasizing that there is nowhere to run and nowhere to rest in this seemingly infinite space. The placement of the caravans in the extreme corners of the hangar required the actors and the mob to traverse huge distances at the beginning of each of these more private scenes as well as during transitions to the next location and moment of action. The physical energy expended by the viewer/participants in these transitions was often determined by the actors, who moved alternately with confidence, stealth, anger, or fear between interactions and locales.

Coriolanus's banishment from Rome and his defection to the Volscians both play out within the confines of vehicles: the citizens' van in the first instance and the interior of a sedan in the second. Again, we watch, peering through the windows and doors of the vehicles and/or on the screens, all the while hearing most intimately the arguments set forth by the characters via our headphones. The enclosed environment of the vehicles offers an illusion of intimacy and privacy for the characters, which is shattered by the cameras and audio mix. However, the demonstrated mobility of the van and cars suggests that escape/change could be imminent, illustrated forcefully the moment the newly banished Coriolanus bursts from the back of the van, blaming us, the citizenry, for his expulsion. These "interior" scenes are moments of arrested movement but are certainly not moments of relaxation.

The visceral nature of movement created an immediacy of response that was constantly being challenged by the distancing effect of seeing the action unfold on the screens, which in turn was complicated by a physical intimacy or distance between the performers and other audience/viewers. This was problematized by the use of headphones, which offered an intimate and immediate connection to the performers' voices, all the while providing us with a musical soundtrack to the event. The accretion of these contexts created the rhythm and flow of the action. Our own choices of where, when, and how to move based on these multiple contexts informed and framed our experience. As Peter Primavesi states: "*Coriolan/us* balances the sublime elements of size, disruption, tragic pathos, failure and loss of control with rather playful and relational elements allowing for a certain sense of freedom in self-positioning as a spectator. In confronting the sublime elements of the text and the space with the interplay of individual movement and behaviour, the audience starts its own performance, crossing the space of dramatic conflict by participating in a casual and dispersed choreography."[19]

While my experience at the beginning of the performance was very similar both evenings, my experience of the battle between the forces of Rome and Antium changed dramatically from my first engagement with the production to my second (figure 2). My choice the first night to linger behind the crowd and continue to watch inside a caravan after a scene officially ended meant that I missed the battle. I couldn't find a place to see the action live, as opposed to mediated on the screen, because the conflict was confined to the narrow, two-and-a-half-meter corridor made by the concrete block walls in the center of the hangar. The

Figure 2. *Coriolan/us*. The Battle. Photo: Mark Douet/National Theatre Wales.

next evening, knowing what was coming, I chose not to follow the crowd to the bright, vertical fluorescent lights at one end of the concrete block corridor that switched on following the caravan scene and instead to go to the darker end of the corridor. I then found myself traversing the darkened hallway as performers jumped off the burned-out cars and lights flickered as they moved in front of them, unable to see the video screens while the soundtrack and voices of the battle raged in my ears. That evening, I was in the middle of the fighting, unsure of what was going to happen next, immersed directly in the moment, unable to get away. As my breathing quickened, my eyes strained for clues, and my heart started to race, I found myself wanting to stop and stand still, to fade into the concrete wall, or to race ahead and extricate myself from this danger-filled, shadowed environment. I was frightened.

In speaking about audience participation and immersion, Gareth White suggests that the term "immersive" refers not only to the spatial arrangement of the environment but also to a visceral experience of that event. He writes, "The suggestion of being inside that comes with the idea of the immersive has resonances with the experience of being able to take action within the work, and with the changed point of view that is gained through the experience that I suggest are the special characteristics of audience participation. To be inside the work, not just inside its physical and temporal space but inside it as an aesthetic, affective, phenomenological entity gives a different aspect to the idea of a point of view, and of action."[20] The aftereffects of this experiential, visceral inclusion in the battle, generated by my own choice, then made me much more engaged and invested in the rest of the story. I celebrated my safe emergence from the battle. I was appalled by the ferocity of the fighting. I was determined to find a secure place in this world, which was rapidly spinning out of control. I reengaged with the mob, finding safety in numbers, less willing now to go it alone. I found no release in the ultimate death of Coriolanus, as it represented more of the violence I had experienced. While my participation and immersion in this moment were solely mine and my presence in the corridor didn't change the course of the story, my point of view was radically changed, and by viewing myself as an "aesthetic, affective, phenomenological entity," my identity as an active and affected citizen of Rome was solidified.

Much of the brilliance of this production lies with Brookes and Pearson's choice, even as we were deliberately cast in the role of the mob, to allow us to rattle around the space on our own, making our own choices. We learned to dance within the intricate choreography of the performers and their vehicles, following, watching, and engaging according to our own impulses and circumstances. Our bodies were continually engaged as we chose how to move through the site and, as Brookes envisioned, found ourselves "within a 'field' of activity where ideas and individuals might meet and locate themselves in actuality."[21] Brooks and Pearson provided multiple ways by which the audience/participants could engage and disengage. Their creative team created a sense of intimacy that was continually challenged and that ultimately led to unique, inspiring, and thought-provoking encounters that exposed the play *Coriolanus* in a new and contemporary light wherein I played a crucial role in the telling of the story.

Notes

1. Additional design by Simon Banham and soundtrack composed by John Hardy.
2. Mike Brookes, "Shaping *Coriolan/us* in program, *Coriolanus*" (National Theatre Wales, 2012), np.
3. Mike Pearson, "National Theatre Wales *Coriolan/us*: A 'Live' Film," in *Experiencing Liveness in Contemporary Performance*, ed. Matthew Reason and Anja Mølle Lindelof, 284–88, 285 (New York: Routledge, 2016).
4. Pearson, "National Theatre Wales *Coriolan/us*," 285.
5. Brookes, "Shaping *Coriolan/us* in program, *Coriolanus*."
6. Brookes, "Shaping *Coriolan/us* in program, *Coriolanus*."
7. Patrick Primavesi, "Performing the Audience: The Politics of Relation and Participation

in *Coriolanus*," in *International Politics and Performance: Critical Aesthetics and Creative Practice*, ed. Jenny Edkins and Adrian Kear, 161–78, 172 (New York: Routledge, 2013).

8. Brookes, "Shaping *Coriolan/us* in program, *Coriolanus*."
9. Pearson, "National Theatre Wales *Coriolan/us*," 284.
10. Brookes, "Shaping *Coriolan/us* in program, *Coriolanus*."
11. Rose Biggins, *Immersive Theatre and Audience Experience: Space, Game and Story in the Work of Punchdrunk* (London, Palgrave Macmillan, 2017), 179.
12. Biggins, *Immersive Theatre and Audience Experience*, 179.
13. Bruce MacConachie, *Theatre & Mind* (London: Palgrave Macmillan, 2013) 23, Quoted in Biggins, *Immersive Theatre and Audience Experience.*
14. Biggins, *Immersive Theatre and Audience Experience*, 179.
15. Pearson, "National Theatre Wales *Coriolan/us*," 286.
16. Blair and Truscott, 1989, quoted in *Performing Site-Specific Theatre: Politics, Place, Practice*, edited by Anna Birch and Joanna Tompkins (London: Palgrave Macmillan, 2012), 5.
17. Primavesi, "Performing the Audience," 165.
18. Mike Pearson, "Haunted House: Staging *The Persians* with the British Army," in *Performing Site-Specific Theatre: Politics, Place, Practice*, ed. Anna Birch and Joanna Tompkins, 69–83, 83 (London: Palgrave Macmillan, 2012).
19. Primavesi, "Performing the Audience," 2013.
20. Gareth White, *Audience Participation in Theatre: Aesthetics of the Invitation* (London: Palgrave MacMillan, 2013), 16–17.
21. Brookes, "Shaping *Coriolan/us* in program, *Coriolanus*."

A Walk in the Park

David Levine's *Private Moment* and Ethical Participation in Site-Based Performance

—SEAN BARTLEY

I: Context (*Cruel Intentions*)

Two young women share a picnic along the Gapstow Bridge in Central Park on a warm Sunday afternoon. Kathryn, dressed in a chic black suit, oversize sunglasses, and a massive black sunhat, brushes the hair of Cecile, dressed in pastels with a cardigan tied across her shoulders. Cecile is stretched across the picnic blanket on her side and is propped up on her elbow; she munches on a grape. When their conversation turns to a mutual admirer, Kathryn abruptly jerks her confidant's hair back. When Cecile admits she has "never even got to first base with a guy," Kathryn suggests they practice kissing on each other. After a relatively tame smooch with eyes closed, Kathryn removes her sunglasses, looks directly into Cecile's eyes, and utters the movie's most famous line: "Ok, let's try it again. Only this time, I'm going to stick my tongue in your mouth. And when I do that, I want you to massage my tongue with yours. And that's what first base is."

Many members of Generation X will immediately recognize this iconic kissing scene, first performed by Sarah Michelle Gellar and Selma Blair, from the 1999 pulpy teen drama *Cruel Intentions*. When the scene was shot for the film, this grassy section of Central Park, nestled alongside the Pond and Bird Sanctuary, was closed to the public and populated with a handful of extras in the distance. But when it reappeared in David Levine's *Private Moment*, which ran on Saturday and Sunday afternoons for six weeks during the summer of 2015, dozens of everyday park-goers surrounded the action, largely unaware that two actors were reperforming the *Cruel Intentions* scene (figure 1). On the Sunday afternoon I attended, more than fifty picnickers and sunbathers shared the small

Figure 1. Audience members watch a *Private Moment* scene. Photo courtesy of David Levine.

section of park with the kissing women. One couple set up their towels and relaxed in the sun less than fifteen feet away. Hundreds more passed the scene on a nearby concrete walkway in the few minutes I spent watching. Besides the two actresses, only four people seemed cognizant that a self-conscious theatrical event was taking place on the picnic blanket: myself and three others standing and watching the scene from a safe distance, clutching our programs, and applauding politely, if discretely, at the completion of the scene.

Commissioned by the Central Park Conservancy and curated by Creative Time as a part of *Drifting in Daylight*, a series of public art projects at various locations in the park, *Private Moment*, according to its program description, "takes iconic Central Park movie scenes and infiltrates them back into their original locations, quietly transforming the park into a backdrop where any given moment could be read as a film."[1] Their verb "infiltrates" suggests a furtive, secret process of transformation. Performers repeat these site-based scenes on continuous loops for six hours. Though Levine had hundreds of major-release films with Central Park scenes to choose from, *Private Moment* features just eight: *Bullets over Broadway* (1994), *The Royal Tenenbaums* (2001), *Marathon Man* (1976), *Symbiopsychotaxiplasm* (1968), *The Out-of-Towners* (1970), *Six Degrees of Separation* (1993), *Portrait of Jennie* (1948), and, finally, *Cruel Intentions* (1999). A map of the park highlighted the scenes inside the *Drifting in Daylight* program and labeled them "A" through "H" moving from north to south. According to my activity tracker, I walked more than seven miles to see all eight scenes in one afternoon. In each location, the phenomenon I noticed at the *Cruel Intentions* picnic held: If there were any audience members at all searching out and watching the scenes, aware that Levine had staged these dialogues for their enjoyment, they were dwarfed by the number of everyday park-goers who, if they noticed these encounters at all, read them as part of just another normal day in Central Park.

This essay seeks to document the ethical and spatial challenges that Levine's *Private Moment* and other contemporary site-based works present for audiences, scholars, and historians. First, I'll explore the ways that *Private Moment* recontextualizes Central Park and invites individual audience members to do the same. Second, I'll theorize how site-based works like *Private Moment* challenge audiences to explore ethical action by moving through space. Finally, borrowing from Jacques Rancière's concept of "dissensus," I'll propose the possible use of contemporary site-based practices to invite reexploration of public space and reorientation of the individual to their social and spatial surroundings.

Though this study will focus on *Private Moment*, let me briefly contextualize it by introducing some of the other pieces that constituted *Drifting in Daylight*. In *Sunset (Central Park)*, Spencer Finch re-created the orange and red hues of a sunset over the park that he had painted through the unique medium of soft-serve ice cream cones, dispensed to passersby for free from a cheery truck. Alicia Framis's *Cartas at Cielo*, an enormous reflective ball decorated with postcards and mail slots, invited park-goers to write and send messages to "those who have no earthbound address."[2] With *The Lamppost Weavers*, Nina Katchadourian suspended a series of unusual bird nests on street lamps along North End West Drive, juxtaposing natural nesting materials with manmade items such as high-top sneakers and string.[3] The *Drifting in Daylight* project inserted new aesthetic objects and sensory elements into the experience of a weekend stroll through the park, encouraging tourists and New Yorkers alike to lose themselves along the path of performances and objects strung through the park.

This process of losing oneself, for Michel de Certeau, is an inherently ambulatory one. In his "Walking in the City" chapter of *The Practice of Everyday Life*, he noted the ways that charting a walk through New York City on a map might downplay the agency the individual takes in the sensory particulars of that journey: "The operations of walking can be traced on city maps in such a way as to transcribe their paths (here well-trodden, there very faint) and their trajectories (going this way and not that). But these thick or thin lines only refer, like words, to the absence of what has passed by. Survey of routes miss what was: the act itself of passing by."[4] *Private Moment* offers a map but no prescribed paths or trajectories for the individual audience member to take. The individual explores their agency in the theatrical event by moving and by noting the experiential effects of the trip. Their ambulatory "passing by," as Certeau notes, becomes "the act itself."

Central Park is highly citational. An individual can explore the eight-hundred-plus acres of the park much like a Hollywood backlot tour, noting the settings for famous film, television, and music video scenes at nearly every corner.[5] According to *Drifting in Daylight* cocurator Cara Starke, "Central Park is like a big screen. It's primed for viewing and being viewed. It also acts like a mnemonic device: So many of the park's locations are recognizable, that it's hard to walk through without triggering a memory. And it's fun to add to that by bringing work that people will remember."[6] Even though I had never been to Central Park before and was ostensibly following the *Private Moment* map to the eight specified sites, I found myself constantly stopping, rerouting, and exploring spots that felt eerily familiar from other films. Strolling past Bow Bridge, I half expected to see Spider-Man, disguised as mild-mannered Peter Parker, wooing Mary Jane. A footpath near Bethesda Terrace made me linger, slowly realizing this was where the titular couple in *When Harry Met Sally* shared a scene among the autumn leaves. Once I had reached the Terrace and Bethesda Fountain, the references to final film sequences began to pile on top of one another. This was where Kevin McAllister had outsmarted the Sticky Bandits in *Home Alone 2: Lost in New York*; where Prior Walter faced the camera and wished the audience more life in *Angels in America*; and where the strapping superheroes of *The Avengers* met before going their separate ways at the end of their adventure. If I were a different age (or if I had simply grown up with a different set of movies replayed on Saturday morning television), I might have had a completely different set of connections and references, searching for Gordon Gecko from *Wall Street* in the Sheep Meadow or remembering *Breakfast at Tiffany's* as I walked past the Bandstand.

When crafting *Private Moment*, David Levine negotiated the highly personal ways in which individual audience members as ambulatory agents frame this vast film set for themselves, striking a balance between historical eras, genres, and relationships that might speak to diverse experiences in different audience members among the scenes he included. While the map and the looping scenes he presents do recontextualize the space and focus the attention of the audience members, they can do so only in broad strokes. Too many factors rest outside the director's control. Individual audience members' familiarity with and impressions of each film shape the narratives they create. When I approached the conversations from *Cruel Intentions* and *The Royal Tenenbaums*, I paid less attention to the familiar dialogue and compared the actors in the park to the well-known Hollywood celebrities who originated the roles. I looked incredulously at the park-goers around me, wondering why they hadn't picked up on the references yet. "She's wearing the Sarah Michelle Gellar hat! He's twirling the umbrella just like Gene Hackman!" I mused to myself. While watching *Symbiopsychotaxiplasm* or *Portrait of Jennie*, which I knew only as important works from film history, I moved in closer, attempting to catch every word and to glean the nature of the characters' relationships.

When I was less familiar with a film on the program, I often went through a process of trial and error trying to locate the actors. Could this smartly dressed couple in the Conservatory Garden be the characters from Woody Allen's *Bullets over Broadway*? Which of the many joggers running around the reservoir is playing Babe, Dustin Hoffman's character in *Marathon Man*? Even the other public art projects that constituted *Drifting in Daylight* invited filmic possibilities. When I walked past Ragnar Kjartansson's *S.S. Hangover*, in which a brass sextet on a wooden boat played loudly and circled the Harlem Meer, I quickly scanned my *Private Moment* map, certain I'd stumbled upon a scene from some obscure Wes Anderson film. The experience of moving through *Private Moment* continually invited me to consider two questions. When, as I explored my ambulatory agency by moving through the park at my own pace, I encountered a notable or exceptional exchange that was not on Creative Time's map, I wondered: "How on earth is this *not* a movie?" When I successfully found one of Levine's eight scenes, I marveled and asked, "How on earth is everyone around me missing this reference?"

The frequent contextual clues that Levine provides and the extreme attention to replicating physical detail that his actors achieve reinforced my sense of "being in on the joke." This feeling helped me understand myself as an agent, capable of connecting scenes spread across miles of urban space and decades of film history into a cohesive performance through my ambulatory choices. The scenes themselves are filled with anachronistic language and references. As he frets about his play, David, the protagonist from *Bullets over Broadway*, calls his own dialogue "turgid."[7] The young lovers from *The Out-of-Towners* search for a Travelers Aid Society office. Outdated costume pieces abound in *Bullets over Broadway* (1920s), *Six Degrees of Separation* (1990s) and *The Out-of-Towners* (1960s). In perhaps the most striking example, the young artist at the center of *Portrait of Jennie*, dressed in Depression-era suit and overcoat, chats with a young woman dressed from the end of the nineteenth century. Remarking at how quickly New Yorkers dismissed these outdated choices, I wondered if *Private Moment* might function differently in a less fashion-forward location.

Does Central Park represent a unique site for period film costume and fashion-forward couture to blend into one another?

According to Levine, these frequent collisions between time periods and the porous boundaries between theatre, film, and everyday life are at the heart of *Private Moment*. In an interview with James N. Kienitz Wilkins for *BOMB Magazine*, Levine describes the ways that his scenes mix into their surroundings: "You start experiencing certain places as possessed, where one person has been swapped for another, or one fiction for another, or one era for another, and no one notices or mourns. That's the idea behind *Private Moment*'s reenactments of movie scenes shot in Central Park. They take place at the original locations, they loop all day, but they're unmarked—and unremarked. Like ghosts that don't know they're dead. They just blend in."[8] Individual audience members in *Private Moment* explore an increased sense of agency as the performance uniquely positions them to remark on scenes that, as Levine notes, go largely "unmarked."[9] By moving between the scenes and following (or not following) the tracks of the actors, audience members assume a perspective and gain an awareness of ways that Central Park recontextualizes these scenes that both the performers and the park-goers around them might lack. This awareness of the unmarked exchanges they observe informs each individual audience member's ambulatory choices and awareness of agency (in their route to pursue the action, their recognition of the action, and proximity and physical relationship to the action) as they move to other scenes.

David Levine's work maintains a complicated relationship with traditional theatrical conventions and, indeed, with "theatre" as a classifying term. In *Actors at Work* (2006), Levine filed contracts with Actors' Equity for union performers to go to their day jobs, reframing bartending and office work as performance. In *Habit* (2010–2012), he meticulously constructed a one-story ranch house inside a series of art galleries, allowing museum guests to peer in the windows and witness professional actors performing a scripted play about domestic life by Jason Grote on a continuous loop for eight hours a day.[10] Conscious of how theatre, film, and everyday urban life meld and refigure one another in *Private Moment* and the unique ways that ambulatory performance can facilitate an investigation of individual agency through a unique use of space, Levine chose a number of movies with strong connections to theatre history and lore among his eight selections.[11] *Bullets over Broadway*, a portrait of a struggling American playwright, is filled with scenes of rehearsals gone awry. *The Out-of-Towners*, originally written as a curtain-raiser for Neil Simon's play *Plaza Suite*, was cut by director Mike Nichols in rehearsal and ultimately reimagined by Simon as a stand-alone film. In *Six Degrees of Separation*, adapted for film by John Guare from his own play, a supposed film version of *Cats* directed by Sidney Poitier initiates the action. *Private Moment* references Central Park's theatrical history even outside the eight scenes it features. Each of these three examples invite individual audience members to make connections between commercial, proscenium-based theatrical performances and the unique form of performance they are actively participating in through their movements. When heading from the *Marathon Man* scene to the *Symbiopsychotaxiplasm* exchange on the Oak Bridge, the connection between the park and theatrical tradition is even more explicit: Audience members pass the Delacorte, home to decades of open-air productions by the Public Theatre.

Ultimately, the scenes that Levine provided in *Private Moment* serve only as a jumping-off point for each individual audience member's ambulatory narrative. The significant physical distances each person must cover force them to interact with other settings and sightseers, crafting narratives out of the interactions they observe. Seeking out these additional scenes not only provides the individual with an increased sense of personal agency but also alters their relationships to the eight prepared *Private Moment* scenes. As Levine proposes in the program, anything the individual encounters can be interpreted like a film scene, blurring the lines between the eight scenes included on *Private Moment*'s map and the everyday activities. This exercise of framing alternative sites facilitates the individual audience member's understanding of agency: Not only their physical path but also their perceptual processes help to create meaning. Because of this muddling effect and the lack of formal explanation of the world of the performance, audiences must learn on the go how to act and react appropriately within the *Private Moment* framework.

II: Ethics (*Symbiopsychotaxiplasm*)

A woman in a floral print dress walks across the Oak Bridge and looks out on the lake. A man in a blue blazer and khaki slacks chases after her, shouting "Alice! Alice!" Once Freddy reaches Alice, they spar in a circuitous, loud argument. Alice declares that she has "really just put up with [his] escapades long enough." Groups of tourists, one of them using a selfie stick, nestle on either side of the couple to take pictures of themselves with the lake behind them. Finally, Alice drops the bombshell: "I saw you. I saw you looking at him. And he was looking right back at you. I saw that whole thing. . . . A little faggot that everybody knows all about." Trapping Freddy against the railing of the bridge, Alice notes that she now understands "why you never want to have any children." After Alice accuses him of making love "like some Nazi stormtrooper," Freddy escapes and storms off the bridge. Following him to exclaim a final "fuck you," Alice storms off down the footpath in the opposite direction. Those around the couple, if they took notice of the fight at all, quickly go back to their strolling, chatting, and picture-taking (figure 2).

In *Theatre & Ethics*, Nicholas Ridout defines ethics in terms of dramatic action: "'How shall I act?' is one succinct way of posing the question of ethics. It is also, as you will, of course, have noticed from the very beginning, a theatrical question."[12] Ridout uses the central example of Neoptolemus in Sophocles's *Philoctetes* to describe the protagonist's struggle with action. As constructed in a great deal of Western dramatic theory, the audience is removed from the ethical struggle of the play, safe to abstractly consider the implications of the actions of Medea, Othello, or Willy Loman for their own secure lives. Herbert Blau describes a prevailing theoretical understanding of "an audience which has delegated itself to the stage," allowing the characters to choose actions on the audience's behalf.[13] In *Audience Participation in the Theatre: Aesthetics of the Invitation*, Gareth White notes that "performers usually retain authority over the action, while the spectators usually retain the right to stay out of the action, and to watch and hear it."[14] The audience ponders the question without actually having to answer it. Safely removed from the ethical stakes of the world of the play, the audience invites the characters to assume the "I" position of Ridout and Sophocles's "how shall I act?" construction on their behalf, judging their successes and failures from a distance.

But in *Private Moment* and many other contemporary site-based works, particularly in this heated exchange from *Symbiopsychotaxiplasm*, the ethical question of "how shall I act" is asked of the individual audience member as well. By choosing which scenes to seek out, how long to observe each scene, and what stops to make outside the guidelines of the performance map, each audience member participates in the creation of a highly individualized narrative. Though many ethical inquiries arise for the individual, I'll focus on three questions here: How shall I interact with each scene spatially? How shall I signal my reactions to the performers? How shall I perform the role of audience member for the thousands of others in Central Park?[15]

The process of voyeurism that individual audience members exercise in *Private Moment* involves a constant stream of spatial choices. When first encountering a scene, I decide how close to get to the action, but the movement patterns of the actors through their "loops" necessitate a constant process of readjustment. When Alice and Freddy storm off in opposite directions, should I follow one of them? If so, which one? Is it rude to nestle up next to them on the railing

Figure 2. Park-goers observe (and disregard) a scene from *Private Moment*. Photo courtesy of David Levine

of the bridge as their confrontation builds? Should I aim to keep the distance that other tourists and park-goers are maintaining? Should I be closer or farther away? Several of the scenes (those from *The Royal Tenenbaums*, *Six Degrees of Separation*, *Marathon Man*) feature characters who move in a circle and naturally return to where they began just in time to repeat the scene. In other scenes (from *Portrait of Jennie*, *Symbiopsychotaxiplasm*), actors move in a more linear pattern and stop to retrace their steps and "reset" themselves before beginning again. In these instances, I often feel several steps behind: Just when I've found a place that seems ideal to watch the action, the actors move farther away, and I begin the search again.

Private Moment offers the individual audience member no guidelines for etiquette or procedure. In some situations, and surroundings, like the dialogue from the *Royal Tenenbaums* scene, applauding after the scene is over and thanking the performers seemed only polite. In others, such as *Symbiopsychotaxiplasm*, congratulating the actors for their viciousness and brutality toward one another somehow felt less appropriate in a public park than it might have inside a proscenium theatre. Expressing my interest in the bigoted insults Alice threw at Freddy not only broke the social contract of the park, where an individual keeps their head down and affords those around them a measure of privacy, but also drew attention to me, spoiling Levine's "unmarked" effect and making those around me wonder why I was so invested in the strangers' fighting. Much of what I determined to be inappropriate audience behavior was gleaned from watching the few other program-wielding individuals I saw at each location. At my first stop, *Bullets over Broadway*, I silently criticized an audience member conspicuously taking pictures of David as he poured his heart out to Helen on a park bench. Moments later, to my amazement and disdain, a particularly daring audience member actually sat beside them on the bench, turning his body in to face the actors as if he were a part of the conversation. By the second or third stop on the *Private Moment* map, I'd developed a set of ground rules for how to approach and interact with the performers. Yet I wondered, perhaps even more pressingly: How was I supposed to deal with everyone else?

The number of New Yorkers and tourists enjoying Central Park unaware of *Private Moment*'s existence dwarfed that of the performers and program-toting audience members at any given moment. By *Marathon Man*, the third stop, I realized that the performance gave me the authority to highlight the repeated performances for those around me. The ultramarathoner playing Babe and jogging around the reservoir in 1970s sweats became much more conspicuous *because* I was searching for him and watching him intently. By the next stop, *Symbiopsychotaxiplasm*, I became aware that my spectatorship invited those around me not only to focus on the performers but also to make assessments about *me*. Why on earth, they might ask, was I staring intently at this heated argument, following closely behind the couple as their relationship reached its breaking point? Was I a voyeur, a weirdo, a creep? I quickly realized that I had no ability to explain away my prurient interest in these characters. Trying to clarify to the sightseers taking selfies that this was really "only a play," a piece of self-conscious performance by professionals, and that I was simply a respectful audience member would, it seemed, have generated even more derision and confusion in those around me. I found that using my agency to move around the scenes while secretly observing them made me feel like I had a part to play in the experiment of the performance itself. I became more than an audience member.

Though the performance offers no explicit direction to this effect, I eventually felt implicitly that part of my role as audience member was to help the actors blend into their surroundings. For me, the profoundest pleasure of *Private Moment* was the feeling of being *in on the game* that those around me did not understand. As I moved from scene to scene, I learned techniques for blending into my surroundings and watching the performers *without looking like I was watching them*. Keeping my sunglasses on allowed me to inconspicuously look directly at the scene while my body faced another direction. Wearing my headphones without actually plugging them into my smartphone helped me play the part of a disaffected everyday New Yorker even more convincingly. By the final few scenes, I had learned to tuck my *Private Moment* program into my pocket before I approached the action. Like an action hero in a film of my own, I covertly completed the objectives on my list. Once I was convinced I had made myself completely discrete, I embraced a new challenge in my own performance: Could I watch an entire scene without the performers themselves knowing I was paying any attention to them? Was the performance somehow more authentic if the actors felt similarly inconspicuous? Was this discretion one of the goals of the performance?

If, as *Private Moment*'s program suggests, the piece recontextualizes the park as "a backdrop where any given moment could be read as a film," it also creates an expanded field that includes the individual audience member as an active agent and participant. *Private Moment* invites the audience member to *infiltrate* (to return to Creative Time's terminology) the private scenes themselves instead of simply operating as a spectator. Rather than "delegating itself" or maintaining a "right to stay out of the action," as Blau and White describe, this audience must act. And action, in *Private Moment*, takes the form of a series of ambulatory choices made by the individual audience member (as agent) from a vast range of potential options.

III: Dissensus (*The Out-of-Towners*)

George runs barefoot beneath the Trefoil Arch in a tattered suit to snatch up his box of Cracker Jack, left behind by the dog that had absconded it. Gwen follows close behind, apologizing for being slow and noting that she was delayed by George's wing tips, which she is wearing. The couple sits on the steps beside the arch and greedily munches on the few remaining pieces of Cracker Jack. When Gwen reveals that a man stole George's watch as they slept on a park bench, George leaps up and storms back toward the arch. As the couple face each other and intensify their argument, a family of four tourists, decked out with cameras and fanny packs, walks directly between them and stops to admire the architecture. The performers do not acknowledge their presence. After George discovers he has chipped a tooth on the Cracker Jack and offers Gwen her shoes, which he has kept in his pocket, the beleaguered couple lock arms and climb the steps in search of help (figure 3).

In his essay "The Ethical Turn of Aesthetics and Politics," Jacques Rancière offers a complex definition of ethics and reframes the concept in terms that particularly inform contemporary discourses on site-based performance: "Ethics, then, is the kind of thinking in which an identity is established between an en-

Figure 3. Tourists and New Yorkers alike ignore a *Private Moment* scene. Photo courtesy of David Levine.

vironment, a way of being and a principle of action."[16] He sees individual action as a central component of ethics. But he also offers two additional mechanisms that apply to *Private Moment*. First, for Rancière, ethics are particularly situated in and bound by their spatial environments. An action that proves ethical in one location might be decidedly less so in another. Shouting for help and dialing 911 on a cellphone, for example, could be noble alongside a stranger at a bus stop but highly inappropriate when Gertrude succumbs to poisoning in the final moments of a *Hamlet* performance. Like George and Gwen in *The Out-of-Towners* or the real out-of-towners who so rudely split their scene apart, one must learn the lay of the land before acting. Second, Rancière notes that individuals create an "identity" and sense of self by examining the ethics of the actions they complete in various environments, just as I had done when realizing that the best way to use my agency was to help the performers blend in and maintain their audience segregation between the park-goers and the program-carrying *Private Moment* attendees. The "individual" Rancière references might be an audience member rather than a performer. After debating how to move and act and developing a course of action, they reflect on what these actions say about them and their place in social orders, determining if they are the sort of person who might act admirably or inadvisably. This "thinking," as Rancière calls it, is an embodied knowledge investigated through the physical exploration of ambulatory agency in the park. *Private Moment* offers individual audience members a unique laboratory for exploring Rancière's formulation.

By visiting and interacting with specifically curated environments, characters, and narratives, *Private Moment* helps the audience member to test their own agency. After first discovering how their presence and movement through each environment shifts the dramatic event, the individual learns through the performance how to alter their movements, actions, and reactions to achieve desired results. Crucially, this learning process of making strategic decisions to explore one's own identity and agency is not limited to the eight *Private Moment* scenes crafted by Levine. The character an individual creates for themselves through their movements extends to the dozens of other interactions they have between each scene. Stopping to purchase a bottle of water from a cart vendor, I kept on my sunglasses, headphones, and quiet, disaffected demeanor. When asked by a group of tourists for directions to the Conservatory Garden I had visited to see *Bullets over Broadway*, I tried to casually point out the way, suggesting that I was a New Yorker simply walking through the park who knew my surroundings intimately, pleased they had mistaken me for a local who could help. Unlike the performers bound in one film re-creation, the individual audience member might present him- or herself in all eight environments and many other settings between. Ultimately, this self-reflective process of site-based exploration might well continue after the performance has ended.

The informed sense of individual agency in a wide range of audience members that *Private Moment* creates might well be dubbed an aesthetic "dissensus." Coined by Rancière in the late 1990s, the term "dissensus," which he consciously contrasts with "consensus," describes "the presence of two worlds in one. . . . It places one world in another."[17] These two collapsing frames, rather than a problem to be solved, represent for Rancière a productive challenge to consensus, or "the reduction of . . . various 'peoples' into a single people identical with the count of a population and its parts."[18] In *Private Moment*, the individual audience members explore their own understandings of self by moving consciously between the frameworks of a stroll through the park and the self-conscious scenes of *Private Moment*, analyzing those around them under the broad umbrella of performance. By reorienting the performance conditions away from an abstract consensus or "audience" and toward the spatial choices of the individual, *Private Moment* enacts Rancière's state of dissensus across a range of urban spaces.[19] As a particularly rich complication of the notion of a preexisting, delegated audience, it invites individual audience members to consider the possibilities for contemporary site-based works to shift an individual's understandings of how they perform selfhood and interact with the civic spaces around them.

IV: Private Moment

David Levine drew his piece's title from the classic Private Moment acting exercise developed by Lee Strasberg to help performers blur the distinction between offstage behavior and onstage action. The exercise challenges the acting student to present a "private" action they would normally complete alone in front of their peers, eliminating their potential feelings of inhibition by re-creating the private space in their minds and investing the everyday activity with importance and introspection. By brushing their teeth, listening to music, or doing their dishes for their observant classmates in an acting workshop, students might stop self-analyzing their work and simply *do*, quite literally acting as if no one was watching.

Private Moment combines the goals of this stage acting exercise, realized on a large scale, with rich cinematic references to blur the lines between the disciplines of film, theatre, and contemporary ambulatory performance. The performance ultimately conflates these forms to force the individual audience members to explore their own agency through movement. Levine stages a continual process by which these different artistic mediums, to use his own words, become "unmarked—and unremarked" in public space.[20] By moving through Central Park on their own, audience members see everyday conversations that might well be film scenes and re-created film scenes that might well be everyday conversations. Gradually aware of these processes of unmarking and unremarking, the individual audience members also realize that their own performances complicate the course of *Private Moment*. They not only watch actors stage private moments but also potentially make these private moments more public through their own observation of and participation in the performances. Even once the performance is over, the audience member negotiates performing their public selves in the acts of leaving the park and traveling home.

Ultimately, *Private Moment* teaches the individual audience member not about theater, or film, but about the self. Once they have begun observing the performers and park-goers around them, they begin to develop not only an ambulatory plan of action but also a complex character for themselves. To borrow from Gareth White's definition of agency, they have stopped being "led to perform" and giving "performances that have been conceived by theatre practitioners" and have begun to "give performances that they invent themselves: the agency of the participant as the inverse, the flipside, of the control of the theatre practitioner."[21] The character I developed in *Private Moment*, a sunglass-wearing sleuth who discretely watched the eight scenes while partly turning away and listening through his headphones, was certainly inspired by the performance, but it was also a unique creation. The eight scenes Levine had created did not contain a perceptible through line or narrative, but my character's trip throughout *Private Moment*, which included a series of pauses and detours, certainly did. I had gone from a confused audience member, trying to learn the conventions of the performance and understand my agency through ambulatory trial and error, to, by the final *Cruel Intentions* scene, an expert able to navigate the unique state of dissensus provided by the performance's multiple frames.

In the process of moving through and watching the recontextualized and "unmarked" film scenes, I found myself becoming the protagonist of *Private Moment*. I met each performer for only one brief scene, but my own experience encompassed a complete, if individualized, version of the performance. Whereas the performers possessed firsthand knowledge of their own particular scenes, my ambulatory choices and the sense of agency they gave me allowed me to take a look at the larger picture. The personalized *Private Moment* narrative I created for my secretive protagonist drew not only on the eight scenes but also on the ways they were marked and unmarked through the reception of those in the park and by my own additions and mental connections, as if I were continually watching and rewinding a spool of 35-millimeter film. The acting exercise that Levine invokes in *Private Moment*'s title serves as an invitation to the individual audience member rather than to the professional actors in each scene. What private parts of the self does each of them choose to bring to the presentation in the park? Through an increased consciousness of their responsibility to the performers and the ways their physical attitudes and movements influence others, the individual audience member turns their own "private moments" into a fully realized public performance.

Notes

1. Creative Time, "Drifting in Daylight," performance program, 2015. According to Creative Time's website, these performances "tempted visitors to transcend their busy lives, losing themselves along a playful trail of sensory experiences." See http://creativetime.org/projects/drifting-in-daylight/.
2. Creative Time, "Alicia Framis." http://creativetime.org/projects/drifting-in-daylight/artists/alicia-framis/.

3. Creative Time, "Nina Katchadourian." http://creativetime.org/projects/drifting-in-daylight/artists/nina-katchadourian/.
4. Michel de Certeau, *The Practice of Everyday Life*, trans. Steven Rendall (Berkeley: University of California Press, 1984), 97.
5. Many tour companies offer pedicab "film tours" of Central Park as well.
6. Michael Barron, "'Drifting in Daylight' Floats Free Art and Performance into Central Park," *Vice*, https://www.vice.com/en_us/article/gqmbky/creative-times-new-drifting-in-daylight-exhibition-brings-free-art-and-performance-to-the-park.
7. *Private Moment*, directed by David Levine. Central Park, New York, June 20, 2015.
8. James N. Kienitz Williams, "David Levine," *BOMB Magazine*, https://bombmagazine.org/articles/david-levine/.
9. As Peggy Phelan notes, "Representation is almost always on the side of the one who looks and almost never on the side of the one who is seen." See Peggy Phelan, *Unmarked: The Politics of Performance* (New York: Routledge, 1996), 26.
10. Like Marcel Duchamp, Levine elevates the mundane aspects of home life into art through their insertion into the gallery.
11. Adam Alston helpfully calls this "entrepreneurial participation," emphasizing the role that personal initiative plays in the content of the theatrical event for each audience member. See Adam Alston, "Immersive Theatre and the Aesthetics of Decadence: On the Ruined Worlds of Punchdrunk, SHUNT and Hammer Film Productions," *Theatre & Performance Design* 3, no. 4 (2017): 199–217.
12. Nicholas Ridout, *Theatre & Ethics* (London: Palgrave Macmillan, 2009), 5–6.
13. Herbert Blau, *The Audience* (Baltimore: Johns Hopkins University Press, 1990), 10.
14. Gareth White, *Audience Participation in the Theatre: Aesthetics of the Invitation* (London: Palgrave Macmillan, 2013), 4.
15. In Keren Zaiontz's construction, this impulse is fundamentally "narcissistic," wherein reception of the performance is "a thing that participants not only consume, but own." See Keren Zaiontz, "Narcissistic Spectatorship in Immersive and One-on-One Performance," *Theatre Journal* 66, no. 3 (2014): 424.
16. Jacques Rancière, *Dissensus: On Politics and Aesthetics*, trans. Steven Corcoran (London: Continuum, 2010), 192.
17. Rancière, *Dissensus*, 45–46.
18. Rancière, *Dissensus*, 197.
19. While it is conventionally thought of as a public space, Central Park is a privately managed park. Private donations fund the Central Park Conservancy's operations, and Creative Time designed *Drifting in Daylight* to commemorate twenty-five years of the conservancy.
20. James N. Kienitz Williams, "David Levine."
21. White, *Audience Participation in the Theatre*, 27.

"I Want You to Feel Uncomfortable"

Adapting Participation in *A 24-Decade History of Popular Music* at San Francisco's Curran Theatre

—DAVID BISAHA

Chapter 4 of Taylor Mac's *A 24-Decade History of Popular Music*, presented on Sunday, September 24, 2017, at San Francisco's Curran Theatre, began even more unusually than the previous chapters had. The audience was a mix of full-series die-hards, for whom this was our fourth concert in ten days, and new initiates, some of whom were only first encountering judy's raucous "radical faerie realness ritual" (Taylor Mac uses "judy," lowercase, as a gender pronoun). To open, Mac sang a mash-up of The Byrds' "Turn! Turn! Turn!" and the *Peter Gunn* theme while sporting 1960s pastiche drag: a bloody pink suit, a pillbox hat, and a boa made of Campbell's soup cans (figure 1). Then, judy uttered a sentence that—I had learned by then—meant something unexpected was coming: "This is what's gonna happen." The Friday night before, chapter 3 had ended with an audience-participatory reenactment of white flight, in which white audience members were told to vacate the center sections of the audience and crowd into "suburbs" on the periphery. People of color were invited to take the better center seats. Mac threatened public humiliation to those who resisted and preemptively mocked those concerned about giving up their more expensive seats. Since we had left the theatre in this arrangement on Friday, we would need to set the scene again. Not ten minutes into Sunday afternoon's concert, judy sang a spooky, slow cover of "I Put a Spell on You." Trancelike, I and other white audience members "ran" to the periphery in exaggerated slow-motion.[1]

At Sunday's performance, the reenactment of white flight prompted an interruption. Several audience members in the mezzanine above the house floor

Figure 1. Taylor Mac in the 1956–1966 decade of *A 24-Decade History of Popular Music* at St. Ann's Warehouse, New York City, 2016. Photo by Teddy Wolff.

refused to give up their seats, and while judy didn't spend more than fifteen seconds directing audience attention to them ("You didn't move, and you look white to me . . ."), the progressive values of Mac's ritual were made abundantly clear to those who had missed the previous three concerts. In that moment, audience members stared at the immobile white men. Were they confused? Angry? Taking a stand? We pondered. Mac, however, quickly directed the audience's discomfort back onto itself. More participation, set to pop: as Mac sang "Please

Don't Let Me Be Misunderstood," the "suburbs" were to make exaggerated vocal and physical gestures of performative white guilt: shrugs, apologies, repudiations. Eventually we were allowed to return to the center section, though we were instructed not to demand our old seats back: "Don't gentrify!" Reflecting on this sequence, reviewer Peter Lawrence Kane noted that Taylor Mac "brandished the very seating chart of a proscenium theater as a weapon, mocking the 'bourgeois crisis' of having to accept an inferior seat to the one you bought, just because there was now a person of color sitting in it."[2] The remainder of the fourth chapter, like the three prior, hinged on such moments of audience participation, walking a line between joy and discomfort.

For my purposes here, I call attention to Mac's self-adaptation of the *24-Decade* project to the large proscenium house of the Curran Theatre. Judy's adjustments of the performance, some planned and some improvised, created a new performance whose sited dramaturgy capitalized on the architecture and social codes of a proscenium theatre space. As Mike Pearson notes in *Site-Specific Performance*, "the auditorium is itself a site, equally susceptible to conceptual readdress" as performances that take place outside of purpose-built theatres.[3] How did the "white flight" episode above, or any of the more than seventy-five distinct participatory elements Mac deployed over twenty-four hours of performance, change as a result of its translation into a three-tiered, 1,600-seat proscenium house?[4]

Mac used the limitations of the space as a metaphor for the uneven terrain of history. By aligning the themes of the performance with the topographical and social codes of the theatrical space, Mac made us embody our literal standing in and against history. Moreover, as compared to the original twenty-four-hour production, which occurred in St. Ann's Warehouse's Steinberg Theatre, at the Curran performance Mac mapped physical distance onto historical separations, subverted typical vertical and horizontal hierarchies in the theatre space, and manipulated the space to raise up individual identities within heterogeneous groups.[5] Whereas the flexibility of the previous warehouse space had allowed for a radical approach to participation using audience movement and reorganization, the Curran Theatre consolidated audiences into ready-made units, defined by permanent seating, focal emphasis on the stage, and difficult-to-access balcony and mezzanine levels. Mac worked within these limitations, playfully critiquing history's uneven terrain and celebrating individuals and groups facing oppression. This second full performance of the project therefore challenged the idea that history is an act of spectatorship by constructing an active, informal audience in a very formal theatre space.

Each hour of the concert corresponded to a decade of history from 1776 to 2016, in which Mac performed songs popular in the United States during that time. Some had playful, performative formats, such as a boxing match between Walt Whitman and Stephen Foster (1846–1856), in which they competed for the title of Father of American Song and the audience "voted" by throwing ping-pong balls at the loser. Periodically, Mac suspended or stopped songs altogether to accommodate commentary drawn from judy's research or personal life; Mac discussed everything from judy's upbringing as a Christian Scientist to back-room sex parties, and most interruptions radically recontextualized the song's original meaning. Often, these incorporated participatory elements as well. For instance, in the decade between 1916 and 1926, Mac brought men aged eighteen to forty onstage—to simulate the trenches of Europe—while judy sang period songs to those left "at home" in the auditorium, including "Keep the Home Fires Burning" queerly reworked into an ode to lesbian sex. Later, after a spoken word/jazz performance of the 1926 song "Masculine Women! Feminine Men!" we were instructed to intentionally mis-gender our neighbors with verbal compliments, showering each other with appreciations, and a few cat-calls, that defied our gender presentations. During a "junior prom" version of the 1975 Ted Nugent hit "Snakeskin Cowboys," Mac told us to find someone of the same gender and dance with them, to kill Nugent's homophobia through ritualized appropriation. With such activities, Mac used playful participation to remake the world, even temporarily, into something just a bit queerer.

By placing Mac's establishment and management of participatory frames in the context of theoretical work on participation and showing how the Curran site crafted new meanings out of audience embodiment, I suggest that Mac's dramaturgy extended participatory aesthetics and ethics away from reductive hopes of producing democracy or citizenship through participation alone, hopes notably critiqued by Claire Bishop in *Artificial Hells*.[6] Rather, Mac's management of participation and site play inflated the space with the potential for community by acknowledging difference, distance, and identity. The divisions prompted by and sustained within the space—immobile chairs, large balconies, a single endstage, groups of audience members pitted against each other, pairs of participants struggling toward common goals—constructed the performance at the Curran as more formal and structural than the space in New York. Furthermore, under Mac's care, audience participation invited us to queer the space, to embrace personal and political discomfort, and to subvert the spatial codes of traditional proscenium theatres. By adapting judy's own work in this way, Mac created site-specific, participatory performance: work rebuilt for a new container, the proscenium space.

The Proscenium Theatre as Site

John Lutterbie, reading phenomenologist Edward Casey, reminds us that the relationship between space and place is first and foremost "experienced in movement. The ability to conceptualize space is made possible by the actions and interactions of the tactile-kinesthetic body, that is through being in place." Movement is the basis on which we understand the dramaturgy of spaces, and playing with these expectations is critical to site-based work. By including movement and participation in judy's popular song performances, Mac made history tactile-kinesthetic. Gareth White, discussing participation, further acknowledges that "participation is a bodily activity, in which the location of the body and its relationship to the organization of space is fundamental, and the experience of audience participation is an experience of changes in spatiality." Taylor Mac certainly encouraged bodies to move differently in the Curran production. Because of the Curran's Beaux Arts style and traditional architecture, audiences were more reluctant to actively participate than in other performances I had witnessed, but the reward was different and perhaps greater. As a result, while the marathon, twenty-four-hour performance in New York City emphasized community, fatigue, and coming together, the temporally and physically separated performances at the Curran emphasized distance, hierarchy, and the work necessary to overcome disconnection.[7]

Some of these thematic shifts emerged from the architecture of the Curran theatre. St. Ann's Warehouse proved a much more flexible space; chairs could be removed, the floor could be taped, and the large space could hold the six to eight hundred freely mobile audience members.[8] Among the challenges presented by the Curran were fixed audience seats, the tiered audience (balcony, mezzanine, and orchestra), the difficult travel between audience levels, which could only occur through staircases in the lobby, and a relatively small stage. This lack of flexibility necessitated certain adaptations from the original performance. For instance, at St. Ann's, Mac took away audience chairs for several hours in the mid-nineteenth century, and audiences sat on the floor. A reenactment of the Oklahoma Land Rush (1889) took place on this flat surface.[9] The open warehouse space also afforded easier transformations of audience shape, such as when a conga line occurred during the twenties ("Happy Days Are Here Again") and or an audience member was hoisted atop shoulders during Judy Garland's "funeral" in 1969. Such processions took on a more organized, formal quality in the Curran owing to its clearly defined aisles and seating banks; rather than winding through one large audience, in the Curran one's position in the aisle or in the seats helped mark one's willingness to engage, dividing participators from bystanders. Finally, the Curran audience was at least twice if not three times as large as the St. Ann's audience. Rather than resisting these limitations of the transfer, Mac used them to reinforce production themes. By adjusting instructions, judy spontaneously turned the struggle to accommodate the audience into an analogy for the difficulties of communication, progress, or movement in history.

At the Curran, audience movement was limited owing to the height of the mezzanine and balcony, and this created some aesthetic compromises and a new subtheme based around breaking the rules of formality prompted by the space. At times, whole sections of the audience were precluded from moving, owing to the risk of falling. One decade included a game of musical chairs, which occurred during a full hour with the audience blindfolded, in acknowledgment of the blind community and the invention of braille. The mezzanine and balcony remained seated throughout this section. But, rather than ignore the obvious metaphor of privilege, hierarchy, and class status, Mac worked with it. Judy adapted by having volunteer ushers push through seated audience members in the balcony, to provide "the feeling of people pushing past you." The land rush (using air-filled balloons as "land") was also decidedly more limited than it had been in St. Ann's, where the scramble to grab a balloon and occupy a taped square on the floor spread over the whole auditorium. On the Curran balcony, I could reach only so far before balloons fell off the balcony onto other audience members. Mac reminded those of us in the balcony to grab balloons as fast as we could, since, after all, the American dream is a fleeting thing.[10]

Mac used the fixed audience seating and the relative lack of open space in the house to draw attention to minority or oppressed communities. Several times, judy invited those with bad seats or those from oppressed identity groups (people of color and queer people, mostly) to take seats in the orchestra pit, moving them from the worst to the best seats in the house. At other points, members of particular groups were invited to stand up within the audience house for a song or two, performing some role or action while the unmarked remainder of the audience watched. In these moments Mac transformed the concept of the audience as a homogenous mass into a collection of individuals, singling out some identities and temporarily destabilizing oppressive hierarchies. This opened possible conditions for symbolic restoration. When the young men returned to their seats after being brought onstage during World War I, Mac cautioned the returning "soldiers" that if a woman had taken his seat while he was away, he should NOT ask her to move. Just find another seat! Earned hierarchies and rights to a place in the theatre (or in history) were simply less important to Mac than the work of building community by acknowledging past oppression based on gender, race, sexuality, or class. Mac showed that even simple actions in the theatre—where to sit, when to participate and how, when to move and when to defer—reflect one's relationship to history. Could performances such as this become practice for generosity, empathy, or even restorative justice? Mac did not claim that these spectating practices would actually change the world ("metaphorical poverty is not actual poverty," we were told in judy's Depression-era "soup kitchen" cabaret), but a small window could be opened for "perpetual consideration."[11] In the words of another San Francisco critic, "Mac aired our sordid history not to absolve us of it but to make each of us feel in our bodies, in our relationship to the other bodies in the Curran, our greatest shames and our nonetheless great potential to write a history we might be prouder of in coming decades."[12] Judy's ability to get us to "feel in our bodies" entailed careful management of space, movement, and our attunement to each other.

Mac also subverted typical audience behavior as conditioned by tradition and reinforced by theatre architecture. In a typical Western theatrical event, an audience would sit in a tiered house, in one assigned seat, arranged (perhaps) by the amount each had paid for a ticket. The production would proceed in darkness and silence. Movement during the production would be discouraged, the ushers would aid movement and seating with efficiency and a minimum of distraction. Bathroom breaks are best taken at the intermission. The full attention of the audience is to be placed on the performers, who rarely if ever acknowledge the audience except at the curtain call. Cell phone use, talking, eating, and other "disruptive" audience behavior is discouraged and policed by the ushers or other conscientious patrons. Importantly, the audience is conceived as a mass divided by economic class, and the individual characteristics of audience members are to be forgotten while one "suspends disbelief" or "loses oneself" in the performance. Finally, these expectations are consistent throughout the performance; inappropriate behavior in the first act is still inappropriate behavior in the last minutes of the production. These norms are conditioned by past experience, supported by both explicit and internalized directions, and kept in check by social pressure. The architecture of theatres coevolved with this mode of theatregoing; narrow aisles and long rows of seats make it difficult to get up in the middle of an act, whereas more capacious lobby areas (with bathrooms, bars, and more comfortable seating) are for addressing one's social and biological needs.

A 24-Decade History of Popular Music, by contrast, overturned each of these audience behavior expectations. Audience members sat in the tiered balcony, yes, but were forced to give up their seats, sometimes to those who may have paid less than the original seatholder, and were repositioned based on their race, gender, sexual orientation, or willingness to participate. The production oscillated between moments of darkness in which Mac sang in spotlight and other moments when bright spotlights illuminated the house. The audience sang, jeered, and yelled at each other and at Mac, often at judy's behest. Audience movement, as in the white flight section or the Judy Garland processional, was not only permitted but also crucial. There were no intermissions, and Mac explicitly told us to choose our own moments to take a break: "I don't know how to take care of you. You take care of you." Action was distributed throughout the theatre, both by Mac's movement through the house and through the participation of the audience. We were given food and drink, in our seats, and encouraged to use cell phones, especially to record and post to social media. At the end of each act, the floor was a mess of ping-pong balls, paper, food wrappers, and other props. Some of these shifts were not radical in and of themselves, but together, they primed the audience for engagement, movement, and risk-taking.

In the move from St. Ann's Warehouse to the Curran, the topography of the site changed radically; what could have been an obstacle to a faithful transfer only further deepened a story of conflict, confrontation, and struggle. White flight was made stronger through embodiment, because people climbed over each other, jumping chairs and stepping on toes as they moved. Metaphorical emigration from the balcony of Eastern Europe to the stage ("America") in the early 1900s only heightened the distance between the Old World and the New. The long trip down the lobby stairs, going "off to war" with the rest of the younger men in the audience, became a journey through and past the rest of the audience, providing a real sense of departure and the risk of loss. During "Snakeskin Cowboy," I realized that I have never been in a room so full of "queer" couples, dancing on balconies and staircases and aisles and onstage, and doing so as a matter of (temporary) normalcy. In straight or mixed spaces, queer dancing still can be performative, often "onstage" and rarely "in the house." In the Curran, it was everywhere. When approaching the new production, Mac handily adapted the original production to one that could accommodate the four-day structure, a vertically oriented audience house with fixed seating, and the traditional behavior implicated by the Curran theatre interior decor.

Discomfort and the Ethics of Participation

One of the most striking aspects of Taylor Mac's style was judy's gentle but firm control over audiences. Mac invited, cajoled, and gently guilted audience members into one potentially uncomfortable participation event after another. Judy lightly mocked us for our initial resistance, and as the performance continued, individuals were brought up onstage, or singled out in the audience, and more forcefully called upon to engage. Judy viewed audiences not as passive vessels but as coparticipants in the work; this is a long-standing concept for Mac and particularly important to the *24-Decade* project. In performance, Mac explained that judy always hated audience participation, because "it feels like people forcing their fun on you," but then, judy ironically explained that "it's different when I ask you to do it . . . I *want* you to feel uncomfortable."[13] Discomfort, risk, and the embodiment of physical challenges are crucial to the project of building up through breaking down that Mac put before the audience.

Thematically, the performance's negotiations over appropriate and inappropriate use of space also questioned the role propriety holds in maintaining an oppressive status quo. Frequently, Mac blurred the line between appropriate and inappropriate action: "Whatever you're feeling is appropriate." Mac repeated this sentence several times, especially as particularly challenging moments emerged. However, unlike feelings, not all *actions* were appropriate; but, rather than shutting down confrontational participation, Mac incorporated hecklers (and other distractingly resistant attendees) into the "art in the room." More than once, Mac responded to talkative audience members by recasting their interruption as simply a desire "to be a part of the show" and explained that judy had learned to work with hecklers because judy came up in gay nightclubs. By repeatedly demonstrating that deviant responses would not derail the performance but rather feed back into the production thanks to the performer's virtuosity, Mac created a strangely liberating sense of both care and inescapability. Mac's facility with the hecklers and unconventional participation actually freed the rest of the audience to consider making their own transgressions against the space or, perhaps, the dominant narratives of history[14] (figure 2).

Several times during the production, Mac aligned our reluctance to behave outside of theatrical norms with conformity, passivity, and dominant culture. Mac has described judy's drag aesthetic as a "conversation about homogeneity and heterogeneity," and in the *24-Decade* project "standing out" was always celebrated.[15] While the distinction between the mass and the individual has always been a part of the performance, in the proscenium space of the Curran, the resistance to standing up, speaking, dancing, or making a scene in the auditorium was architecturally reinforced. But, as this was not a space normally used for such behavioral interruptions, doing so was doubly freeing, queering the space as well as history. Staying silent or refusing to participate was choosing security through conformity. In one performance, Mac gazed over the audience and chided the number of men in H&M clothing; if all dress is drag, judy wondered,

Figure 2. Taylor Mac and audience at the beginning of *A 24-Decade History of Popular Music* at St. Ann's Warehouse, New York City, 2016. Photo by Teddy Wolff.

then why had so many men made such a boring choice? At other moments, Mac mocked resistance to engaging in "bad" audience behavior as simply a "bourgeois crisis"—not actually a real problem. And what better place to challenge conformity than a space of neatly arranged, bounded audiences, accustomed by tradition and architectural semiotics toward silent acceptance of a performance? By casting conformity with passivity in the face of history, Mac accused nonparticipators of accepting the (majoritarian, straight, white, male) history as written, rather than seeking out newer, queerer ancestors.

For Mac, individuality and heterogeneity are the keys to queer liberation and "dreaming the culture forward." Participation replaced complacency. We did not "lose ourselves" in the performance but rather were encouraged to identify ourselves, or even experiment with different versions of self. By setting up a few rules early on, changing behavior expectations periodically, and skillfully incorporating inappropriate responses or interruptions, Mac unhinged practiced expectations of being auditors in a theatre space. Over time, and with repetition, social expectations "fell apart" and possibilities emerged over the hours-long concerts. Nonetheless, some restatement of norms had to occur at the beginning of each new act, as some portion of each audience was new to Mac's performance for the first time. Perhaps this interruption of new attendees explains the white flight "resistance" with which I began this article. The Curran performance was distinguished by its continual need to reteach and manage behavioral expectations, owing to the divided, four-day performance. When this was successful, as Mac eventually was most often, audience behavior reinforced the overarching themes of the production. American history, too, Mac argued, is based on expectations, familiar narratives, and the things that "everyone knows" but hides. Partway through the performance, Mac explained that judy is "not a teacher; I'm a reminder. I'm just trying to remind you of things you've dismissed, forgotten, or buried."[16] Mac's participatory theatre embodied estrangement, allowing play with other possible selves and possible relations.

Our discomfort wasn't only played for laughs, though; Mac demonstrated that the humility of awkwardness and failure is a prerequisite for the act of reaching toward others. San Francisco reviewer Lily Janiak reflected on the role of participation in the Curran production, which she described as "a party, a circus, a religious awakening, a free-for-all": "It's uncomfortable, and it's supposed to be. Is there any other way to feel when Mac uncovers a verse of Kentucky's state song that includes the word 'darkies'? Mac is an expert scorer of discomfort: acknowledging that the audience is probably feeling it, without letting them off the hook for it."[17] Here Janiak pinpoints the source of Mac's sneakiest strategy. It would have been far easier to explain away the racist songs of the Confederacy or the oppressive consequences of white flight if not for the fact that we had just reached toward these historical perspectives through playful reenactment, using our own bodies and voices. As often as not, Mac then undercut the joy of participation by directing our attention to uncomfortably racist lyrics (as above) or other oppressive historical contexts associated with the song. Mac implicitly asked, what were you just up to? If you were having fun, then can that fun, that joy, also fuel reaching out toward the Other? By first staging a historical context such as war or social conflict through audience activity, and then complicating the ethical entailments of that arrangement by subverting the narrative while the audience was still invested with their bodies, Mac used audience participation to ask deep questions of historical ethics.

But why might it be useful to put the audience in this position? Mac might say that there is value in simply prying open space between the usual and queered interpretation of historical events. Claire Bishop and Nicholas Ridout, speaking from divergent perspectives, agree that confrontation without insisting on a specific final interpretation is a commonly successful technique. Bishop, reviewing the political hopes of participatory art across the twentieth century, notes that "most striking projects that constitute the history of participatory art unseat all of the polarities on which this discourse is founded (individual/collective, author/spectator, active/passive, real life/art) but not with the goals of collapsing them." Ridout, reading philosopher Emmanuel Levinas's ethics alongside the work of Peggy Phelan and Hans-Thies Lehmann, finds that postmodern performances constitute the self through a confrontation with the Other rather than through "a philosophical emphasis on being." Put another way, certain postmodern performances attempt to stage the encounter with the Other, a binary held in tension through becoming rather than being. They draw the potential for ethical questions from that encounter rather than from a meditation on the qualities of the self.[18]

The unusual requests of the last chapters of the performance structured potential ethical engagements with unfamiliar Others most strongly. For most participating audience members, Mac's impish "perpetual consideration" allowed for riskier play as the performance continued through its chapters; the fun turned into an exploration of one's own complicity in structural oppression. For instance, one moment in chapter 3 moved me deeply. During the 1950s decade, after the first white flight, the decade ended when Mac invited all the gay men and women in the suburbs to return to the inner city; as white queers descended on the few people of color in the audience, we were told "Don't gentrify!" But, as Mac covered Chuck Berry's "Promised Land," we did exactly that; the tension between the joy of meeting other queer folks but displacing the people of color already in the "cities" stuck with me. While dancing back to the city, I questioned, what was my responsibility toward that part of the community's history?

Ridout and Bishop, as critics, share an emphasis on a fundamental confrontation of contradiction inherent in postmodern work, and in Bishop's case, in participatory artwork. Both acknowledge value in the difference emerging from confrontation and potential discomfort. I believe that Mac is working within both of these frames; the ethics of the participatory experiment lead toward several confrontations with fictional and actual Others in the final chapters of the performance. The task was not to decide who we were but rather to allow the encounter with the Other to hold open the conditions for (temporary) personal change. Mac did not attempt to subsume all into a single community; rather, participation became a way toward more meaningful community-making. Being together in the room constituted the performance community, and each audience member figured out how to manage confrontation, discomfort, and historical guilt in his or her own way.

Encounters with the Other frequently result in failure, an aesthetic Jack Halberstam has aligned with queer, anti-normative, anti-capitalist power. Mac continues in this tradition. Ridout, too, considers that failure may be constitutive of theatre's power and that gaps in perfect mimesis ("corpses" and "collapses") may in fact be a source of performative power: "A certain failure of relation in this encounter lies at the heart of the theatrical experience . . . its properly placed ineptitude . . . might lie in an under-investment in mastery, technique, and perfection and a counter-investment in some kind of failure to master the techniques of perfect representation." Mac would perhaps agree with Ridout, extending the idea of the performer's "under-investment in mastery" and applying it to whole audiences. On the large scale, the project itself is so large that failures, gaps, and interruptions are inevitable. To partake in the ritual, one must embrace failure and the potential that failure opens between the performer and the audience member, or even between two audience members. At the Curran, the failure to perform white flight correctly, as the resistant men did, or to dance the Ted Nugent prom without giggling pervading the room (and it did!) was both meaningless (how would one fail at that?) and exactly the art that Mac aimed to produce. It's nothing more polished than that, for as judy reminded us, "perfection is for assholes." The freedom to be imperfect is also the freedom to blur binaries, to (perpetually) consider, to stage prickly questions without coming to a definitive opinion for any longer than the moment of participation. And, in the face of failure, Mac preached resilience and continuing forward; the ethical choice facing all of us in our current world is, as judy sang in the final song of the performance, to "lie down or get up and play." Mac challenged us to embrace recovery, humility, empathy, and perhaps activism. Judy insisted on discomfort and failure as constitutive of judy's art. "It's about we're all in this room together and we happen to have this history on our back. . . . How do we deal with it?"[19]

Finding Community by Sacrificing Self

"I don't want it to feel like Oprah," Mac says, "where everyone is agreeing and applauding. I want people to be a little lost. I don't want them to feel like they're satisfied with their purchase."[20] By taking durational group discomfort as a large part of the performance itself, but working with and through displeasure, joy, control, resistance, and submission—a distinctly queer sensibility—Mac set up the conditions to be lost, and to be lost in community. Being confused, being unsure what to do or how long one is going to be performing an action, being unsure about what's going to happen next, or being pushed to transgress were all part of the game. This has been a part of the production from its inception, but as the original performance became a touring series, new spaces and new audiences compelled further evolution of Mac's original vision.

In the *24-Decade* project, Taylor Mac reinterpreted history through the views of forgotten or overlooked communities and wondrously called them into being through play and reenactment. Most of the wonder should be attributed to Mac and judy's collaborators; each was working at a high level. The production's flexible structure, entirely dependent on Mac at the microphone calling the shots, allowed for the up-to-the-minute adjustments that kept the adaptation working. Mac has honed the skills of observation, of audience work, and of pithy phrasing. Judy has the ability to tell, "in high drag-queen style . . . a profound truth disguised as a flip rejoinder."[21] Such openness was infectious and encouraged the audience to be similarly loose and open to revision as the performance unfolded. Unlike other immersive or design-heavy spectacles, Mac's performance prized the potential of spontaneous community, despite failure, above the deadness of the preplanned. Mac could call for changes in the song list or lighting cues or could extend segments that were going well, a particular benefit of the concert style over a more mimetic performance. The innovation here is that, through the frame of the performance art concert and the overwhelming mastery of the material held by Mac, arranger-music director Matt Ray, and other collaborators, the landscape was clear for confident, improvisational play with a large audience. I have never experienced structured play in a theatre that was so freeing; and paradoxically, the need to surrender to Mac's aesthetic vision only made it freer.

In San Francisco, Mac faced new challenges of adaptation: a larger audience, a larger and more formal space to fill, a larger cast of musicians and assistants, and larger gaps between acts and performances. Could the community feeling of the first chapters extend to the last? Could the performance be successfully translated into a proscenium theatre like the Curran? Likely, yes; however, Mac's adaptation to the Curran resulted in a newly envisioned work, not simply transferred but adapted to the space. Judy understood the ways that the auditorium afforded certain types of movement and hampered others. A proscenium stage, fixed seats, vertical hierarchies, and processionals through the aisles became core parts of the San Francisco iteration, obstacles turned into opportunities. Because of the formal setting and audience arrangement, participation was both more difficult and more radically liberating when it did come. By challenging audiences with many opportunities to engage in "inappropriate" or unusual audience behavior, Mac structured encounters with discomfort and the Other that were only heightened by the Curran's architectural formality. Mac was right; participation did feel different when judy asked me to do it. In this, the *24-Decade* project staged site as problem, participation as solution, and radical faerie realness ritual sacrifice as a subjective, hopeful, and challenging response to the pressures of being an American living in community.

Notes

1. Mac's performance invokes the Radical Faerie movement, a group founded in 1979 to create an earth-centered, nontheistic spiritual community that explores aesthetic, sexual, and political alternatives to the then-emergent mainstream gay culture. See Joey Cain, "Who Are the Radical Faeries?" http://eniac.yak.net/shaggy/faerieinf.html, and for application to the Curran performance, Andrew Sean Greer, "A Radical Sense of Beauty," Curran, https://sfcurran.com/the-currant/articles/radical-beauty/. On pronouns, Mac explains: "I was getting introduced onstage and written about, and some people would say 'he' and others would say 'she' and neither really felt right for the art I was making. . . . I'm an artist, and it's part of my job to make people think outside their norms a little bit. And I wanted a gender pronoun that was fun, and that immediately emasculates you—because you can't roll your eyes and say 'judy' without being camp." Alex Needham, "Taylor Mac on Queering History: 'Someone Like Me Doesn't Normally Get to Represent America,'" *Guardian*, September 12, 2017, https://www.theguardian.com/stage/2017/sep/13/taylor-mac-on-queering-history-someone-like-me-doesnt-normally-get-to-represent-america.
2. Peter Lawrence Kane, "24-Hour Fitness: Taylor Mac's *A 24-Decade History of Popular Music*, Ch. 4," *SF Weekly*, September 26, 2017, http://www.sfweekly.com/culture/24-hour-fitness-taylor-macs-a-24-decade-history-of-popular-music-ch-4/.
3. Mike Pearson, *Site-Specific Performance* (Basingstoke: Macmillan Education UK, 2010), 16.
4. According to my recollection and notes, there were at least seventy-five elements of "participation" in the performance. Mac has released no script, song list, or other official record of the performance as of August 2018.
5. The *24-Decade* project began five years before the premiere as a collection of workshops, concerts, and presentations of increasing duration. The premiere at St. Ann's occurred on October 8–9, 2016, in one twenty-four-hour marathon. It was preceded by a two-week series of three-hour concerts at the same venue, in which Mac performed the decades in chronological order. At the time of writing, the project has been performed in its entirety six times: twice in Brooklyn (2016), and once each at the Curran and the Melbourne Arts Festival (2017) and Los Angeles and Philadelphia (2018). The project and its critical legacy are in progress. See David Román et al., "Subjective Histories of Taylor Mac's 'Radical Faerie Realness Ritual' *History*," *Theatre Journal* 69, no. 3 (September 2017): 403–15; and a book project in progress at the time of printing, *Get Up and Play: Taylor Mac's "A 24-Decade History of Popular Music*," ed. Sean F. Edgecomb, David Román, and Dan Venning.
6. "Participatory art is not a privileged political medium, nor a ready-made solution to a society of the spectacle, but is as uncertain and precarious as democracy itself; neither are legitimated in advance but need continually to be performed and tested in every specific context." Claire Bishop, *Artificial Hells: Participatory Art and the Politics of Citizenship* (London: Verso, 2012), 284.
7. John Lutterbie, "Phenomenology and the Dramaturgy of Space and Place," *Journal of Dramatic Theory and Criticism* 16, no. 1 (Fall 2001): 126–27; Gareth White, *Audience Participation in Theatre: Aesthetics of the Invitation* (Basingstoke, UK: Springer, 2013), 167.
8. As described by reviewers, as well as the author's conversations with attendees. Jennifer

Parker-Starbuck et al., "The Queer, Resistant, Historical Bodies of Taylor Mac's *A 24-Decade History of Popular Music*: A Curated Conversation," (panel discussion, American Society for Theatre Research, Atlanta, November 18, 2017).

9. At St. Ann's the chairs taken away for the land rush returned as the 1950s decade began, only to have the seating changed yet again when the white flight sequence occurred minutes later.
10. In subsequent performances, such as in Philadelphia in June 2018, the land rush was cut entirely. Mac explained from the stage that the change was because the performance began to transfer into theatres where "they nailed the seats down." The Curran performance began the process of adapting to proscenium sites, but the piece continued to change in future iterations.
11. Mac, in performance: "In performance art there is no failure, only perpetual consideration."
12. Lily Janiak, "Taylor Mac's History Lesson: Create," *SFGate*, September 27, 2017, http://www.sfgate.com/performance/article/Taylor-Mac-s-history-lesson-create-12230116.php.
13. Mac quoted in Ethan Philbrick, "Ten Things I Learned about History from Taylor Mac," *Helix Queer Performance Network*, http://helixqpn.org/post/110066363227/ten-things-i-learned-about-history-from-taylor-mac.
14. "One of the things I learned from performing in the clubs is that if something is threatening to take the story away from the storyteller, then you have to incorporate that threatening thing into the story, at all costs." Taylor Mac in Garth Greenwell, "Hero's Journey with Taylor Mac," *Paris Review*, June 25, 2018, https://www.theparisreview.org/blog/2018/06/25/heros-journey-an-interview-with-taylor-mac/
15. Tre'vell Anderson, "For Taylor Mac, the Stage Show Is Just Part of the Fight for the LGBT Community," *Los Angeles Times*, March 11, 2016, https://www.latimes.com/entertainment/arts/la-et-cm-taylor-mac-los-angeles-20180314-story.html.
16. Taylor Mac, "I Believe," lecture at the "From Where I Stand" Symposium at the Under the Radar Festival, Public Theatre, New York, 2013, http://www.taylormac.org/i-believe/.
17. Lily Janiak, "Taylor Mac's Ferocious Epic Traces American History Through Music," *SFGate*, September 19, 2017, http://www.sfgate.com/performance/article/Taylor-Mac-s-ferocious-epic-traces-American-12209408.php.
18. Bishop, *Artificial Hells*, 277–78; Nicholas Ridout, *Theatre & Ethics* (Basingstoke, UK: Palgrave Macmillan, 2009), 52.
19. Jack Halberstam, *The Queer Art of Failure* (Durham: Duke University Press, 2011); Nicholas Ridout, *Stage Fright, Animals, and Other Theatrical Problems* (Cambridge: Cambridge University Press, 2006), 31–32; Alexis Soloski, "Taylor Mac: How a 24-Hour Pop Odyssey Redefines American History," *Guardian*, September 19, 2016, https://www.theguardian.com/stage/2016/sep/19/taylor-mac-24-hour-pop-odyssey-redefines-american-history.
20. Soloski, "Taylor Mac."
21. Hugh Ryan, "How Taylor Mac's 24-Hour Performance Encapsulated the Experience of the AIDS Crisis," *Vulture*, October 18, 2016, http://www.vulture.com/2016/10/taylor-mac-performance-encapsulated-the-aids-crisis.html.

Navigating Neverland and Wonderland

Audience as Spect-Character

—COLLEEN RUA

According to W. B. Worthen, *Sleep No More* "immerses its audiences in a paradoxical practice: we write our individualized plotlines in our own movements, but are constructed within the spectacle as realist voyeurs, watchers, and readers, not agents."[1] This may be true for productions like Punchdrunk's *Sleep No More* or Third Rail Projects' *Grand Paradise*, in which audience members are primarily followers who share physical space with actors. This element of on-the-sidelines participation can be appealing, as audience members are often voyeuristic witnesses to taboo activities. As the level of participation increases, through one-on-one interactions, for example, audience members may feel their status move from watcher to agent. Much scholarship has questioned audience agency in immersive productions. In *Artificial Hells*, Claire Bishop points to "the contradictions between intention and reception, agency and manipulation" as "central problems in the contemporary discourse of participation," challenging the idea that audience participation is equivalent to choice, empowerment, or free will on the part of the audience member.[2] Keren Zaiontz argues that in immersive and one-on-one performance, "consumptive engagement produces a narcissistic spectatorship," one that is "self-managed."[3] The complicated nature of participation in these types of experiences has prompted more recent immersive productions to recontextualize and renegotiate the place of the audience member as participant.

Here, I use two case studies to elucidate how a recontextualized audience participatory element was devised: first, in *An Awfully Big Adventure* (2016) at Bridgewater State University (Bridgewater, Massachusetts) and, again, in *Alice in Wonderland* (2017) at Plimoth Plantation (Plymouth, Massachusetts). As the conceiver and director of these two productions, I will discuss the aims of the production team, our creative process, and my observations, with a focus on the "spect-character," my terminology for the audience member. In doing so, I propose one way to consider the audience-actor relationship and hope to add to the discourse around participation in immersive experiences.

The scope and limitations of this study should be noted here. As conceiver and director of both *An Awfully Big Adventure* and *Alice in Wonderland*, I was present throughout the entire process: conducting research, attending production meetings, devising/creating the script with student collaborators, attending all rehearsals and performances, and conducting interviews with actors and audience members. My discussion of each process describes how the production team set out to create actor-audience interactions in the context of multiple story lines and considers the role of the audience member *from the perspective of the creators*. The methodology I used in assessing the outcomes of audience experience unfolded over the course of the creative process, through direct observation of actor-audience interactions, through feedback from audiences, performers, and technical staff, and through personal experience. With this methodology, I follow Gomme in "embrac[ing] the subjective account as our principal mode of access to spectator experience."[4] My data, of course, does not amount to a large-enough sample to draw conclusions about the nature of the "spect-character" in general. Further research would need to be undertaken to determine whether the characteristics of the "spect-character" are evident across a wider sample of productions and whether such a sample would result in a complete definition of "spect-character" in immersive performance.

Spect-Character

Both *An Awfully Big Adventure* and *Alice in Wonderland* fit Gareth White's working definition of immersive experiences as ones that include "dialogue with in-role facilitators; surrendering oneself to an experimental process; mak[ing] use of a physical interior, engag[ing] the whole body of the spectator/participant, and creat[ing] an ambiguous situation whereby it is unclear whether the work is happening around, to, or within the spectator/participant who is invited to explore points of view in relation to the performance and setting. The implication of the term 'immersive' is that it has a special capacity to create deep involvement and commitment from the audience."[5] These experiences created multilayered identities for participating individuals who moved beyond spectators, voyeurs, and the concepts of Boal's "spect-actor," or Brecht's distanced bystander, to become emotionally invested spect-characters.[6] I introduce the term "spect-character" to refer to audience participants in these two case studies who functioned as both spectators and characters within each production. These experiences called upon spectators to *become* characters in navigating interactions that required self-reflection and resulted in a performance of their own humanity. In *An Awfully Big Adventure* and *Alice in Wonderland*, spect-characters were immersed in the world of the play not only through designed physical environments but also through their own roles in each production. Each spect-character followed an assigned story line, but through their interactions with actors and the completion of specific tasks, spect-characters moved in and out of their dual roles, experiencing them alternately or simultaneously as the play unfolded. To delve into the stories moving within and about them, spect-characters engage with intersections of their past and present experiences and solve problems that require immediate and intimate interactions, leaving them vulnerable and prone to complicity. Such high-stakes situations can lead to highly emotional states. Surrender to the process is necessary to fully experience the production and to shift from spectator to character and back again in an immersive space. When functioning as character, the spect-character may actually serve as a way for the *actor* to become further immersed in performance.

In "Participations on Participation: Researching the 'Active' Theatre Audience," Matthew Reason notes, "In film and media audience research, the description of active and passive audiences has the particular connotation of spectators being either subservient . . . or transformatively active" and proposes that immersive practitioners view "an active audience [as] good and a passive audience [as] bad."[7] Must either the spectator or the participant be privileged? In influencing *how* a story is told, can the audience participant support the intentions of the creators while creators afford the participant status as cocreator? Commenting on Jacques Rancière's ideas about the emancipated spectator, Reason argues that audience participants in immersive experiences are "engulfed within the work . . . no longer able to see the work, no longer able to question its principles."[8] It's true; the spect-character does not have the ability in the moment to apply a critical lens to a production. But does the traditional spectator who sits in a theatre seat, emotionally engaged in a performance, have this ability? Is analytical distance fully accessible in these moments? Rancière argues that "being a spectator is not some passive condition that we should transform into activity."[9] If we consider *all* audience members as active, we can better understand the position of the spect-character. The activity of audience members, whether in a seat or on their feet, includes responses both internalized and externalized and whose interactions with the play extend to the adoption of a critical lens, often after the performance ends. Must the intention of the creators of participatory theatre equivocate a powerless audience or is there a space where actors and audience coexist, one responsible for where the story is going, while the other contributes to how it gets there?

I propose that the spect-character functions as both spectator and character, with neither being privileged over the other. During performance, the spect-character exists in a continuous loop of giving and receiving, taking in information through all five senses, reacting, and putting out information in response to the sensory experience. This new information is then picked up by actors who react in turn. In the spect-character, we see an audience participant that supports the actors' storytelling by becoming, from the actor's perspective, a scene partner.

One way in which the spect-character is able to take on this role is through prior exposure to source material, or what I refer to as a "rehearsal." A spect-character's "rehearsal" includes any foundational knowledge they bring to a production that has prepared them for entry into a participatory world, consciously or subconsciously. This may be through a shared text, collective memory, or written or visual materials available to the audience before or at the start of the performance. Such texts create a common language between audience and actor before the performance begins. This may prove particularly useful for immersive situations in which storytelling is not always linear and the burden is often on the receptor to fill in bits and pieces unseen. Additionally, the degree of familiarity with a text may shape the spect-character's expectations of what she will experience during the performance. Rand Harmon argues that engagement with a site may provide a similar shaping of experiences that "not only grounds the individual's cognitive interpretation of the performance, but . . . also might impart clues as to the role an audience member might play in the event. The more apparent and integrated the role, the more readily the audience member may experience emotional connections."[10] Therefore, a spect-character's initial investment in the process and their ability to experience themselves as a character in the play may be directly related to and influenced by her knowledge of the text.

An Awfully Big Adventure

In summer 2015, I conducted field research in London and New York City, studying the work of production companies including Punchdrunk (*Against Captain's Orders, Sleep No More*), Third Rail Projects (*Then She Fell, Grand Paradise*), Secret Cinema (*Star Wars, Back to the Future*), Dreamthinkspeak (*Absent, The Rest Is Silence*), and Speakeasy Dollhouse (*The Bloody Beginning, The Illuminati Ball*), with the aim of creating an immersive production with my own students. I selected J. M. Barrie's 1911 novel, *Peter Pan*, as the foundational text for what would become *An Awfully Big Adventure*, hypothesizing that the spect-character experience would be more successfully constructed upon the foundation of a familiar text. I determined that in addition to adapting stories from the novel, we would also include Barrie's life as a source.

Twenty-six actor-playwrights began the devising process with spect-character as our focus. *What character(s) would the audience become? What role would they play?* We determined that our audiences were intended to move fluidly between roles of spectator and character(s) within six simultaneously presented story lines, called "tracks": Peter Pan and Wendy (track 1), Captain Hook (track 2), Tinkerbell (track 3), Tiger Lily (track 4), J. M. Barrie (track 5), and the Lost Boys (track 6). Rehearsal exercises were aimed at identifying which scenes would become a part of each track and what participatory activities spect-characters would engage in to accompany each scene. Exercises in identifying strong imagery, physicality, objectives, and theatricality yielded a long list of potential scenes that could be included. From there, we considered how spect-characters might engage with actors and environments. It was ultimately determined that the audience would be introduced as classmates to the Llewelyn Davies boys, with whom Barrie had a close relationship, and would then become Lost Boys along with the Llewelyn Davies children. Depending upon which track each group of audience members set out on, spect-characters then became, at times, pirates, parents, or members of Tiger Lily's army. Spect-characters engaged in a variety of participatory activities and one-on-one encounters, including: dressing Wendy, poisoning a cake with pirates, tucking Lost Boys into bed, playing cards with Tinkerbell, and being initiated into Tiger Lily's army.

The production, which ran for thirteen performances in April 2016, utilized sixteen distinct playing spaces, eight of which were built for the production and eight of which were classrooms and other spaces in the theatre wing of BSU's Rondileau Campus Center building. Spect-characters were guided by multiple actors as stories unfolded in a variety of locations, including a Victorian classroom, a nursery, a pirate ship, a Neverland lagoon, Tiger Lily's mountain retreat, the underground home of the Lost Boys, and J. M. Barrie's office. While the majority of scenes were unique to a specific track, there were times when more than one track experienced the same scene, and all six tracks shared the same opening and closing scenes.

The spect-character experience began as soon as participants arrived at the Rondileau Campus Center building and received a ticket with an illustration of one of the Llewelyn Davies/Lost Boys on it. Upon entering the space, spect-characters found the correct boy, who presented them with some information about the subject they had been studying. A dramaturgical device was required to set boundaries for audience expectations. The Headmistress, stern and no-nonsense, who would later appear as Captain Hook, delivered a set of rules to the "schoolchildren." Preview audiences were helpful in shaping this introductory scene. These audiences were exclusively unfamiliar with immersive theatre and proposed that a more complete set of rules, in particular ones that outlined how they were able to participate, would be helpful to audience members in navigating their way through the production. At performance, spect-characters were advised that they may speak when spoken to and were encouraged to answer questions and engage in dialogue. They were also told that they may participate in activities as they were able and partake in food/drink as they desired and were warned not to stray from their group (figure 1).

As the creative team anticipated, our audience's unfamiliarity with immersive theatre presented some challenges in actor-audience interaction. Similar to the audience anxiety and discomfort around their expectations that Uwe Gröschel describes in *People in Glass Cases Shouldn't Throw Stones*,[11] some of our audience members admitted to feeling "afraid" to participate, for fear that they would "mess up the show."[12] During these performances, I observed that spect-characters were willing and eager to participate in specific activities that were accompanied by directions (i.e., playing a card game, frosting a cake, painting a picture). However, when invited to engage in improvised dialogue by an actor, fewer audience members were as willing or confident. When I asked spect-characters how they felt in response to each of these parts of the experience (participatory activities versus improvised dialogue), many claimed they felt "safer" engaging in participatory activities. One audience member said, "I know how to frost a cake, so that wasn't scary. I wasn't sure what to say when an actor wanted to have a conversation and I didn't want to throw them off."[13] When I asked if they felt manipulated in their roles, most spect-characters felt a sense of responsibility to the production. "I did not feel manipulated but felt obligated to complete tasks to keep things moving."[14]

Figure 1. *An Awfully Big Adventure*, Bridgewater State University (2016). Photo courtesy of Matt Greene.

In addition to reseating the audience/actor relationship—suggesting a role for participants other than Boal's spect-actor, El Teatro Campesino's worker-actor, or Bread and Puppet's prerehearsed audience volunteers—immersive theatre departs from other forms of participatory drama in its use of performance space in which the actors and audience participants exist within the same world, rather than one in which spectators in the actual world observe actors in the world of the play. In this shared world, an audience member crosses the threshold into the realm of character. In these environments, audience autonomy is still limited, as it is largely determined by a set of rules outlined by production facilitators. Theatre practitioners largely maintain control of the space and guide the audience into their roles. In several instances during *An Awfully Big Adventure*, audience participants were required to make choices that would affect their own personal story, while in others, they were guided to complete tasks that affected the outcome of the overall story. In one scene, the audience finger painted with Tiger Lily and her army. One member of the army guided the hand of a spect-character to complete the phrase "Hook is dead." This message, delivered in each of the six simultaneous story lines, was essential to the overall story and moved the action of each along to the finale. Yet, it is the endowment of these roles upon the spect-character that engage active involvement and a sense of investment and responsibility to the production.

A greater sense of responsibility and investment was present when actors cast spect-characters in a very specific role. An example of this was during a scene in which each boy invited a single audience member to play catch. During the game, each boy delivered a monologue explaining Peter's thoughts about fathers. As the spect-character walked away from the game, the boy cried, "thanks, Dad." In that moment, for each Lost Boy, the audience spect-character became a father and was endowed with the associated traits and responsibilities. One audience member experienced his transformation in this way: "When I was playing catch [with a Lost Boy], I was actually playing catch, so it felt normal and natural to have a conversation. Then he called me 'Dad' at the very end, and I realized who I was supposed to be and I felt like I wanted to go back and give him a hug, so I did."[15]

Specific moments of self-identification as a character took place in moments like this. In my experience, the transformation of the spect-character could be very effective when a spect-character experienced what has become at many such productions a highly sought-after "one-to-one" encounter. These moments of intimacy typically involve an interaction between a single actor and a single spect-character in a private space. Such interactions may range from morally or intellectually challenging to sensually stimulating. One-on-one experiences push the boundaries not only of identity but also of what becomes personally acceptable in the safety of a theatrical setting.

In *An Awfully Big Adventure*, one-to-one interactions required that spectator/participants demonstrate vulnerability in high-stakes situations that were explicitly tied to identity. In one such encounter, Peter Pan brought a spect-character into a tiny room, where he sat across from her as though looking in a mirror and asks why *she* abandoned him. Over the course of Peter's monologue, the participant learns that s/he *is* Peter's lost mother. One spect-character who experienced this interaction found herself "completely emotionally invested. The actor, the small set, did indeed immerse me totally in the moment, such that a good deal of sobbing was induced from me. A truly moving experience."[16] Another spect-character claimed she felt like a character in the production because "people were so delighted to see me when I entered a room" and "felt central to the storytelling, specifically when looking at a message in a bottle with Captain Hook."[17] Responses to one-to-one interactions were often visceral, eliciting high emotions. The actor who played *An Awfully Big Adventure*'s Wendy remembers, "I think it made many people the best kind of uncomfortable. Being inches from rejection, death, love, truly forced people to look at their own relationships. If being at a distance makes you think, then being up close makes you feel. . . . There are so few opportunities where it's okay to just feel with another person."[18] The state of the spect-character is a most vulnerable one. Yet, it was in moments of one-to-one interaction between an actor and a single participant that spect-characters felt most invested. In these interactions, for both actors and audience, borders became permeable, flexible, and open as they collaborated in the moment. The actor who played the role of Peter Pan commented, "We didn't know how any audience member would react at any given moment and those possibilities were infinite. I couldn't 'act.' I couldn't think of the best way to make something work, I just had to make it work. I had to be Peter Pan and problem solve as the audience and I moved through Neverland. The actors didn't have more power; the audience didn't have more power. We shared it."[19]

Alice in Wonderland

The success of *An Awfully Big Adventure* led to another devised project of an immersive nature in which the spect-character was central. In summer 2017, the BSU Theatre Department, in collaboration with Bridgewater's Arts for Youth program and historic Plimoth Plantation, presented forty performances of *Alice in Wonderland*, created as a part of my Children's Theatre Tour course (figure 2). Sixteen students, under my guidance and direction, devised and scripted an immersive and site-specific adaptation of Lewis Carroll's most famous work. While Plimoth Plantation is best known for its living history sites, which host thousands of visitors each year, *Alice* took as its performance space the plantation's Hornblower House and Garden. This beautiful location allowed for scenes staged in fifteen distinct spaces including the kitchen, dining room, front and rear porches, two auxiliary rooms, an alcove under the stairs, a formal English garden, the koi pond, wooded paths, various clearings, and a short stone wall. As the performances were in July and August, the gardens were in full bloom and provided a convincing backdrop for Wonderland.

This production was geared toward a family audience, inviting spect-characters to travel along one of four "tracks," Diamonds (track 1), Hearts (track 2), Clubs (track 3), and Spades (track 4), on a quest to save Wonderland from the Red Queen. Familiar characters in this production included Alice, the Queen, the King and Knave of Hearts, the White Rabbit, the March Hare, the Mad Hatter, the Dormouse, Caterpillar, and Tweedledee and Tweedledum. Two additional characters, Humpty Dumpty and the Cheshire Cat, were puppets, each manipulated by the same actor. *Alice* was completely guided, with one actor-guide (as a Playing Card) assigned to each track. In each of these experiences, young spect-characters became collaborators in the process as they made active choices, engaged in dialogue, and crossed borders to move in and out of multilayered roles. The most significant outcome of this experience was that I found that the role of spect-character may be useful as a pedagogical tool in the engagement, teaching, and learning of young children.

The process for creating *Alice in Wonderland* was similar to that of *An Awfully Big Adventure*. Once again, I chose a text that would be familiar to audience members before attending the production, providing inside knowledge, or "rehearsal," for our spect-characters. Proof of this inside knowledge was evidenced by the many young audience members who arrived at the production dressed as Alice or the Red Queen. The knowledge that many audience members would be children shaped how the experience of the spect-character was constructed. While *Alice in Wonderland* steered away from the darker elements of the life of Lewis Carroll and his controversial relationship with the young Alice Liddell, it did anchor its audience experience in the familiarity of croquet games and courtroom trials while exploring the largely unseen relationships among the playing cards and the reason why the White Rabbit must never be late.[20] Bringing groups together for select scenes also reminded spect-characters that other participants were seeing entirely different, simultaneously occurring stories.

Throughout the creative process, we paid particular attention to the limits of participation for young spect-characters, who would have a hand in setting their own boundaries. This shaped our approach to designating the specific role of the spect-character. We determined that owing to the large number of children attending accompanied by parents, families would stay together on the same track, with spect-characters led by one consistent actor-guide throughout the entire process. This meant that each suit of cards would enlist spect-characters as members of their cause: Diamonds and Spades in aiding the Queen; Heart and Clubs in organizing a rebellion against her (figure 2).

In *Alice*, the creative team provided fewer opportunities for one-to-one interactions owing to the practicalities of separating a mixed audience of children and adults. There was, however, one particularly impactful one-to-one interaction between the Red Queen and a single, adult audience member. In this interaction, the spect-character watched the Queen as she gazed at her own reflection in a mirror. Here, she revealed her fear of growing old and came to the realization that she, in fact, had already aged past her ability to travel in innocence to Wonderland. In the mirrored interaction, the spect-character simultaneously saw his own reflection in addition to that of the Queen. The Queen delivers her monologue in the second person, effectively rendering the spect-characters simultaneously themselves and iterations of the Queen. The spect-characters, then, are faced with their own mortality and loss of innocence.

Figure 2. *Alice in Wonderland*, Plimoth Plantation (2017). Photo courtesy of Ethan Child.

The actor playing the Queen commented, "One man, on Diamonds track, was by himself and he started crying. For one minute he could relate, he *was* the Red Queen."[21] Another adult audience member witnessed the same scene and commented, "The Queen talked about her experience of aging. But it was my experience of aging, my experience of time passing."[22]

Generally speaking, children are more freely enticed to create and participate in embodied, imaginative worlds than are their adult counterparts. *Alice*'s synesthetic experience was determined largely by the natural environment coupled with the participatory activities planned for each space. Spect-character as pedagogical tool was employed in the creation of these activities for our young soldiers or rebels. Working within Gardner's theory of multiple intelligences, actor-playwrights incorporated various embodied experiences across each track. These included: kinesthetic experiences (spect-characters played croquet), linguistic experiences (spect-characters read poetry), spatial experiences (spect-characters drew pictures), musical experiences (spect-characters sang a song), natural experiences (spect-characters identified plants), logical-mathematical experiences (spect-characters completed math problems), interpersonal experiences (spect-characters engaged in dialogue with characters), and intrapersonal experiences (spect-characters reflected upon their own journeys). This design led to an interesting outcome. Through observation I found that unlike the audiences of *An Awfully Big Adventure*, *Alice*'s younger audiences were more than willing to initiate their own transformations from spectator to character through engagement in activities/tasks, as well as through improvised dialogue. Young audiences were more vocal and demonstrated a greater sense of control over the play's outcome than their adult companions. While the overall structure of the entire story remained unchanged, individual scenes were sometimes altered by young audience members who felt empowered to make decisions and guide scenes in their preferred direction, typically away from anything scripted. Of course, permission to run wild with the imagination is much more easily granted to children than to adults. However, the investment of the young spect-characters in the production and in their own role in it was highly impactful not only for the spect-characters but also for the actors. The actor who played the White Rabbit remembers one encounter with a young female audience member immediately following the Tea Party, where she learned that March Hare was on a desperate search to find her son, a white rabbit with a pocket watch: "As soon as I got there, a little girl who was already active with the story told me, 'you just missed your Mom! Where is she? You need to find her!' I improvised my way through the scene. I didn't want to ignore her curiosity and focus. I entertained her notion about the mother and eventually improvised my way back into the scene. But the situation left me with an increased level of urgency. 'Where's my mom? I have to find her!' I was happy that she was really invested in the story. The adults were more like spectators and the children were more like characters."[23] Young people's consumption of *Alice*'s dramaturgy was a mode of scaffolded learning. For example, in the three-scene sequence preceding the aforementioned spect-character's interaction with the White Rabbit, the spect-character: 1) assists the March Hare in finding pieces to a puzzle that, when completed, shows them a photograph of her son, the White Rabbit; 2) meets the White Rabbit and assists him in recognizing that it is time for the Tea Party; and 3) attends the Mad Hatter's Tea Party where they reencounter the March Hare, participate in the tea, and learn that this is the place where she was supposed to meet her son. Here, young spect-characters engage in spatial learning, interpersonal learning, and musical learning and synthesize these activities to solve the problem of a separated mother and son. At the close of *Alice in Wonderland*, all participants were given the opportunity to reflect upon their experiences as a group, allowing them to decompress and process the events of the play. An actor playing Alice's mother, who had set spect-characters off on their journey at the start of the play, asked them about their experiences down the rabbit hole. It was striking to hear many young spect-characters confidently announce what they had done to solve the problem faced by their group. Through authentic, embodied experiences, the spect-character in immersive-based activities, both in and out of the classroom, may serve to promote interdisciplinary learning for children, particularly at the elementary school level.

Spect-Character as Accomplice

One outcome shared by both *An Awfully Big Adventure* and *Alice in Wonderland* was the finding that the spect-character experience is shaped by actions in which they may be complicit. These interactions may be one-to-one or group-based. *An Awfully Big Adventure* and *Alice in Wonderland* required that spect-characters share complicity in questionable situations, but there was some degree of choice offered in their participation. Most often, these interactions were carried out in a three-step process: the "set-up," the "reveal," and the "consequences." In *An Awfully Big Adventure*, spect-characters witnessed a set-up: Tinkerbell's seduction of Tootles, ensuring that Wendy would be shot. It was with this knowledge that spect-characters were offered the opportunity to hand Tootles his weapon. If a spect-character choose to do so, she became complicit in the action. In the consequences step, the spect-character in question was encouraged to stand with Tootles as he admitted his crime to Peter. Again, the spect-character chose whether to take responsibility.

In the final moments of the trial scene in *Alice in Wonderland*, during which the Knave of Hearts is accused of stealing the queen's tarts, Hearts claims guilt, standing, holding up his playing card, and announcing, "I ate the tarts!" In what came to be jokingly known as the production's "Spartacus Moment," spect-characters followed, each standing and exclaiming, "I ate the tarts!" Audience members were not encouraged to join in but chose whether to participate. Most did, rising to exclaim their guilt and save the Knave. Some did not. Specifically, those who were on the Diamonds and Spades tracks were reluctant to participate, having been enlisted to serve the Queen, while those on Hearts and Clubs tracks were eager to advance the cause of the resistance. Investment in the process was embodied at the close of the trial scene through a negotiation of complicity between saving oneself or acting in the interest of the greater good.

The collaborative team of *Alice in Wonderland* strove to create a family-friendly yet sophisticated piece. In doing so, they created a world filled with anticipated fun and whimsy but did not shy away from asking young spect-characters to take part in decision-making and self-reflection. This experience was similar to that of Boal's spect-actor in that they were, at times, asked to make a decision that may change the outcome of a scene, situation, or problem. Alyssa

Germaine, who played the title role in *Alice*, noted that some children were conflicted when issues of complicity arose. In one scene, Tweedledee breaks her brother's rattle, thrusts it into the hands of a spect-character, and asks them to keep mum about it. Later, Tweedledum questions the audience member. Germaine observed, "Kids wanted to defend Tweedledee; they didn't want to throw her under the bus. So I threw them under the bus. They may have been afraid because on top of hiding the rattle, they could get caught in a lie. That's a big dilemma for a kid."[24]

The request for spect-character silence functions in two ways. First, it lends itself to a sense of voyeurism whereby seeing interactions not meant to be seen become an arousing experience. Second, the assumption of imposed silence leaves the spect-character with the ethical dilemma of choice: when to break the rules for their own, or the greater, good. In a structured environment, volumes of storytelling potential open for the spect-character who now structures an entire world within themselves. They may ask, "What choices do I make as the agent of action (or inaction), as protagonist in my own story?"

Ethical Considerations and Caring for the Spect-Character

When constructing the identity or participation of the spect-character, as was done in each case study discussed here, the ethics of immersive and site-responsive experiences are invoked. What responsibility do the artists and producers of such experiences have in guiding spect-characters toward a prescribed final outcome? In instances of one-to-one interactions that are intimate and immediate, leaving spect-characters in vulnerable situations, what must the process include to ensure not only the physical safety of the participant but also her/his mental and emotional security? In my experience, the best traditional theatre experiences elicit emotional and intellectual responses from an audience who are left with memories of moments that resonate long after the final curtain. In immersive and site-based experiences, audience participants who experience an interaction with a performer up close and personal, without an opportunity for distance, may retain resonances of that moment in their memory long into the future. The creators must consider this in their rehearsal processes and provide opportunities for participants to mitigate this condition. Various productions have attempted different ways of doing this. Third Rail's *Then She Fell* allows ample time for participants to be alone in a space before a new scene begins, allowing them time to process what has occurred and prepare for what is to come. During this time alone, participants are encouraged to explore the material space. Outfitted with a skeleton key that opens closets and drawers, participants uncover elements of the story and acclimate to the new space.[25] Les Enfant Terribles's *Alice's Adventures Underground* takes a different approach, always having a guide present, though this guide may change as groups are handed off to different characters.[26] I took a similar approach in *An Awfully Big Adventure*, as audience groups were led by various characters, depending on their "track," and each playing space was staffed by a crew member. With this method, participants are always accompanied and always have access to a crew member, should they feel the need to exit a space. This handing-off technique also allows flexibility in the creation of multiple story lines and affords actors time to travel behind-the-scenes. In *Alice in Wonderland*, a single guide was ever-present, establishing a relationship with his group. Particularly in a production where many participants were children and young adults, this created the most secure of scenarios, as these participants had a clear role to play and tasks to perform, as well as the freedom to engage in improvised conversation with their guide. In addition, stage management staff were stationed in a second-floor room of the Hornblower House, allowing unimpeded and constant visual access to the outdoor playing spaces, close physical access to the indoor spaces, and verbal communication with each guide over a headset. Should an audience member require assistance, a member of the stage management staff was sent to accompany the participant to a designated assistance area.

The creative teams of *An Awfully Big Adventure* and *Alice in Wonderland* spent substantial time during the process attending to "caring for participants." Techniques employed in the rehearsal room included learning to hold the gaze of the spect-character, leading them gently through the physical space, and negotiating when to encourage participation and when to move in another direction. In cases where spect-characters were asked to participate as accomplices, they were afforded the opportunity to make choices, and actors were ready to adjust in the event selected participants were unwilling. In many instances, spect-characters were encouraged to use their voices, engaging in improvised dialogue with actors.

Conclusion

An Awfully Big Adventure and *Alice in Wonderland* provide examples of how we might recontextualize the role of audience participant as one that privileges neither the experience of the spectator nor the experience of the character. For the spect-character to contribute to and thrive within immersive dramaturgy, there must be great care taken to ensure that actors and spect-characters coexist in a space of simultaneous giving and receiving. Through the transformative act of becoming a character, a strong level of trust must be reached between actor and participant. In *An Awfully Big Adventure* and *Alice in Wonderland*, the foundation of this trust was the rehearsal exercises and performance practices that focused on caring for the physical and emotional safety of the spect-character. This was particularly effective in *Alice in Wonderland*, where young audience members found themselves in a safe space that allowed them to engage freely in dialogue and decision-making within the world of the play. This supported engagement across a variety of learning styles may indicate the potential for the experience of the spect-character to be used as a pedagogical tool, engaging students in interdisciplinary activities that promote independent and critical thinking. In *An Awfully Big Adventure*, the relationship between actor and spect-character was one in which audience participants supported the storytelling by becoming, from the actors' perspective, a character in the production. At times when spect-characters could be seen as accomplices to an action, many were willing to accept blame. The fluidity with which spect-characters could move in and out of roles allowed for collaboration with the actors. In the two case studies presented here, the majority of spect-characters were invested and eager to perform their roles in each production.

In the transition from observer to participant, the spect-character may engage in dialogue and physical activity that propels the plot forward and possibly develops character relationships. The spect-character is neither wholly themselves nor completely a character, and yet is simultaneously both and neither. Spectators become characters in support of actors as they enter a dialogue with text and space, a pastiche of fantasy and reality or past and present. The fluidity of spect-characters' roles in these productions made perfect (non)sense in the worlds of Neverland and Wonderland, liminal spaces where anything may happen and real-world norms are abandoned. Whether on a flight to Neverland or on a trip down the rabbit hole, the spect-character is changed.

Notes

1. W. B. Worthen, "The Written Troubles of the Brain: *Sleep No More* and the Space of Character," *Theatre Journal* 64, no. 1 (March 2012): 79.
2. Claire Bishop, *Artificial Hells: Participatory Art and the Politics of Spectatorship* (London: Verso, 2012), 73.
3. Keren Zaiontz. "Narcissistic Spectatorship in Immersive and One-on-One Performance,"

Theatre Journal 66, no. 3 (2014): 405–25, accessed September 18, 2018: https://muse.jhu.edu/.

4. Rachel Gomme, "Not-so-Close Encounters: Searching for Intimacy in One-to-One Performance," *Participations Journal of Audience and Reception Studies* 12, no. 1 (May 2015): 283.
5. Gareth White, "On Immersive Theatre." *Theatre Research International* 37, no. 3 (2012): 221–35.
6. I first used the term "spectator-character" in an earlier draft of this paper titled "Navigating Identity and Agency in *An Awfully Big Adventure*," at the American Society for Theatre Research Conference Panel "Site-Based Theatre as a Trans-Contextual Experience" in Minneapolis, Minnesota, November 2016.
7. Matthew Reason, "Participations on Participation: Researching the 'Active' Theatre Audience," *Participations Journal of Audience and Reception Studies* 12, no. 1 (May 2015): 272.
8. Reason, "Participations on Participation," 272.
9. Jacques Rancière and Gregory Elliott, *The Emancipated Spectator* (London: Verso, 2009), 17.
10. Rand Harmon, "Site-Based Theatre in 21st Century Britain: Conceptualizing Audience Experiences," University of Colorado at Boulder, 2015. https://scholar.colorado.edu/cgi/viewcontent.cgi?article=1036&context=thtr_gradetds.
11. Uwe Gröschel, "Researching Audiences through Walking Fieldwork," *Participations Journal of Audience and Reception Studies* 12, no. 1 (May 2015): 349–67.
12. Lauren Germaine, interview with Colleen Rua, October 22, 2017.
13. Sharon Alicandro, interview with Colleen Rua, September 10, 2017.
14. Chris Germaine, interview with Colleen Rua, October 22, 2017.
15. Matthew Lundeen, interview with Colleen Rua, September 10, 2017.
16. Ruth Barnwell, interview with Colleen Rua, April 27, 2016.
17. Samantha Mueller, interview with Colleen Rua, May 20, 2016.
18. Emily Borges (Wendy), interview with Colleen Rua, May 15, 2016.
19. Frank Iaquinta (Peter Pan), interview with Colleen Rua, May 15, 2016.
20. Martin Gardner's *The Annotated Alice: The Definitive Edition* (Lewis Carroll, *Alice's Adventures in Wonderland & Through the Looking-Glass* [New York: W. W. Norton, 2015]), which provided a wealth of information to student playwrights, similarly steers away from the Carroll/Liddell controversy. Conversely, Maria Tatar's *The Annotated Peter Pan* (J. M. Barrie et al., The Annotated Peter Pan [New York: W. W. Norton, 2011]) investigates in depth the allegations surrounding J. M. Barrie's relationships with Sylvia and the Llewelyn Davies boys.
21. Richard Pickering, interview with Colleen Rua, September 20, 2018.
22. Marissa Stanley, interview with Colleen Rua, December 1, 2017.
23. Michael Eckenreiter (White Rabbit), interview with Colleen Rua, December 1, 2017.
24. Alyssa Germaine (Alice), interview with Colleen Rua, December 1, 2017.
25. *Then She Fell*, Third Rail Projects, August 28, 2015, Kingsland Ward, Brooklyn, NY.
26. *Alice's Adventures Underground*, Les Enfants Terribles, August 11, 2015, Waterloo Station, London.

Ethics and Site-Based Theatre

A Curated Discussion

—GUILLERMO AVILES-RODRIGUEZ, PENELOPE COLE, RAND HARMON, AND ERIN B. MEE

Operating outside of the conventional theatrical space with its normalized precepts of behavior for both performer and spectator, site-based (or site-specific, site-responsive, or immersive) performance blurs the boundaries and redefines the social conventions of the viewer/performer/site relationships. By erasing the perceived safety of the theatrical auditorium, site-based works force a range of proxemic relationships that confront issues of cultural difference, inclusion, exclusion, physical agency, hierarchy, and entitlement, among others. The human body displayed on the distant and distinct stage has a very different power than a human body sharing the space of the viewer/participant. Whether it is the protagonist in Cora Bissett's *Roadkill*, who pleads with individual viewers to help her escape from the sex traffickers who hold her, or the terror of the implied potential violence in Hydrocracker's 2011 *The New World Order*, participants are challenged to respond without a script and outside of both social and personal norms, thus opening the potential for aesthetic and ethical conflicts.

Furthermore, the emphasis on a visceral experience embedded in site-based work often assumes a certain type of viewing body and that the viewer can, and will, be mobile, regardless of the topography of the site. Productions that require participants to climb a steep hillside after dark, such as NVA's 2012 production of *Speed of Light*, on Arthur's Seat in Edinburgh, or San Francisco's We Players's *The Odyssey* in 2012, which was enacted along a five-mile trek around Angel Island, pose serious questions regarding the experiential aesthetic of these productions for those who are differently abled.

In an effort to begin to address some of the ethical issues surrounding the creation and consumption of site-based work, we invited two theatre scholars and artists to join us in a discussion of how and when the aesthetics of site-based theatre performance come into conflict with ethical considerations. Guillermo Aviles-Rodriguez, of Los Angeles, and Erin B. Mee, of New York City, joined Penelope Cole, of Golden, Colorado, and Rand Harmon, of Denver, Colorado, on May 20, 2018, for a lively conversation on the ethical challenges unique to site-based work. In 2016, Cole and Harmon organized an ASTR working group titled "Site-Based Theatre as a Trans-contextual Experience." Mee and Aviles-Rodriguez, also participated in that initial working group where in the concluding moments of that conference session many of these ethical questions entered our discussion.[1]

Each artist/scholar led one portion of the discussion. To begin each segment, the individual artist related an experience, as either a participant or a creator of site-based work, which prompted them to question the ethics of that interaction, which led to further interrogation of ethical dilemmas of site-based work in general. Based on that personal experience, a question was composed to prompt dialogue. The group then shared experiences and perspectives in an effort to identify possible best practices for creators of site-based theatre to consider.

It was not our intent in this discussion to be prescriptive or to suggest that our potential solutions to ethical problems are one-size-fits-all. Nor are we discounting the many companies, creators, and productions that succeed in creating safe yet challenging spaces for interaction. However, we acknowledge that even in the hands of the most experienced and/or well-intentioned producers, problems can, and do, arise. Ethical concerns that we addressed include postcolonial issues of intrusion and appropriation, physical accessibility/mobile versus immobile participants, accessibility versus aesthetic choices, implied contracts of trust between producer/participant and participant/performer, and participant dangers and risks. We would like to note that in the following transcription, we frequently use the terms "colonization" and "power." In these we are referencing projection on multiple social and cultural levels: race, gender, economy, interpersonal relations, and ability.

Postcolonial Intrusions and Appropriations

Discussion Leader: Guillermo Aviles-Rodriguez

Guillermo: I have a story about an incident that happened during an experimental opera titled *Hopscotch: A Mobile Opera for 24 Cars* that I consulted on and translated for in 2015.[2] This transit-oriented site-responsive opera was performed inside and around limousines in various locations in Los Angeles. My story focuses on one of the many locales and communities in which the opera took place. Of all the locations, only a few presented problems, but I think that all the problems had the same cause. This particular incident happened in Hollenbeck Park, in the community of Boyle Heights. It was here that the performance sparked protests from community members who accused *Hopscotch* of being just another example of the rampant gentrification, or "neo-colonization" as it is framed, taking place in Los Angeles's communities. This particular performance was intended to enrich and enliven, but it ended up driving a wedge between the outside audience and the local residents who felt that the art was a thinly veiled attempt to open the community up to more economic exploitation.

The main group protesting at this site was Serve the People–Los Angeles, a neo-Marxist group that hands out food and supplies at the park once a month. One of their food distribution events coincided with a *Hopscotch* performance. As they observed the performance unfold and saw what the piece was doing, and how it was doing it, Serve the People took issue with three aspects: with the representation of the community; with the performers and their perceived ethnic makeup; and with opera in general, as an activity associated with higher income brackets. *Hopscotch*'s producers decided to meet those Serve the People's questions with assertiveness and pushed back. This struggle caused a dangerous and ultimately unfortunate battle in the community that left no participant unscathed.

Ethically, the ultimate battle that the show had with the residents of that neighborhood leads us to the question of how much responsibility the producer of site-responsive performances has and, conversely, how much responsibility does the community have in terms of the manner in which the piece is being presented? How much responsibility do they owe to each other when conflicts arise? And I will add that, in my observation, this issue or dilemma hasn't gotten as much traction from the theatre community as I think it should. The ultimate question is who has the right to the city during these site-responsive performances: creators or residents? Henri Lefebvre's concept is that the city belongs to everybody, not just the institutions, or the well-heeled, or the people we conventionally understand to run the city.[3] The city belongs to all of us, including the people who don't have the economic means, whose legal status is not established, and so on. *So, if you look at this issue through that lens, then a question arises: When a creator of an intended site-based performance event enters a site, do they have to ask permission from anybody other than the city council or administrators who manage that site?*

Rand: I appreciate you offering this anecdote to start us off because I think it cuts to one of the basic components of why successful, or impactful, site-based theatre elevates the audience's experience above a piece of dramaturgy merely set against a really pretty real-world backdrop. What makes a site-based audience experience really visceral is that the dramaturgy intersects with the contexts of the site and the audience is actually immersed in, interfacing with, and reacting within the contexts that they understand they're interpreting from the site. Any site is going to present a multitude of resonances, whether architectural, spatial, economic, political, historical, or cultural, as you referred to with this particular performance incident. And beyond that, every participant will bring a different personal spectrum of knowledge of that site to their participation. Some people that participated in *Hopscotch* might have gone to Hollenbeck Park before. Some people might have had some sort of prior knowledge of the park, or some people might have responded to something political that had happened in Hollenbeck Park twenty years ago; all of those associations are going to affect how they participate. These resonances are elevated even more so when the site is a live site, a real-world site that people actually inhabit and perhaps use to exchange in commerce, so, the site is ongoing, and transient, and living. In my opinion, there has to be a level of respect for that living community within the contexts to be unlocked by the dramaturgy for the ultimate performance to also live within that site.

I really responded to your referencing Lefebvre and the right to the city because there's a sense of privilege that is inherent when people, as we are going to refer to this, colonize a site for their own dramaturgical purposes, as opposed to perform upon that site in collaboration, or at least cooperation, with the community. I think about my own study of the Common Wealth Theatre in England, and their production *Our Glass House* in 2012–2013, a multilayered site-responsive performance exploration of spousal abuse created from several actual case studies.[4] These case studies predominantly came out of public housing developments, or "council estates." People apply to and are placed in these units, which are owned by the local government and are appropriately sized for their needs as a family. It's not that spousal abuse is so aligned to particular economic classes; it's just that the prevalence of these case studies that Common Wealth ultimately used as foundational material came from council reservations like this. Thus, Evie Manning and Rhiannon White built this production to play in various council estates around the United Kingdom. My understanding is that the first time they did this piece, a lot of questions arose within the surrounding community, like: What are you doing? Where do you come from? Is this meant to be a comment on us? Manning and White emphasized to me that the performers' collaboration with the residents of that first council estate significantly enriched the ultimate production.[5]

When I experienced the production, I felt a palpable sense of the audience intruding into the council estate as part of the experience. The audience group for each performance embarked from the edge of the estate, and as you walked through the neighborhood to the site of the performance, there were residents who would come out on their front stoop and look at you. There was a very real sense of being an outsider, of trespassing in this council estate before you then were admitted into one particular house and experienced the production. At the end of the performance, when you see the protagonists of this production then "escape" that environment, and "escape" their abuse, you really feel engaged in what this community is experiencing. So, I think considering the successes of that production, it perhaps indicates what could be done to not "colonize" the site, but conversely, to actually build a piece within the site to try to ensure positive community engagement. Who are the people who live in this place and what are their stories? How do those stories interface with the dramaturgy and therefore with the experience that the audience is intended to have?

Erin: I want to respond, first, to what Guillermo said and then to something you said, Rand. Guillermo, whenever you tell this story, I think about Peter Brook's book, *The Empty Space*, and the fact that nothing is ever an empty space. When someone decides to do a performance in what might look to them like an empty space, they need to take into account that that space may well be rich with a history, a set of lived experiences, and a set of associations that must be researched. I think that site-based performance loses a lot of its strength when it uses the site simply as a backdrop or a set piece, rather than making the site the central character, or the central theme, or, in fact, responding to what is actually there—which includes the resident community. Some people think of "site" as referring only to the physical space but, Guillermo, what you bring up is the fact that all physical locations exist within communities, plural. There are many ways people have of engaging with these sites, and people have many relationships to these sites, and, Rand, as you say, to fail to take that into account is to lose the opportunity to delve into the richness and depth of what could—and should—be part of the production. I'm the artistic director of This is Not A Theatre Company, and we did a piece called *Ferry Play*, which is a site-specific audio play for the Staten Island Ferry. For tourists, the Staten Island Ferry is a tourist attraction, but for people who live in Staten Island, it's a way of getting to and from work. For the drunk guys that were hanging out on the ferry, it was a place where they could hang out all day. The site had a very different life for each group of people riding it; when you take that into account, the play is much richer and more nuanced, and you're not colonizing someone else's space and saying, "We don't really care about your relationship to this space; we just want to use your space." Not caring about the people who use the space is equivalent to somebody walking into my apartment and saying, "I want to do a play in your apartment, but I don't care that you're living here." Well, if I'm living here, you need to care.

Penny: I like very much, Guillermo, that you talked about Lefebvre and how the city belongs to everyone. However, there is a flip side of this issue that we need to acknowledge: The city may belong to everyone, but the stories do not. The city is made up of individual stories, and it's those stories that we need to bring to life, that need to be honored within the landscape of that city. *Hopscotch* imposed a story on the people in the park, with a disregard for the story of the people in that park, which was an act of colonization and set up an ethical conflict.

Other questions to consider are: What is the intent? and What do these theatre companies want to achieve? I think part of our responsibility is to understand the goal of the performance and to ask if that goal is appropriate for this community, to discover the community's goal, and to determine where these goals come together.

Erin: Yes, Penny, what you are saying is that *Hopscotch* embodied an attitude of "We are bringing this very lovely cultural production to your neighborhood," which implies they thought that neighborhood didn't have a culture. Where is the responsibility for taking into account that communities have cultures of their own and stories of their own?

Guillermo: Absolutely. I also think that this is not only a site-responsive problem. It is not a problem specifically manifested with people who produce site-based theatre, but it does need highlighting. A problem seems to be approaching this type of work by focusing on our motives in a given community. The community knows nothing about our motives and looks only at our actions. I think this was definitely true with *Hopscotch*. I am very comfortable in saying that they had the best intentions when they produced this piece. Now, the actions they took were, in many cases, ham-fisted and shortsighted; however, I don't think that the response the event received was something unique to them. There might be many productions that get away with a similar exploitation because the community in which they perform may not be as politically activated as Boyle Heights. We need to go into a situation knowing not only what we want to do but also how we plan to engage residents who may already have a very rich culture and creative engine running. I think the real problem here is the difference between what the creators meant to do and what they actually did, which are two different things.

Another important concept is Barbara Kirshenblatt-Gimblett's social pornography.[6] Sometimes there exists a privileged audience that wants to penetrate a community and be a part of a show because of a desire to consume or possess an exotified other. But a hypothetical privileged audience wants to do so safely, because they cannot just drive their hypothetical Bentley through our hypothetical neighborhood. And, because this hypothetical audience would have a lot of people around them during a performance, they would feel safe. I think that is the motivation that a lot of audience members brought to this show in Hollenbeck Park. I think the people there felt it and reacted as you would react if somebody organized a safari into your community. I think in wrapping up this phase, we need to think about the audience who lives in that community, the accidental audience, and what they might feel when the production's audience comes to see the piece housed in their community.

Rand: I'm thinking from a producer's standpoint now and about how some dramaturgies lend themselves to being enriched by the accidental and some dramaturgies don't. I think a prudent practice might be to acknowledge that these potential tensions exist and to caution potential creators to at least investigate before deciding on the hard boundaries of the production's engagement with the site.

Erin: But doesn't it also have to do with a level of homework? What I think I am hearing is that this producer did extensive research on Hollenbeck Park, what it looked like and what it felt like, but not sufficient research into the resident communities. So, I think it's a question as well of the amount of research, the depth of research, and the focus of the research: One has to consider the communities in which that site exists as part of the research.

Guillermo: Yes, but again to go to Lefebvre, one step beyond that is to acknowledge and embrace the fact that sites are constructed and consistently recreated by the people who inhabit and embody that space. So, if site-based practitioners can embrace that concept, then they'll never merely approach a park thinking that the permit from the city is enough, because they'll know that, yes, that does create space for the performance of the site but so does the churro vendor who makes her living in the park. The people who manage a space are not necessarily the same as the ones who inhabit it. I think that the way to honor the complexity of this issue is to frame it thus, because it's easy to theorize about the need to research a site, but in practice I think it's difficult to have to ask permission from the homeless person who sleeps there if I'm not going to use that part of the park. I do understand the difficulties of what we're asking a practitioner to do, but I think the price that you pay for not doing that is much greater, as we've discussed. Furthermore, I think this issue is going to arise more frequently as

Figure 1. Caitlan Lattimer and Richard McBride do the Dance of Crayons with two audience members in This Is Not A Theatre Company's *Café Play*. Photo by Maria Baranova-Suzuki.

site-based theatre productions continue to spread into communities where they might not need to lease a space, where the permits are easy to acquire, or where the community's people are less upwardly mobile. In Los Angeles, gentrification is a very, very hot topic and is very controversial. Site-based theatre production will not be able to exist independently of a conversation about gentrification any longer, whereas ten years, even five years, ago gentrification wasn't as big of an issue. Now it's very much an issue and will continue to be. So, these cases, this example of *Hopscotch*, could be the first of many more examples like it, at least in California, but I'm sure all over the country very soon.

Erin: Guillermo, in an earlier discussion, you brought up the question of how artistic directors and producers want to treat site-based theatre with the same amount of control that they wield on the conventional proscenium stage. In *Hopscotch*, you've got the churro seller, the homeless person, and many others—the site is the churro seller's place of business, it's someone's home, and you can't kick them out. When we did *Café Play* (figure 1) at the Cornelia Street Café,[7] I thought, during one rehearsal, "Can we ask everybody to handle the dishes in the kitchen really, really quietly?" because the clanging of the dishes was so loud (figure 2). And of course, being the control freak that I am, I went to the owner and asked, and he said, "Well, everybody's doing their job. This is a place of work

Figure 2. *Café Play* by This is Not A Theatre Company. Photo by Maria Baranova-Suzuki.

for these people, so they're just going to have to continue." And, of course, after a bit I realized that the sounds of the dishes were actually an integral and important part of the play. I think that there's a politics to displacing people, but it's often bound up in the attempt to control a site or space in the same way you would try to control a conventional theatre space. I think there's a political component to the aesthetic choices.

Accessibility: Ethics versus Aesthetics and the Responsibility of the Creators

Discussion Leader: Rand Harmon

Rand: Erin, I think that bringing up the issue of control presents a great segue. My question grows out of my long-standing relationship with We Players in San Francisco. They produce what they call site-integrated work, which is bringing a classical text—a new adaptation of a Shakespeare text, mostly, but other classical texts, too—and staging them in historical locations by integrating the site and the spatiality of the site, and the cultural and historical resonances of the site, into moments of the dramaturgy.

Figure 3. *The Odyssey* on Angel Island (2012). Nathaniel Justiniano as Zeus and Henry Hung on trumpet. Photo by Tracy Martin.

The issue that I want to discuss concerns the ethical responsibilities of the creators of site-based experiences with regard to accommodating potential physical limitations in the audience as they conceptualize and design the audiences' made experiences. The issue really came to prominence for this particular company with their production of *The Odyssey* on Angel Island in 2012.[8] When I attended, I was somewhat aware of the controversy, but I didn't realize the extent of what happened until after I interviewed Ava Roy, We Players's artistic director. I have continued to follow this issue and their subsequent attempts to provide as much accommodation as possible at their productions.

For *The Odyssey* on Angel Island, they designed a nearly five-mile, on average, five-hour trekking experience (figure 3). As an audience member, you arrived at the landing on Angel Island at the historic, nineteenth-century quarantine station in Ayala Cove. As we arrived at the ferry landing, we were instantly cast as visitors to the court, celebrating a local holiday. The oracles were telling Telemachus of Odysseus's delayed return. Telemachus decided to go on a quest to find his father, and he enlisted audience members as his band of explorers to accompany him. We were provisioned with bags that contained a map, snacks, water, and other items that we might need on our journey, and off we departed on a nearly five-mile trek around the island. At various locations, we encoun-

Figure 4. *The Odyssey* on Angel Island (2012). James Udom as Telemachus. Photo by Tracy Martin.

tered different stories from *The Odyssey*: We were serenaded by the Sirens, we explored a bunker where the Minotaur had been slain by Odysseus's troops, we climbed Mount Olympus to observe Zeus and a council of the gods, and we were guided by underworld spirits through the House of the Dead. However, for the entire journey, we were members of Telemachus's merry band. He addressed us by name. We encountered obstacles and addressed them together as a team, participating at a very high level of physical engagement (figure 4).

All throughout that trek, however, there was a white twelve-passenger van with a wheelchair lift (that conveyed nonambulatory patrons) following behind our walking group. At each stop the production would pause, momentarily, while those patrons were allowed to unload from the van and then make their way to the performance site. Our walking experience of the trek embodied a nearly five-hour constant engagement; however, the van riders' experience became episodic owing to the isolating nature of their conveyance.

The promotions for *The Odyssey* on Angel Island clearly communicated that the patrons would be required to walk around Angel Island for extensive distances over uneven terrain and be engaged in physical activity. However, that did not deter a few less mobile people who wanted to have that experience from purchasing a ticket and taking the ferry to Angel Island. We Players felt obligated, and generously and kindly provided the conveyances needed, to transport these less ambulatory audience members around the course of the production.

I believe, in our society, we feel, whether or not it's a legal obligation, that if someone has a particular need, we as presenters must do our best to accommodate that need. In 2017, I saw We Players's production of *Midsummer of Love*.[9] It was their aesthetic choice to produce this event in two different locations; it provided two different settings and atmospheres in which to explore the themes of the play. However, an added benefit was an opportunity to provide for the range of physical abilities of their audience. One location, Kennedy Grove, in a public park in El Sobrante, outside of Berkeley, did require thirty minutes of strenuous physical exertion by the audience, up a significant elevation gain, to reach the performance site. They advised people with medical conditions or mobility needs of their limitations in providing accommodation and encouraged them to attend performances at another site in Golden Gate Park, on Strawberry Hill, which required a less strenuous climb. The Strawberry Hill performance required about ten minutes to climb to the site, not strenuous exertion, and also had a road to the site where We Players could provide egress for people requiring wheeled conveyance. Much effort was made to communicate these differences in experience and to direct patrons to performances appropriate to their ability levels. Yet, We Players had patrons that either didn't heed, or underestimated, the warnings and choose the more rugged approach, which ultimately required a couple of emergency responses for patrons over the run of the production.[10]

I'd like to explore the question of what responsibilities creators of site-based performances should concern themselves with regarding providing for all ranges of potential audiences' physical limitations. Again, I'll reiterate that generally we feel obligated to provide for our audiences' needs; however, should that obligation extend to designing equal aesthetic experiences for the ambulatory and nonambulatory potential audience members? We normally provide for interpretation of performances for the non-hearing and non-sighted audiences. Legally, new performance venue construction and renovation is legislated and regulated to provide access and accommodation for all, but when we produce in a real-world site, those accommodations may not necessarily exist. *What ethical responsibilities lie with the creators for providing these accommodations, and how much responsibility is there to make sure that the experiences provide parity between the mobile and mobility-impaired experiences, the sighted or non-sighted experiences, or is there a responsibility to make all experiences available for all levels of physical interaction?*

Guillermo: This is an issue close to my heart. One side of me who produces feels one way, and the other half of me that goes to site-based theatre feels another way. I directed a piece called *Alicia in Arroyo Land*, an adaptation of *Alice in Wonderland* set in a Latino context.[11] It was performed at the Audubon Center in Lincoln Heights, which is a community in North East Los Angeles, hilly, very verdant. The sites I chose to stage the piece in put the second half of the show in a natural clearing at the top of a hill. It felt like an aesthetically brilliant choice to use this location until the issue arose of how to transport our eighty-year-old patrons up there or our patrons in wheelchairs. The easy answer, the answer we were given by park administrators, was that we were exempt from the Americans with Disabilities Act (ADA) because our show was sited in a space considered a trail. In California, nature trails and outdoor sites are not bound by ADA regulations. The producers of this performance had a conversation concerning being within legal and safety limitations and felt that somehow artistically we were justified, but that somehow socially, or politically, we were not exempt. We considered options ranging from telecasting the happenings up at the site to a lower level where people could watch them via video to transporting them along another path, which would however require them to miss the first third of the play because of the increased length of that path. This is why this question is fraught; there are only degrees of virtuousness. Regardless of your intention, your solution is not going to accommodate all. Let's say, by definition, that the site is exempt from the ADA, and then I excluded differently abled people because of my artistic choice. To tell you the truth, I was not thinking about that population when I was making that piece, and that was my mistake. Since that experience, I've learned that if we're truly going to make theatre for the people, then we need to utilize places that are welcoming and accessible or make those sites as welcoming and accessible as possible to all.

Erin: My father is in a wheelchair, so I think about this every day, and I will say that some of the worst wheelchair-accessible spaces are proscenium theatres. For example, to get him into the Park Avenue Armory in Manhattan, we have to go around to the back, in through the freight-loading door, and make our way over cables, around light stands, and other backstage equipment. So, to be fair, I think this is an issue with all theatre, not just site-based theatre.

Proscenium theatre predominantly uses only two of the five senses, sight and sound, so if you have difficulty seeing or difficulty hearing, you're excluded from experiencing a large percentage of the play. Site-based theatre is inherently multisensory because the perfume of the person next to you, the texture of the things you touch, the feel of the wind on your skin are all integral to the production rather than being outside the frame of the production. You can experience that in a wheelchair or if you have trouble seeing. Therefore, there are aspects of site-based theatre that I think open the audience to wider modes of participation and experience and perhaps make site-based theatre open to more people.

Maybe what we need to think of is not how to conceive for different abilities but how to explore further and extend the audience experience to include the five senses. Perhaps if we think of this as an opportunity to further explore multimodal experiences, then site-based work would be more open to more people. In one of our earlier discussions, we were talking about how if there are two or three scenes happening at the same time, not all participants are going to have the same experience anyway, so perhaps the utopic way to think about this is not to think about parity but to think of this question as an invitation to conceive many ways of engaging the participant, and then to allow the audience member to engage in the way that they choose, through the modes that are available to their particular needs.

Penny: Erin, I was also thinking of our earlier discussion about the individuality of experience as a participant of site-based performance, as well as about the portion of the question about the ethics surrounding providing parity of experience. I think it harkens back to an idea that we try to control the experience for everyone, much like you, Erin, wanted the dishwashers not to clank dishes while *Café Play* was performing. I'm not convinced that parity is possible even in a traditional theatre space, let alone in a site-based space. It's not that we ignore that this experience shouldn't be similar, but no two experiences are ever going to be exactly the same.

I also really responded, Guillermo, to your comment that in choosing a site you need to own up to the fact that you're the one who chose it and that that site caused certain problems, such as when you acknowledged you excluded a particular population. While we may think that one site is absolutely the perfect, and only, site for our production, as we are researching that site, building the dramaturgy, and understanding what the site gives us in terms of the dramaturgy, as creators when we realize we have excluded a group of people, we then need to rethink our attachment to that site.

Guillermo: Beautifully put.

Penny: We have flexibility, as creators, to say, I want a place that's on a mountain top. It'd be perfect, but it's perfect for very specific reasons. Another site might be perfect but give me a different kind of dramaturgy, right? How can the story be unlocked in a different way, or maybe the question is can it be unlocked in the same way even though the site is different? I like the example you gave, Rand, of We Players and their production of *Midsummer of Love* on two different hills; the hill was what was important to the dramaturgy. It seems as if, based on the dramaturgy of the production, it didn't necessarily matter which hill hosted the performance. I'm sure they had some things in common, such as a wooded area, some elevation gain, open space to play on, but, important to this issue, they offered two different accessibility points for differently abled audience members and thus included more of the population. In my opinion, this is a really wonderful way of negotiating and compromising in a good way; compromising to be as inclusive as possible. We need to ask, "How can the site be accessible and also give me what I need dramaturgically?"

Guillermo: I think we should first invite wholeheartedly, appropriately, and persistently. If we are guided by the idea that differently abled patrons may not want or be able to experience this particular show, then you're going to make that a reality—an unfortunate reality. However, if we say, I'm inviting everybody to my site-based work, and you build it in such a way that everybody is invited, then I think you will be able to attract those typically marginalized populations. I use "marginalized populations" because I'm thinking that the same social mechanism is in play when people ask why don't "Hispanics" come to our plays, why don't black people come to our plays, why don't Asians? It starts with the work, and we may not be creating work in places that invite anybody other than the typical audience, which, by the way, is fast evaporating. So, a more articulate way to say it would be that site-based work offers us a unique opportunity to invite people who are too often forgotten and have frequently not been invited. Oh, and let's do it in a more complete, real, and organic way because we have that possibility available to us.

Erin: Guillermo, what you're saying reminds me of Howard Gardner's book *Frames of Mind*.[12] As educators, we know we have some kinesthetic learners, some visual learners, some interpersonal learners, and so on, and in our teaching, we invite students to learn in different ways. When I teach, I'm always conscious of including a number of different ways to approach the material and engage with it. I try to do the same as a director. Site-based theatre can offer different modes of engagement, whether you are walking, or in a wheelchair, or smelling, or touching, or tasting your way through a piece (babies learn by tasting things, which is why they put everything in their mouths). I think site-based theatre already invites other approaches through the multimodal, multisensory nature of the work. And if we would lean into that, into those different frames of experiencing, then, as you say, Guillermo, we'd be inviting all kinds of people into our work.

Rand: Well, I appreciate everybody's input on this and I feel that, again, from a creator's standpoint it comes back to that issue of control and how much we are intending to harness the experience of the site, as opposed to open up the experience of the site. I think it echoes back to a theme that we've been developing this entire conversation about the multitude of potential interpretations that can happen within a site, as opposed to trying to restrict and limit the experience to hard boundaries. I really like the idea of exploring and intersecting different modes of participation and interrogating the site for accessibility to a wide spectrum of modes of participation, as opposed to narrowly accessible experiential journeys, as are frequently produced. I remember immersive experiences that I've had where I've been blinded because there's not been any light in the space, and I've had to rely on other senses, resulting in a deeper emotional engagement, or a more visceral engagement. I've thought of site-based experiences where I was not ambulatory, where I was being transported, and I had given up my personal agency of being able to walk where I wanted to walk. I think there exist all kinds of methods that, because this is an experiential form, the creators can use to expand upon their dramaturgical concept. Very good discussion everyone, thank you.

Trust and Consent in the Interaction between Performer and Participant

Discussion Leader: Penelope Cole

Penny: When I was in London, in 2013, I had the opportunity to see Punchdrunk's *The Drowned Man*.[13] I purposely did not research the production or the company, so other than what I had heard, or read a bit of, I didn't know much about the story of *The Drowned Man* or of Punchdrunk's specific production style. For example, I didn't really understand how the one-on-one aspect of their work was embedded within the entire experience. I paid extra to experience the preshow to the show in order to get as much out of the experience as possible. I spent a lot of the preshow wanting to sit back and watch in order to engage in my own time and in my own way. I was a little taken aback at first by the other people in the room who were jumping in, giving opinions, and telling secrets. A male performer started demanding answers of me. I didn't feel invited. I didn't feel that my answer was important. I was uncomfortable and experiencing a bit of peer pressure in that space.

And then we got our masks. The mask, for me, was very isolating. It made me feel very vulnerable with no one to support me. I felt there was no way that I could make a connection with another human being, and so that also set me on edge during the experience. But I appreciated the different spaces. I took myself on a journey and explored the scenography, which was absolutely glorious. There was one space I really wanted to get back to and experience, alone, honestly, as opposed to alone in a crowd. I was moved out of that space by one of the ushers because I was not supposed to be in that area at that point in time.

By virtue of these interactions, I was feeling fairly coerced throughout the entire experience, which came to a head toward the very end. We were all being ushered down toward the lower floors of the building, the location of the final scene that Punchdrunk has in many of their shows, where everybody comes together in one communal experience. As I was making my way down, a male performer grabbed my wrist and started dragging me down an empty hallway. He actually grabbed my wrist and started pulling me along. At that moment I dug in my heels and refused to go with him. I'm a "yes, and ..." kind of person, but (in my memory) this happening in a dark hallway; it was narrow, I didn't know where exits were, and I was being pulled away from where I could hear the crowd was. I had no sense of being given any agency in that moment in time. So, I took it. At which point I, yet again, felt judged as the performer threw up his hands, sort of pushed me, and said, "Go back to the crowd." I have very little recollection of what really happened in that final piece of the performance because, as a woman alone in a situation where I felt negated as a human being, I felt like I had just escaped a highly dangerous situation. I also felt negated because I didn't know the rules, hadn't done the research. The question sparked by this experience is: *What are the ethical considerations that theatremakers should bear in mind while managing the specific performer-viewer interactions in their work? How much should the physical and emotional safety of the audience be taken into account, and how can transformative experiences be created that are also not abusive?*

Erin: Penny, I think that's a fantastic question and I want to start my response with an anecdote of my own, which led to some of the rehearsal modes I use with This Is Not A Theatre Company. I was in one of the test audiences for *Queen of the Night*,[14] and early on in the evening an actor read my palm, tracing my palm in a seductive way. Because it was my palm, and because I have been trained in the "yes, and . . . " mode of improv engagement, that was fine. However, toward the end of the play everyone danced together, and the same guy came up, invited me to dance, and then took me in his arms to slow dance with me. I had consented to dance, but I had not consented to slow dance, and the way in which he was dancing with me is something I, to be quite honest, associate with foreplay and sex. And so, I kept saying to myself "it's 'yes and . . . ' you have to participate." But I felt compelled to come home and tell my husband what had happened; it was almost as though I felt I had had an affair. I have been making a joke out of this story for years, except I don't think it's that funny.

I always talk to my actors about how you take someone's hand if you want to lead them somewhere: How do you get someone's consent to hold their hand, to touch them, to put your arm around them? There are ways of holding your hand out and making eye contact and reading the situation. I think actors are actually good at that. What they have to do is be reminded by directors/producers that they have to respond to what they see—so that if someone is uncomfortable, you let them go or you give them some space and come back later (or not). But grabbing and pulling—for me, that's absolutely crossing a line. If a man grabs me, I have a particular reaction because of things that have happened in my life; I'm going to pull away. I was talking to someone who referenced an "exciting" performance in which someone pulled a gun on them. To me, that's not exciting. Perhaps that could be exciting to someone who's never had a gun pulled on them in real life. I'm from New York. I lived through the 1970s in New York, and pulling a gun on me is not funny. If I were African American and somebody pulled a gun on me in this particular historical moment, I don't think I'd find that exciting or edgy; I think I'd find it terrifying. I do think we have an ethical obligation to take those possible responses into account. To be honest, Penny, I think it's also an aesthetic obligation, if what we're doing is creating an experience for someone; unless you want to traumatize them, you want to think ahead about the kind of reaction they might have and the kind of invitation that you're offering and, in fact, the way in which you're offering the invitation.

Guillermo: I think that there are many shows that push that boundary. I think the responsibility is on the producer and on the director to inform the people before they engage. Before the show begins, absolutely inform people you will be touched, you will be positioned, whatever it is that that show is going to do. I don't see why site-specific theatre should be any different than a haunted house where you are notified about aggressive, potentially traumatic interactions and are given a waiver to sign before entering. Also, in this site-specific world, you do have to be ready to be kicked in the genitals when you grab a woman and try to drag her into a dark hallway. If aggressive behavior is something that you're going to incorporate, then you have to be prepared for the consequences.

Rand: Gareth White writes that he thinks, to a great extent, that theatre is an institution that is understood by the attending public and that there are levels of implied consent when people buy a ticket to go to a theatrical engagement.[15] Our understanding of implied consent is mediated by our horizons of expectations. We know that conventional theatre has somewhat long-established horizons of expectations. However, when we're talking about an unconventional theatre, when we're talking about inviting an audience into a site, then all basis for spectator conventions is negated and new conventions will be established by how we invite the audience to participate in the site and the dramaturgy. Even though there's an implied consent, there's a responsibility on the producer's part to describe the horizons of engagement, not a responsibility on the particular participant to research and find out what they're in store for.

I also attended *The Drowned Man* in London; however, I never encountered any aggressive behavior toward me. I was at one point pushed back because I was too close to a performer for that particular engagement. There is also an unspoken spectator convention in the culture of attending immersive theatre that if you want to be engaged you get close to the performers who could potentially engage with you; however, if you're too close they will push you back because they have a performative responsibility. I was also pulled into a private engagement, but there was an invitation extended to me. I was tapped on the shoulder, I turned, there was a gentleman in costume, and he said to me and to the young woman standing next to me, "Would you two like to come with me? I'll give you a particular hint about something that's coming if you'll come with me in private and we can talk." It was an invitation, but I was not aggressively pulled into something.[16] I wish, Penny, that you had reported that to Punchdrunk at the time because I would be curious whether this was a rogue performer. I would be curious as to Punchdrunk's response to your experience; curious from a producer's standpoint, not from a right or wrong ethical judgment. That was definitely an aggressive engagement and dangerous.

I think that Guillermo is absolutely right that there is a responsibility for the safety of the performer and that an aggressive engagement of a participant is only going to cause a particular type of response. There is a responsibility to inform the audience participant of what kinds of engagement to expect. In her February 8, 2018, post on No Proscenium, Leah Ableson says that setting up the rules of engagement isn't only good for protecting the safety of the participant but also for expanding the beneficial experience of the participant. She believes most attendees would agree that they are able to relax and enjoy and imagine the space and beautiful performance if they feel safe while doing so, that there can only be a positive effect of describing to the participant, in advance, the horizon of engagement.[17]

Erin: I think one of the things that we need to talk about is a kind of performer training that has not yet been established for this work. In my theatre company, we treat the invitation as a skill that has to be practiced and rehearsed. How you invite an audience member to dance with you, or draw with you, or look into your eyes for a very long time needs to be rehearsed as much as anything else. It's in the invitation—it's *the way* in which someone holds their hand out to me—that lets me know that I can say no or can't say no. Audience response is part of this kind of work and has to be included as an essential part of the rehearsal process.

To double back to my *Queen of the Night* story: I did report my experience to the director, who was a friend of mine, and I assume she made changes. I also took that experience and made it a part of what This Is Not A Theatre Company does. We never ever open a show without rehearsing with the audience, without sitting with them and getting feedback. We also bring in Jeff Wirth, who is an expert in interactive acting, which is his term for the kind of interacting that happens when a trained actor is interacting with an untrained participant who is not an actor.[18] For example, Jeff Wirth gave us an hour-long rehearsal on how to invite a spectator up onstage to dance with you and how to deal with the numerous moments of consent in that interaction. The first moment of invitation is eye contact. If you get eye contact, then you can offer your hand; if they take your hand, help them stand; then you make eye contact again; then you lead them to the middle of the space. You continue to make eye contact, and basically with the eye contact you're saying, "Is this still okay because now I invited you to stand up, now I'm inviting you to the middle of the space, are you okay with that, now we're going to dance together, are you okay?" In other words, there are, within asking someone to dance, not one but ten moments of consent and you have to break it down very carefully. I think so many of these theatre companies, producers, directors, and even performers, as Guillermo said earlier, are still working with their proscenium-based training. They don't actually have the training to do the ten moments of consent that would have allowed me to feel comfortable in *Queen of the Night.*

Penny: Thank you all. The responsibility of the participant is another topic to consider. Absolutely, as a participant I am responsible for me, and at this age I'm very good at being responsible for me. I think what I responded strongly to in my experience with Punchdrunk was I knew that my twenty-year-old self would have gone with the actor in *The Drowned Man* and would have been scared to death. Part of that is being a female, some of that is the rape culture I've grown up in, some of that's my cultural training as a female in when it's appropriate to take a stand and when it's not. I made the choice to take care of me and probably missed out on something that would have expanded my experience of the story itself. This one-on-one opportunity with Punchdrunk was not presented in a way that allowed me to take that step.

Erin, I love your explanation of the breakdown of the moments of consent within an interaction. It isn't just about the invitation; it's also about moments of invitation that then set up a safety net for somebody to be able to say, "Oops, you have gone past my boundaries that I feel safe with" or "Hell, I'm going to break a boundary today because you've made me feel safe." If we don't pay attention to that structuring of the invitation, we rely on and reinscribe social ways of interaction that, maybe, are not healthy. If we're really wanting a transformative experience, then we need to figure out how to make the invitation, so we can break that boundary together.

Trust and Consent in the Participant/ Performer Relationship: Crossing the Line

Discussion Leader: Erin B. Mee

Erin: When we did *Café Play* at the Cornelia Street Café, we explored the interpersonal dynamics of a restaurant space, many of which were based on power. For example, one character (played by an African American actress) was a customer mistaken for a waitress, so we could confront the microaggressions that occur in restaurant settings. Another character was very entitled and privileged and very rude to the waitress. The audience was "cast" in the play by virtue of the fact that they sat at tables and ate and drank during the show. So, they were implicated in the message. One night there was an audience member who began to exhibit some very odd behavior during the course of the play: He kept leaning forward into scenes and putting his face right into the face of one of our company members. Most of our audiences followed customary "restaurant" etiquette and behavior, but his behavior was not appropriate to the setting—which meant it was therefore not appropriate to the play (because as a director, I was counting on people taking their behavioral codes from the setting and situation). I found out later that he was stalking one of my actresses and had used our show as an opportunity to see her. So the next morning I said to her: "He's not welcome at any of our shows. I'll get his name from our mailing list, I will put him off the mailing list but I'll hang on to his name so that if he ever tries to buy a ticket I'll just keep refunding it and block him from coming to any of our shows." I called and emailed a number of colleagues to ask if they had ever had a similar experience, and if so, had they developed a way of handling it. I found out that there is no protocol. On a proscenium stage, he would have had to stay in his seat and she would have been protected by the proscenium; in this situation, he was sitting right next to her in the café. My question is: *How do we protect performers from unwanted invasive behaviors in site-based work, where the performers and audiences are much closer physically and are often interacting?*

Penny: I think there are multiple ways, some of which have already been mentioned. Rand noted that in site-based theatre, getting close to the performer is often encouraged; getting near the performer allows you to have a particular kind of experience. I think in all instances, performers have the permission to say no, to push participants away and say, "You're too close." That is one way, giving that power to the performer to set their own boundaries.

And that goes hand in hand with training. If we train actors in this kind of work, the training in consent is important. Equally important is the training in how you manage situations much like you were talking about, Erin, by having a test audience. We really need to think through interactions; if you're getting an inappropriate response that places the performer in danger, then depending on the story, the site, and what's going on, possibly another performer can help that performer out. Finding safeguards to build into the performance is very, very important, as is creating our own internal and dramaturgical protocol.

I love this idea of the etiquette of the site as another dramaturgy that we need to pay attention to in order to understand the dynamics and the social power dynamics within the site. Each site is going to have a different social power dynamic, and the etiquette that we expect from one another within each individual site will differ. If we pay more attention to the etiquette of site, just as we need to pay attention to a broader idea of abled-ness, then we've unlocked a very rich texture.

We can also hook this back into a sense of ownership, that when I buy my ticket I own this experience, and that could potentially mean in a site-based performance I own that performer. How the performer is perceived within the interaction in site-based work is important for us to both acknowledge and figure out ways to negotiate.

Erin: Some people go to Broadway to see a certain star and have a sense of ownership, and so, I wonder if some of them bring that agenda into this work—"Oh, I can get closer to this person in this site-based piece"—and so they come not to see the play but to see the person, which is exacerbated by the fact that it's at a site where they are interacting more closely with the performer rather than being glued to their seat.

Rand: All conventions are off when audiences go to a real-world site. I feel that there should always be a protocol for ejecting the unruly spectator from a site-based work. I think that we have to be proactive about protecting our performers. Granted, you're probably going to have spent enough time in the site to identify potential physical hazards for your participants before you have an audience, but I think that in the same way we've got to anticipate what possible things might happen to our performers. In *Elevator Plays*, we had a security guard because we wanted to protect the site; the building was an active office building.[19] However, at the end of that first festival, our security contractor said, "Hey, we need to develop a protocol for ejecting participants because if someone comes and they're really drunk, or they're going to mess with the operation of the elevator, or they're going to mess with the performers while they're isolated in the elevator, we've got to have a system." So, we developed a protocol.

The heart of this is we've got to provide for everyone's security, performer and participant alike; we need to have a safety net for all involved. Just as we need a protocol for ejecting the spectator, we need a protocol for denying admission for someone who's caused problems in the past.

Guillermo: I want to distinguish between someone who is going to the show as an audience member, and somebody who lives, works, or plays where the performance is taking place. That's an important distinction because I can see a world in which a site-specific performer wants to ban the homeless people for the duration of their show, as in "let them find a different place to live in for the time that I'm doing my art!" So, I want to activate that vigilance about who we're allowed to ban and who we should not. Legally, I cannot tell you not to go to the park and have a picnic, whether I'm using it for a show or not. But, if you're my audience member, you bought a ticket and you want to follow the show, then yes, of course I can ban you if you become disorderly.

Hearing Erin's story about the scripted moment with the black performer, I thought, in that moment, we get to talk about how the site-specific mechanism functions inside of racialized places. Well, every place in America is racialized, but I'm specifically thinking of hyper-racialized locations like Hollenbeck Park, which is a politically woke area and definitely sees connections between site-specific work, racism, colonization, and many of the other issues that we've been talking about. We really can't hope to deal with that in the time that we have, but I did want to register that race is a fluid that we are swimming in when we are injecting ourselves into these public spaces that include bodies of color inside of them. Then, I think it's a best practice that has been mentioned and that we have to include, just like when you walk the space for safety for the actors, in that same walk you have to walk that space for safety of accessibility, safety of audience participation. Just like you would for any other performance.

Erin: I feel as though some of the smaller, less corporatized companies have more protocols for things like this. Rand, you spoke of security guards. I think there are ways to do it without security guards being involved. I mean, a security guard wouldn't make any sense in a café or in the play that I do in my apartment. We had life guards when we did *Pool Play 2.0* in the pool; because audiences sat around the edge of the pool with their feet in the water, the lifeguards were there for literal physical safety (in case someone fell in).[20] But also, they were there to enforce the pool rules. As part of that piece, we brought everyone in as guest members of the gym, so they had to read the rules of the gym and the pool and then sign. We did that for insurance, but it also became part of entering the space. But I think, even in situations where it doesn't make sense to have a security guard, you can rehearse what can you do if X, Y, or Z happens.

Guillermo: I wanted to share an experience I remember at a staging of *Fefu and Her Friends* inside of the Hollyhock House, which is a historic landmark in the Hollywood Hills.[21] I went to the show and the audience had to put these booties on their shoes because it's a historical building, and you are not allowed to use your shoes there. So, we went in and there was this older woman whose job it was, I guess, now that I look back, to make sure that you didn't find your way to a nonpermitted area of this historical landmark and pick up a figurine and take it home as a trophy. Why I wanted to share that story is because the last thing I would have wanted to see in that show would be a sort of a Rent-a-Cop there with a side arm waiting for you to do something wrong. I think that in thinking about the security issue, we can also think about how many times less is more, it doesn't have to be authoritarian; it can be more—I don't know what the word is—thematic or benign.

Erin: For *Versailles 2015*,[22] which was set in an actual apartment, we realized that the host of the party should welcome everybody and then, as part of her welcome speech, talk about what was okay and not okay in terms of behavior. We built it into the opening monologue of one of the characters.

Rand: Some of the most creative safety talks I've experienced have been delivered by characters in the play written particularly for the dramaturgy, or the period being portrayed. They got across very succinctly how you're supposed to act, and what you were to expect to happen. To come back around on the security issue, I think that security does not want to be visible; that's going to affect the contextual relationship with the site. However, I think that in all of the We Players productions I've experienced, I've noticed one or two park rangers close by to protect their site, as well as to protect the people performing in their site.

Penny: There's a couple of other things that I'd like to touch on here. Thank you, Guillermo, for bringing up the idea of including bodies of color; understanding that the world is bigger, and our choices can lead to a clash of cultures where a standard of societal behavior and interaction is appropriate for one culture and not the other. We've got to understand the layers of behavior and negotiate each particular interaction and problem.

We've also not mentioned sexual abuse. In the BuzzFeed *Sleep No More* article,[23] it is clear that the scenes that are highly sexualized, where bodies are exposed, are the scenes where performers are more at risk for actual grabbing, groping, or worse. Just as when you do any scene that deals with sexual content on a proscenium or more traditional stage, you must approach it with the utmost of care. But I think you also need to build in extra protocols, because for the site-based participant all expected and tacit conventions are gone. We're (both audience and performers) learning, with every production, a new way of behaving, and in those highly sexualized moments, we have to have an extra layer of protection for those performers.

Erin: Penny, what you were saying reminds me that *Sleep No More* has itself set up a kind of culture of response. When we did *Versailles 2015*, the piece about income inequality in New York City apartments, the first apartment we performed in was my house and I thought "uh oh, everybody's been to *Sleep No More* and they've been encouraged to open the drawers and read everything, so is everybody going to rifle through my underwear drawer?" So, we actually wrote some etiquette rules into the host's monologue, reminding people that while the play was fictional, the home was real. I think many people do bring a sense of entitlement or a capitalist sense of ownership to a play (e.g., I bought a ticket, so I own this). And if you have that mind-set, and you are encouraged to open a drawer and read a "private" letter, then you might apply that logic to the nude body and think, "Oh, well, I've been encouraged to read a private letter, so I'm also now going to reach out and touch that breast because that's an exploration, too." There's this sense of: If I'm invited to open the drawer and read the letter, then I can feel the breast, and I can also take this prop as a memento; this is now mine. I think *Sleep No More* has actually set up a culture of response that many site-based immersive and interactive productions are fighting against, at the same time that they are fighting against "no, I'll just sit here in my chair and not interact with anyone." I think there are two fronts on which we are now educating audiences to the particular performance.

Concluding Remarks

Rand: Gareth White says in his book *Audience Participation in Theatre: Aesthetics of the Invitation* (2013), "The ethics of audience participation, then, aren't as simple as removing all significant risk or ensuring explicit or implicit consent. At times effective participation—and politically challenging participation—will be that which puts participants in compromising situations."[24] In this discussion, we've explored numerous questions across a range of ethical considerations. The four of us have focused our ethical questions around situations when site-based productions put participants, performers, and indeed communities in compromising situations. What are the takeaways you've heard in this discussion? Are there areas where our discussion has too lightly touched, or perhaps even skirted, or where a further "what's next?" query might explore more deeply a particular ethical dilemma, or lead us closer toward articulating better or best practices to be considered or developed?

Erin: I think that we need to train performers, directors, and producers in interactive, site-based, and immersive work. I think we need to train performers specifically in a range of modes and kinds of interaction and different sorts of invitations. I think we need to rehearse with audiences, because, if the audience is part of your piece in performance, then they should be part of your rehearsal process. You should see what the range of responses might be so that you can better anticipate and deal with them.

I would also suggest embracing the multimodal nature (multisensory, multimodal, multi-frames of mind) of site-based, interactive, and immersive work, because I think embracing that and pushing it further provides an opportunity, to borrow Penny's language, not just to accommodate but also to embrace, invite, and welcome. How do we make somebody feel not just tolerated but warmly welcomed and included? I think we can do that if we, in turn, get out of the proscenium mind-set and remember that site-based work is multisensory, multimodal, and often has nonlinear dramaturgical structures. I think if we embrace those aspects of it, then we are welcoming, and inviting, and including, rather than just tolerating, different audiences. Perhaps we also need to hold workshops for our audiences so they learn the skills of interacting with actor-characters in these liminal spaces.

Guillermo: I'd like to highlight the term that Rand used in our earlier discussion, which was "Dramaturgy of Space." I think that's what we need. We're in need of a standardized way to deal with producing art in spaces that were not originally conceived to house them. And we need to remember that all space is a product, and that its construction happens only when everybody who lives, works, and plays in a space contributes. Everyone should have the opportunity to use space to achieve self-presentation and self-representation. To not allow for this creates many, many more problems for your art than any production would be capable of handling.

Penny: I would like to see us delve more deeply into the clash between the expectations of the producer/performer/artist and the participant. We need to think through how our interactions with one another impact the dramaturgy, the telling of the story. I also challenge us to change our perception about what those interactions can be, acknowledging our own social understanding of how the world works, and challenge those expectations through these interactions. Let me just give you one example: At the beginning of *Café Play*,[25] one of the first actors to appear was a young black woman. She was seated in the farthest corner, away from the audience. She immediately assumed that she was being sidelined because of her race, pulled out her phone, and started texting, or Instagramming, or Facebooking: "You won't believe what just happened to me. I cannot get service, I'm seated far away, I can't get a menu, et cetera." And—

Erin: They also asked for her credit card in advance.

Penny: And they asked for her credit card in advance. Suddenly, the lack of appropriate communication in this public space was up front and center, in my face. I assumed I knew the waitstaff's perception of the black customer and expected and supported the black customer's response, but yet I understood these responses in a much more immediate way because of my proximity to the interaction. In a way, I became complicit.

Theatre's always been at the heart of social change, even when part of the ruling hierarchy. It can be subversive, in part, because it's embedded in the human body, and I think the human body in such a close proximity to mine, potentially helping me participate and be part of the story, can make social change. So, I would like to see us really grapple with how to find those moments that bring social norms and expectations into focus through interaction and proximity in order to challenge those expectations and potentially create change. This also implies an examination of whether we're reinscribing bad social behaviors as opposed to challenging them through the work and structuring of the audience/performer interactions.

Rand: I think these have all been great takeaways. I'd like to conclude by calling into focus the number of times we've addressed the culture of the spectator, the culture of the participant. The culture of the participant in conventional theatre has evolved and been discussed over millennia, and, of course, experiential theatre has gone through many cycles and evolutions as well. We've even seen site-based theatre forms before in our history, but this level of site-based theatre production in the United Kingdom and United States is a very recent phenomenon. With the bounty of site-based theatre we've seen produced over the last two decades, outside of a few avid bloggers, there exists little discussion among the spectator population about what it is they're experiencing; it's still a new phenomenon. I would like to see the producers of site-based works nurture discussion among their participants regarding what they experienced: what they liked, what they didn't like, what they observed going on, and so on. I point to efforts in social media and web-based community building that has been done by the National Theatre Wales, where such ongoing discussion nurtures more participation in the development of a site-based theatre culture, where audiences start to know what it means to participate and what's possible when they participate—how it all works.[26] I think it is important to open channels for audience members to provide feedback and to participate in that discussion with the producers so that the producers are learning from their participants instead of just making their best guess as to possible audience responses.

As scholars, we need to accept the responsibility to not just critically analyze these productions but also foster this dialogue surrounding the participants' experience. Let us nurture a dialogue between spectators and creators about what can improve and how the participant can take agency in learning the culture and get their best experience. I feel that as avid consumers of site-based theatre, we four are somewhat holding the entire deck, because we know and have experienced a broad range of site-based works and because we've studied and practiced this theatre form. However, not everyone may be going to these shows with the amount of knowledge we have, and we might know how to unlock something in the experience where someone less experienced will not. We in the academy should cultivate more scholarly investigation into how to further this dialogue between audiences and creators of site-based theatre. I think we need this dialogue, not just with the occasional bloggers—albeit loyal, knowledgeable, really invested bloggers—but also, I think, with performance scholars leading the charge for this interchange, hosting talk-backs, and inviting the audience's feedback and participation in the evolution of the form. As creators, we need to devise ways, as we are developing a new site-based piece, to expand our community of participants to incorporate not only supporters and potential audience members but also inhabitants and users of the site and its surrounding environs, and establish a more vibrant culture of participant/performer/creator intra-communication in this art form.

Again, I think this has been a great discussion. Thank you, everyone, for your stories, your questions, and your insights.

Notes

1. The audio recording of the panel's discussion was transcribed by Becky Roper, a recent graduate of the University of Northern Colorado, BA in theatre arts.
2. Guillermo Aviles-Rodriguez was a consultant for *Hopscotch: A Mobile Opera for 24 Cars*, directed by Yuval Sharon. See https://vimeo.com/151711336.
3. Henri Lefebvre (1996), "The Right to the City," in *Writings on Cities*, ed. Eleonore Kofman and Elizabeth Lebas (Cambridge, MA: Wiley-Blackwell, 1996), 158.
4. Rand Harmon experienced *Our Glass House* on August 22, 2013, at the Wester Hailes

council estate when it was produced by Common Wealth Theatre at the 2013 Edinburgh Festival Fringe. The production was written by Aisha Zia, codirected by Evie Manning and Rhiannon White, and devised by the original ensemble for the inaugural performance in Bristol, UK, in 2012.

5. Evie Manning and Rhiannon White, personal interview with Rand Harmon, August 16, 2012.
6. Barbara Kirshenblatt-Gimblett, *Destination Culture: Tourism, Museums, and Heritage* (Berkeley: University of California Press, 1998).
7. *Café Play* was conceived and directed by Erin B. Mee with scenes by Jenny Lyn Bader, Jessie Bear, Erin B. Mee, and Colin Waitt, and choreography by Jonathan Matthews. *Café Play* ran for seven weeks, from October 4, 2017, to November 15, 2017, at the Cornelia Street Café, New York.
8. Rand Harmon experienced *The Odyssey* on May 19, 2012, produced by We Players, in and around historic structures in Angel Island State Park, in the San Francisco Bay. The production was directed by Ava Roy and devised by her and the ensemble.
9. Rand Harmon experienced *Midsummer of Love* on July 29, 2017, produced by We Players, on Strawberry Hill, in Golden Gate Park, in San Francisco, CA. This production was directed by Ava Roy and devised by her and the ensemble.
10. Ava Roy, personal interview with Rand Harmon, July 28, 2017.
11. Directed by Guillermo Aviles-Rodriguez, *Alicia in Arroyoland* was a site-based adaptation of *Alice in Wonderland*. See https://vimeo.com/229235436.
12. Howard Gardner, *Frames of Mind: The Theory of Multiple Intelligences* (New York: Basic, 1983).
13. Penny Cole attended *The Drowned Man: A Hollywood Fable*, produced by Punchdrunk in collaboration with the National Theatre and directed by Felix Barrett and Maxine Doyle, in July 2013.
14. *Queen of the Night* was conceived by Randy Weiner in collaboration with Murtaz Akbar and Simon Hammerstein and presented in February and March 2014 at the Diamond Horseshoe in the Paramount Hotel, New York.
15. Gareth White, *Audience Participation in Theatre: Aesthetics of the Invitation* (Basingstoke, UK: Palgrave Macmillan, 2013), 90–91.
16. Rand Harmon experienced *The Drowned Man: A Hollywood Fable* on August 16, 2013.
17. Leah Ableson, "Constructing Consent in Immersive," in No Procenium: The Guide to Everything Immersive, February 8, 2018, accessed May 20, 2018: http"//noproscenium.com/constructing-consent-in-immersive-a8d6cfdeeede.
18. Jeff Wirth is the director of the Interactive PlayLab in New York City, where he conducts training, playtests, and prototypes for interactive performance projects. Jeff has consulted for such top-tier clients as Cirque du Soleil, Blue Man Group, and Disney Imagineering. He authored the book *Interactive Acting* and has written and directed more than one hundred interactive shows.
19. *Elevator Plays* was produced by Specific Gravity Ensemble, in the historic Starks Building, in downtown Louisville, Kentucky. *Elevator Plays: Assent/Dissent—Ascent/Decent* ran from January 26 through February 24, 2007, *Elevator Plays 2: Beyond the Norm!* ran from January 25 through February 17, 2008, *Elevator Plays 3* ran from January 30 through February 22, 2009. Short plays were submitted from playwrights around North America

or written by ensemble members. Individual plays were directed by various ensemble directors and guests.

20. *Pool Play 2.0* was produced by This Is Not A Theatre Company and conceived and directed by Erin B. Mee with text by Jessie Bear and Charles Mee.
21. Guillermo Aviles-Rodriguez experienced this performance of *Fefu and Her Friends* in May 2017, produced by A J.U.S.T. Toys Production in association with Circle X Theatre Co., in Los Angeles, CA. The play was written by María Irene Fornés and this production was directed by Kate Jopson. See: http://www.latimes.com/entertainment/arts/la-et-cm-fefu-and-her-friends-review-20170522-story.html.
22. This Is Not A Theatre Company produced *Versailles 2015 (and 2016)* in real New York City apartments. The production was conceived and directed by Erin B. Mee with text by Charles Mee and Jessie Bear, choreography by Jonathan Matthews, and videography by Stefan Hartmann.
23. Amber Jamieson, "Performers and Staffers of *Sleep No More* say Audience Members Have Sexually Assaulted Them," BuzzFeed, February 6, 2018. https://www.buzzfeednews.com/article/amberjamieson/sleep-no-more.
24. White, *Audience Participation in Theatre*, 92.
25. Penny Cole attended a 10:00 a.m. performance of *Café Play* in October 2017 at the Cornelia Street Café, New York.
26. "National Theatre Wales Community," National Theatre Wales, 2018, accessed July 12, 2018: http://community.nationaltheatrewales.org.

Part III

THE ROBERT A. SCHANKE AWARD-WINNING ESSAY FROM THE 2018 MID-AMERICA THEATRE CONFERENCE

Inventing the Tramp

The Early Tramp Comic on the Variety Stage

—MICHELLE GRANSHAW

In their tattered clothes and grotesque makeup, well over a hundred comic tramps staggered across the US vaudeville stage at the turn of the twentieth century.[1] One of the most popular stage types in vaudeville, comic tramps sang, recited monologues, juggled, rode bicycles, and performed in sketches.[2] Although these comic figures are well known in theatre history, to date, the variety theatre's distinctive role in the tramp's performance history remains unrecognized. Two decades before the widely popular vaudeville comic tramp, the figure first stepped onto the variety stage at the moment of the tramp's cultural invention.

Until the 1870s, the word "tramp" existed primarily as a verb in the American lexicon and referred to a long walk or march. When "tramp" emerged as a noun in the wake of the Panic of 1873, it resulted from a collective effort to understand and contain the mobile spectacle of unemployed men traveling across the country.[3] In performance, American and European actors have performed variations on comic vagrants and beggars for hundreds of years, notably in commedia dell'arte, the circus, and minstrelsy.[4] However, tramps distinguished themselves from their predecessors onstage and in American culture through their scale and exceptional mobility, which reflected the extent of the economic distress caused by the Panic as well as improvements in transportation, such as the railroad.

Transformations in mobility captured the popular imagination and offered variety theatre a way to appeal to their audience's fears and fantasies that accompanied the rapid economic and social changes sweeping through the country. Playing for primarily a working-class audience at a time when first-class variety theatres increasingly succeeded at drawing more middle-class audience members, the variety stage comic tramp reflected tensions between the negative caricature in the dominant imagination and the more sympathetic connotations rooted in working-class experience. The early comic tramp of the variety stage reflected the nation's complicated racial, ethnic, gendered, and classed power dynamics that determined who had the privilege, permission, and safety to move throughout the country. In the 1870s, the range of comic tramps illustrates the instability of the tramp figure and the struggle over its meaning. The earliest comic tramps, performed primarily as stage Irish or in blackface, were almost indistinguishable. Aside from reflecting the popularity of Irish and blackface characters on the variety stage, Irish and blackface racial and ethnic comedy created a visual vocabulary that offered a quickly recognizable stand-in for the seemingly invisible crime of lacking means of work.

As the decade progressed, performers portrayed the most popular comic tramps as Irish, aligning mobility with whiteness and turning the comic tramp into a performance of racial privilege, even for immigrant and ethnic groups who faced staunch prejudice. Through the comic tramp's transformation in the 1870s, the comic tramp became a site of cultural "spin" and the rapidly realigning racial hierarchies of the nation after the Civil War. The increasing popularity of the Irish comic tramp demonstrated the North's limited ability to imagine freedom of mobility for black Americans. The Irish tramp, by contrast, may have reflected many negative characteristics, including his wandering nature, his unemployment, and his drinking, but he also showed that the Irish comic tramp could be part of a community and in some instances, even a hero.

The Tramp in the Dominant Imagination

During the economic depression of the 1870s, when mobile, unemployed strangers wandered through towns and cities across the country, people grew anxious over their inability to distinguish between who was unemployed and genuinely searching for work and who was idle and potentially a threat to people and property.[5] The figure of the tramp provided new possibilities for navigating these fears. The emerging image of the tramp in the dominant imagination, especially in the North, focused on an excessively mobile, idle, drunk, and potentially violent man, typically white. Reformers' construction of the tramp demonstrates how they conceived of the mobile unemployed—not as victims of the industrial economy but as criminals. This classification resulted not from any specific acts but from individual, moral faults. Through the cultural production surrounding the tramp, such as dime novels, newspapers, literature, speeches, pamphlets, cartoons, and theatre, the tramp figure reflected views held by reformers for decades that equated poverty with criminality.[6]

By the end of the 1870s, the new tramp laws passed by state legislatures reflected cultural and legal notions of tramping that developed throughout the decade, including the notion that a person with no "visible means of work" committed an arrestable offense. Starting with the first tramp law passed in New Jersey in 1876, the new laws made tramping a crime of status as opposed to a crime of action, distinguishing between tramps and antebellum vagrants. A person only had to *appear* to be unemployed and mobile to be arrested.[7] Placing them outside of social and economic causes for their circumstances, cultural representations construed tramps as consummate performers who survived and obtained charity through their lies. These performances presumed an audience; the tramp performed for people who were intentionally supposed to recognize and witness them to obtain food, drink, or shelter. For the dominant classes, the tramps' startling visibility comprised part of their central identity and threat.[8]

Ethnicity and race became intertwined with tramps' visibility. Without systematic study of tramps in the 1870s, many reformers assumed most tramps were male immigrants. Franklin B. Sanborn, secretary of Massachusetts's charity board, stated, "The two movements, as they show themselves in America—immigration and tramping—are but varieties of the same species."[9] Feeding anti-immigrant and anti-tramp prejudices, the conflation of immigrants and tramps led to biological explanations for tramping and intensified debates over immigration regulation at the state level; in both conversations, the Irish played a central role.[10] Building on long-held anti-Irish prejudices, reformers envisioned Irish ethnicity as representative of the lack of means and desire to work. In spite of anxiety over the newly freed black population after the Civil War, the northern dominant imagination tended not to envision the nation's tramps as black. It is possible this racial representation of the tramp emerged because they still imagined mobility as primarily a white right. At least for a short time, the variety stage blurred these distinctions.

The Comic Tramp Onstage

At a time when many variety theatres changed sketches and afterpieces after only a week in an appeal to novelty, a few months into the Panic, the comic tramp started to appear in songs, sketches, and afterpieces for weeks at a time.[11] From its earliest appearances on the variety stage, the comic tramp navigated the fluid ethnic and racial terrain surrounding the genesis of the tramp. Almost indistinguishable, the use of blackface and Irishness to construct the comic tramp reflected distinct prejudices against black Americans and the Irish that made the performances of their racial and ethnic types a clear visual marker of the tramp menace.[12]

With the dominant classes considering black Americans and the Irish as inherently inferior, their racial and ethnic comic stereotypes provided a visual vocabulary that offered a quickly recognizable stand-in for the tramp's seemingly invisible crime of lacking "means of work" and his failure in proper American citizenship. Early blackface and Irish comic tramps often did not verbally identify themselves, if they spoke at all. In their startling visibility, other characters recognize them on sight. First performed in January 1874 at New York's Olympic Theatre, *Private Boarding* features one of the few rare instances of a female tramp on the variety stage. Performed by a cross-dressing man in blackface, Mrs. Tramp instantly is recognized as a tramp by Mrs. Boardem, the boardinghouse landlady. When Mrs. Tramp asks if the home is a boarding house, Mrs. Boardem replies, "What did you think it was? The station house, or the soup-house?"[13] Another example, the sketch *The Terrible Example* (1874), which starred popular comedian Johnny Wild in the title role as an Irish tramp, Jimmy Lush, focuses on a temperance meeting led by hypocritical reformers. When Lush enters the temperance meeting, no one speaks to him or asks him for the fee to enter the talk. The president of the temperance society, Moriarity, notices and recognizes him on sight. His grotesque makeup and demeanor automatically make him stand out. Without any conversation, Moriarity "throws him out."[14]

Other characters recognize the black and Irish tramp through a visual vocabulary tied to their racial and ethnic comedic stereotypes. Repeatedly, the black and Irish comic tramps demonstrate their lack of bodily discipline while standing, sitting, or walking, in part due to drunkenness. Tom Pepper, the blackface comic tramp in *One, Two, Three* (1874), enters "very drunk, staggering, with an old segar butt in his mouth."[15] When Pepper sneaks back into the office, the servant goes to remove him, but Pepper's legs go out from under him.[16] Similarly, in *The Terrible Example*, Lush "staggers down" and falls against another character when he enters.[17] When the reformers decide to use Lush as their "terrible example" of alcoholism at their temperance meeting, they place him in a chair, but he slides off the chair and falls, repeatedly, sometimes bringing other characters with him. The visual gag grows throughout the sketch, with the entire Thirteenth Ward Glee Club falling over as a result of Lush's collapse.[18] Aside from reflecting physical comedy typically found on the variety stage, the comic tramps' physicality suggests that their flexible, floppy bodies cannot become disciplined enough for the regular, rigid, repetitive machine work increasingly dominating the American economy.

The trouble and chaos created by the comic tramps through their physical behavior also identifies them to surrounding characters. It was not uncommon for sketches and afterpieces, especially those at the Theatre Comique or Tony Pastor's, to end with a melee. In these sketches, the comic tramps instigate fights throughout the performance and the chaos ends the scene or sketch. As a result of their disruptive presence, other characters actively attempt to throw out the comic tramps in an effort to minimize the chaos. These actions highlight a key aspect of the tramp figure in the dominant imagination; the tramps have no place in contemporary society. In *Private Boarding*, Mrs. Boardem chases Mrs. Tramp around the stage, hitting her with a broom and eventually forcing her out the door.[19] The entire rhythm of *One, Two, Three* and *The Terrible Example* depends on the entrance of and the chaos caused by efforts to remove the tramp. Pepper enters, is noticed, is chased, and either is thrown out or exits on his own five times throughout the sketch.[20] In *The Terrible Example*, the reformers attempt to toss Lush out a minimum of four times.[21] In *Down Broadway*, Roger, the tourist, explicitly states that the tramps do not belong: "I can't see why a big city like New York will let those poor men die in the streets without giving them a home in the States Prison."[22] Through his falls, fights, and disruptions, the comic tramp makes his lack of means of work visible through the racial and ethnic caricatures. On sight, it is clear the comic tramp is lazy, drunk, and disruptive, which many intuitively assumed about black and Irish Americans in American society.

As the 1870s progressed, the most popular comic tramp characters on New York's variety stage appeared at the Theatre Comique. The comic tramp sketches with the longest runs and most revivals—*The Terrible Example* (1874), *Down Broadway* (1875), and the *Mulligan Guard Picnic* (1878 and expanded in 1880)—featured Irish comic tramps written by Edward Harrigan, part of the duo Harrigan and Hart, and performed by Johnny Wild.[23] However simplistic, the comic tramp embodied the tension between the negative stereotype emerging in the dominant imagination and the economic realities facing variety's working-class male audiences. Although Harrigan never escaped the tramp as conceived in the dominant imagination or stage Irish caricature, each subsequent sketch increased the positive connotations of the comic tramp, making him more verbal, integrated into the New York and Irish American community, and, on occasion, heroic. The popularity of the Irish comic tramp tied the figure to predominant white representations in the dominant imagination and helped solidify its ethnic white representation on the variety stage.

Lemons, from the *Mulligan Guard Picnic*, is the most vocal of all three Irish comic tramps, and he tells the audience about his employment history in a dialogue with the Mulligans' black servant, Rebecca Allup, played by Hart in blackface. When Rebecca says that she has seen Lemons's face in the police gazette, he claims it is because he was once an inspector. He also explains that he worked as "a jailor . . . and sailor boarding house runner. And I've played in the old Bowery Theatre."[24] By listing a bunch of working-class jobs, Lemons places himself in the same category as many of the men in the audience, who also moved from job to job. Lemons might be a tramp now, but his current situation does not mean he never worked for a living and raises questions about how he fell to his current condition. The dialogue makes clear he likely did not succeed in his many professions, and in line with the stereotype, he chooses not to work in the present moment. Still, Lemons brags to Rebecca, "I stood high once."[25]

Unlike the image of the tramp as a strange invader, Harrigan's Irish comic tramps are New Yorkers with local ties. These portrayals reflect Harrigan's tendency to develop New York Irish types in his sketches. Through their portrayals, mobility does not eliminate the possibility of having a home. In *The Terrible Example*, the characters' recognition of Lush implies he might be a regular fixture in the neighborhood, but his exact status is unclear. *Down Broadway* starts to flesh out the Irish comic tramp, also named Jimmy Lush, in more detail. When the bummers leave Blackwell's Isle, they return to New York, their home. Harrigan also marks Lush's presence through his mobility along with the moving panorama used in the sketch. As the scene changes to a new sight in New York, such as Union Square, Harry Hill's, and the Battery, Lush moves with it. The *New York Clipper* highlighted Wild's appearance as the "drunken bummer who figured in every scene with great fidelity to nature" as one of the show's main attractions.[26] Through this depiction, it is implied that New York is his city and Roger, the tourist, is the stranger.

In the *Mulligan Guard Picnic*, Harrigan makes Lemons's ties to the Irish American community explicit. He also indicates the tramp's capacity for loyalty and compassion, even if the expression of these emotions is inherently silly. When trying to convince Rebecca to give him the food from her basket, he claims a long-standing friendship with Dan, whom he refers to as a brother, and the Mulligan Committee, which planned the picnic. When he runs into Dan, he pleads for a ticket, which Dan denies him because he is a drunk and a tramp. Despite his rejection, Lemons remains loyal to Dan, stating, "So long Dan—No harm done. You can count on Lemons all the time."[27] After jumping on to the boat and following the Mulligan crowd on their picnic, he learns about Dan's fight with the tailor, who cut off his pant leg, and promises revenge on the tailor for Dan. Although this is a ludicrous mission, Lemons does not cause trouble because he is depraved but because he wants to help his friend. The people at the picnic also defend and help Lemons as one of their own. When Rebecca picks on Lemons by giving him soap instead of food to eat, one of the Mulligan Guard tell her to leave him alone.[28] Over Dan's objections, Cordelia, Dan's wife, and Bridget, their neighbor, insist Lemons join everyone at the picnic table because "The poor man is hungry!"[29] They might not condone his drinking or silly actions, but he is part of the community. This depiction of the tramp is not radical, but it portrays a nuance missing from previous representations. The tramp is not an evil stranger; he is someone you might know.

By making Lemons a hero, Harrigan makes the distinction between the Irish comic tramp and native-born, white tramp. Although Lemons drinks, fights, and steals, he never attacks anyone on the side of the Mulligan Guard. In contrast, Gypsy Jack, a native-born white tramp, holds up the picnic at gunpoint, taking clothes and food from the group. Lemons see him, the "Jersey sneak," and realizes that he robbed his friends. Lemons attacks him, easily wins the fight, and gets the food and clothes back.[30] For all his faults, Lemons saves the picnic and the others cheer his heroism.

The increasing prominence of the Irish comic tramp on the variety stage through the popularity of Harrigan and Wild's depictions at the turn of the decade implicitly tied whiteness to mobility. After his revival of *One, Two, Three* in 1874, Wild, a prominent blackface comedian, performed the tramp characters in whiteface. These images suggested that the ability to travel in search of work or idleness remained a right of white Americans. Performers like William Hoey and Lew Bloom continued the connection between whiteness and the tramp in variety performances during the 1880s, bridging the popular performances of Harrigan and Wild and the phenomenon of vaudeville tramp comics at the turn of the century. The alignment of whiteness with tramping on the variety stage did not mean that laziness, drunkenness, poverty, and violence remained the provenance of only white or Irish representations in variety and vaudeville. Blackface comic characters that performers, managers, newspapers, and historians could reasonably call tramps continued to appear on variety and vaudeville stages, but people tended to not label them tramps. As vaudeville historian Douglas Gilbert acknowledges, often in variety and vaudeville "blackface acts were brother comics of the tramps and it is no step at all into their dressing rooms where the grease color and occasional accent will be about the only changes found."[31] This quote follows a section on tramp comics, all who performed in whiteface. Gilbert's history reflected the categorizations made during the performers' lives. The whiteface comic performed tramp comedy; the blackface comics performed something else. The word "tramp" was directly tied to mobility; terms like "poor" or "homeless" did not have the same mobile connotation.

Officials and reformers may not have wanted Irish and Irish American wandering poor, but they implied less of a threat to the racial and social structure than notions of wandering black Americans. Especially since the South continued to rely heavily on black labor, the ability to move asserted not only the tramps' freedom but also their ability to cripple white business with their economic choices. Although it may not have been perceived as an ethnic victory for the Irish to be portrayed as tramps, arguably, it represented another step for Irish and Irish Americans toward claiming all the rights of whiteness in the late nineteenth century.

Notes

1. For a full article version of this conference paper, see Michelle Granshaw, "Inventing the Tramp: The Early Tramp Comic on the Variety Stage," *Popular Entertainment Studies* 9, nos. 1–2 (2018): 44–63. For more on the comic tramp, see also chapter 1 in Michelle Granshaw, *Irish on the Move: Performing Mobility in American Variety Theatre* (forthcoming from University of Iowa Press in Fall 2019).
2. Arthur Frank Wertheim, *W. C. Fields From Burlesque and Vaudeville to Broadway* (New York: Palgrave, 2014), 50–51; Douglas Gilbert, *American Vaudeville: Its Life and Times* (New York: Whittlesey, 1940; reprint New York: Dover, 1963), 269–78; Max Schulman, "Beaten, Battered, and Brawny: American Variety Entertainers and the Working-Class Body," in *Working in the Wings: New Perspectives on Theatre History and Labor*, ed. Elizabeth A. Osborne and Christine Woodworth (Carbondale: Southern Illinois University Press, 2015), 102; Todd DePastino, *Citizen Hobo: How a Century of Homelessness Shaped America* (Chicago: University of Chicago Press, 2003), 152–62; Tim Cresswell, *The Tramp in America* (London: Reaktion, 2001), 130–70; Kenneth L. Kusmer, *Down and Out, On the Road: The Homeless in American History* (New York: Oxford University Press, 2002), 170–73.
3. Paul T. Ringenbach, *Tramps and Reformers, 1873–1916* (Westport, CT: Greenwood, 1973), 3–29.
4. Although this chapter examines the years of the comic tramp's genesis, it does not claim to identify an originator of the comic tramp in variety. Many performers claimed to have performed the comic tramp first, most notably comedian Lew Bloom in 1885, and writers similarly disagree on who performed the comic tramp first and in what decade. The fragmented and mostly absent archive of variety theatre makes this quest in many ways futile. Theatre histories and cultural histories that address previous versions of comic vagrants or beggars include Robert Henke, *Poverty and Charity in Early Modern Theater and Performance* (Iowa City: University of Iowa Press, 2015); and John H. Towsen, *Clowns* (New York: Hawthorn, 1976).

5. Eric H. Monkkonen, *Police in Urban America, 1860–1920* (New York: Cambridge University Press, 1981), 88–93; Kusmer, *Down and Out, On the Road*, 35–56.
6. For example, see Francis Wayland, "Papers on out-door relief and tramps, read at the Saratoga Meeting of the American Social Science Association, before the Conference of State Charities, Sept. 5 and 6, 1877" (New Haven, CT: Hoggson and Robinson, 1877), 10.
7. "An Act Concerning Tramps," *Laws of the State Affecting the Interests in the City and County of New York Passed by the Legislature of 1880* (New York: Martin B. Brown, 1880), 45; Harry A. Millis, "The Law Affecting Tramps and Immigrants," *Charities Review* 7 (September 1897): 587–94.
8. For examples of this in other forms of cultural production, see Lee O. Harris, *The Man Who Tramps: A Story of Today* (Indianapolis: Douglass and Carlton, 1878), 18; STAATS, *A Tight Squeeze or, The Adventures of a Gentleman* (Boston: Lee and Shepard, 1879), 10; Anon., *The Tramp*, ed. Frank Bellew (New York: Dick and Fitzgerald, 1878), 21–22.
9. Franklin B. Sanborn, "The Tramp: His Cause and Cure," *Independent* 30 (1878): 1.
10. DePastino, *Citizen Hobo*, 15; Hidetaka Hirota, *Expelling the Poor: Atlantic Seaboard States and the Nineteenth-Century Origins of American Immigration Policy* (New York: Oxford University Press, 2017), 137.
11. "City Summary," *New York Clipper*, March 21, 1874, 406; "City Summary," *New York Clipper*, October 10, 1874, 222; "City Summary," *New York Clipper*, March 27, 1875, 414; Advertisement, *New York Clipper*, April 3, 1875, 7; Advertisement, *New York Clipper*, May 1, 1875, 35; "City Summary," *New York Clipper*, October 14, 1876, 230; George C. D. Odell, *Annals of the New York Stage*, vol. 10, 1875–1877 (New York: Columbia University Press, 1938), 266; *New York Herald*, April 13, 1877, 11; *New York Herald*, May 4, 1879, 17.
12. For more on the popularity of Irish, blackface, and Dutch acts in variety, see Gilbert, *American Vaudeville*, 37–85. As scholars have discussed, caricatures of black Americans and the Irish often reflected similar prejudices, making the parallels in stage representation not unusual.
13. William Courtright, *Private Boarding* (New York: Clinton T. DeWitt, 1877), 3.
14. Edward Harrigan, *The Terrible Example*, Edward Harrigan Papers, Manuscripts and Archives Division, New York Public Library, Astor, Lenox and Tilden Foundations, np.
15. John Wild, *One, Two, Three* (New York: Robert M. DeWitt, 1875), 4.
16. Wild, *One, Two, Three*, 4.
17. Harrigan, *The Terrible Example.*
18. Harrigan, *The Terrible Example.*
19. Courtright, *Private Boarding*, 4.
20. Wild, *One, Two, Three*, 4–6.
21. Harrigan, *The Terrible Example.*
22. Harrigan, *Down Broadway*, Edward Harrigan Papers, Manuscripts and Archives Division, New York Public Library, Astor, Lenox and Tilden Foundations, 10.
23. For more on Harrigan, see Richard Moody, *Ned Harrigan: From Corlear's Hook to Herald Square* (Chicago: Nelson-Hall, 1980).
24. Edward Harrigan, *Mulligan Guard Picnic* (two-act version, likely 1880), Edward Harrigan Papers, Manuscripts and Archives Division, New York Public Library, Astor, Lenox and Tilden Foundations, act 1, 64.
25. Harrigan, *Mulligan Guard Picnic* (two-act version, likely 1880), act 1, 63.
26. "City Summary," *New York Clipper*, May 1, 1875, 38.

27. Harrigan, *Mulligan Guard Picnic* (two-act version, likely 1880), act 1, 67.
28. Harrigan, *Mulligan Guard Picnic* (two-act version, likely 1880), act 2, 51.
29. Harrigan, *Mulligan Guard Picnic* (two-act version, likely 1880), act 2, 51.
30. Harrigan, *Mulligan Guard Picnic* (two-act version, likely 1880), act 2, 68.
31. Gilbert, *American Vaudeville*, 278.

Part IV

BOOK REVIEWS

Deborah and Her Sisters: How One Nineteenth-Century Melodrama and a Host of Celebrated Actresses Put Judaism on the World Stage. By Jonathan M. Hess. Philadelphia: University of Pennsylvania Press, 2018. pp. 272. $49.95 cloth.

Few nineteenth-century melodramas provide for us in the twenty-first century a window into the historical relationships between cultures or religions. S. H. Mosenthal's *Deborah*, a play about a Jewish woman eventually rejected by her Christian lover, inspired in Jewish and non-Jewish audience members an intense overflow of emotion that typically manifested through tears. *Deborah and Her Sisters* is the first full-length study that examines the history and legacy of Mosenthal's sensational melodrama, which premiered in Hamburg in 1849 and was performed and adapted around the Western world until the early twentieth century. In the book, the late Jonathan M. Hess argues that *Deborah* and its many adaptations invoked in audience members a compassion for Jewish suffering and, as such, functioned as "the epitome of and foundation for liberal feeling" (207). *Deborah and Her Sisters* offers an exposé into a dramatic work that illuminates the relationship between Jews and non-Jews almost two hundred years ago.

Hess expands his study of the *Deborah* phenomenon over four chapters, each carefully constructed, deeply rooted in archival material, and supported with an impressive collection of images. The book's introduction contextualizes theatre practice and popular culture in the nineteenth century. Hess explains that *Deborah*'s success in Germany became appealing to myriad theatrical giants including Augustin Daly, whose adaptation, *Leah*, made waves in the United States. Despite the generous artistic licenses taken within each adaptation, all of them made their audiences cry. Thus, argues Hess, "In an era that witnessed the rise of new forms of political and racial anti-Semitism, theatergoers often celebrated the pleasure taken in feeling the pain of the suffering Jewish woman as the ultimate litmus test for liberal feeling" (7). *Deborah* was, according to Hess, not simply a play that made people cry but one that bridged a divide between Jews and non-Jews *through* tears.

In the first two chapters, Hess investigates the anatomy of the melodrama, traces how and why *Deborah* became an international sensation, and theorizes the meaning behind audiences' emotional reactions to the play. Chapter 1 analyzes *Deborah*'s primary function as a tearjerker. By focusing on the text and reviews of several productions, Hess explains that when audience members came together to witness *Deborah* or one of the various adaptations, they "embrace[d] crying as a collective experience," a moment of community building despite differences in religious background (28). Arguing that the play is a "masterfully constructed melodrama," Hess theorizes that the spectator's tears indicate a thrilling moment of identification with Jewish suffering, thereby deconstructing religious barriers for its audiences (35). Chapter 2 compares *Deborah*'s many adaptations to Mosenthal's original text and production. Though producers were drawn to *Deborah* primarily for its commercial appeal, each adaptation had a personalized effect within the country where it was playing. Daly's *Leah*, for example, forced American Christians to "confront the brutality of their own past with its Puritan-like fanaticism and intolerance" (81).

Hess shifts the focus of chapter 3 from the anatomy of *Deborah*'s text to the function and impact of the actresses playing the title role. Deborah was an alluring part for both Jewish and non-Jewish actresses. This chapter asks, what does it mean to perform Jewishness and what are the intersections between theatricality and authenticity, particularly for a play that allegedly builds bridges between religions? Hess postulates that Jewish and non-Jewish audiences experienced the play as both a theatrical occurrence and an authentic representation of Jewishness, despite the religious background of the main performers.

In his final chapter, Hess most closely engages with his major argument—that the *Deborah* phenomenon "probes the legacy of nineteenth-century liberal culture and its universalist aspirations" (9). Asserting that *Deborah* is an example of philo-Semitism, or "the idealization of Jews and Judaism among non-Jews," Hess contends that the image of Jewishness within Mosenthal's play is not a mirror image of Jewish life (167). Instead, Jews had a direct hand in *Deborah*'s creation and production, "working together with non-Jews in a variety of settings to create images of Jewishness for Jews and non-Jews alike that shaped the relations between them" (168). Despite its rejection by many Jewish scholars of the time as illegitimate, *Deborah* and its adaptations created a space for all people to come together regardless of religion to enjoy a play and sentimentalize the Jewish experience.

Deborah and Her Sisters provides a generous history of a play often neglected by both theatre and Jewish studies scholars. Unfortunately, Hess spends more time exploring *Deborah*'s history than he does drawing direct connections between this evidence and his major argument. Though he often repeats his overarching argument throughout the book, Hess fully engages with it only in his final chapter. More specifically, Hess does not clearly define what he means by "liberal feeling" or how the play fits within larger conversations of liberalism. While it is easy to see from Hess's careful mining of its history that audience members reacted strongly to this play, a deeper analysis of the meaning behind such emotion would be useful.

Despite this one issue, however, Hess offers a beautiful and comprehensive history of "the most popular Jewish drama of the era" and the adaptations it inspired throughout Europe and North America. The text is well-organized and easy to read. Hess's writing is engaging, offering readers quippy anecdotes and stories interpreted from archival material. The book would serve well in undergraduate theatre history classrooms, as well as in graduate-level seminars on Jewish performance. Scholars interested in the intersections of religion and theatre will find it an invaluable resource, as well. *Deborah and Her Sisters* champions the history of an important melodrama often overlooked or forgotten. It is a significant contribution to scholarly conversations in the fields of theatre history and Jewish studies.

—JOSEPH R. D'AMBROSI
Indiana University

Shakespeare's Dramatic Persons. By Travis Curtright. Lanham, MD: Farleigh Dickinson University Press, 2017. pp. ix + 185. $80.00 cloth. $40.50 electronic.

Shakespeare's Dramatic Persons investigates early modern acting styles through the lens of a robust rhetorical tradition. As Travis Curtright summarizes in his introduction, discussions of early modern acting styles—and Original Practice—have long dichotomized the "formalism" of the Elizabethan stage and the "naturalism" of a post-Cartesian world of interior focus (1). Curtright proposes to "renegotiate" this dichotomy by considering "how the classical rhetorical tradition would inform an actor's personation of character in ways that could enhance the illusion of what was 'truly done' upon the stage" (1). The argument proceeds dialectically, as Curtright explores the rhetorical resources available to Shakespeare's actors inscribed in the "dramatic persons" themselves: Shakespeare, well educated in the rhetorical tradition, deploys rhetorical figures, typological conventions, formal delivery and declamation, and the aims of eloquence itself to cue the actor to a lifelike "personation" on the stage. Curtright contends that an awareness of what he calls "the mimetic possibilities of a rhetorical style of acting" will help refashion our understanding of the lifelike or realistic qualities of early modern acting (145).

One of the many virtues of the book is the lucid and focused presentation of the argument over a manageable 155 pages, complete with periodic summaries. The author remains disciplined in his focus and relegates topics of inquiry tangential to the main thesis to five hundred endnotes, as each discreet investigation resists synthetic readings of the plays. Curtright selects five characters that span Shakespeare's career and that touch on the four main "genres" of Shakespeare's plays (history, tragedy, comedy [x2], and romance). Each investigation, while noting certain rhetorical features about Shakespeare's language, proceeds with a necessary modesty of claim. This is a book about the possibilities available to Shakespeare's actors for lifelike personation, and Curtright (rightly) tempers his claims accordingly; as he puts it, "though it is impossible to retrieve all of the original conditions of Shakespeare's Globe or how various actors performed in his plays, we can specify where scripts incorporated the classical rhetorical tradition" (4). Thus, the author's awareness of his own project—its limitations and ramifications—furnishes a refreshing voice in what can be an otherwise contentious conversation.

Each chapter provides a unique insight into a "rhetorical style of acting" as Curtright moves through five of Shakespeare's most famous characters: Richard III, Katherina, Benedick, Iago, and Marina. Two of these studies, however, strike me as particularly important.

Curtright's first chapter, Richard III, challenges the common perception of "formal" or "typological" acting as bombastic, unwieldy, and wooden. This study is important for two reasons. The first is Curtright's emphasis on Thomas More's *History of King Richard III* as a source for Shakespeare's famous hunchbacked tyrant. Curtright cites energeia as the rhetorical technique that "binds More and Shakespeare's art together," and he demonstrates a much closer kinship between Shakespeare's play and More's history. This source study naturally implicates more than Burbage's style of acting and informs any synthetic reading of the play. The second important ramification of Curtright's study involves our conception of character "type." As he traces Richard's "typological genealogy," through More to Tacitus and Terrence, Curtright highlights the self-conscious theatricality in both the historical person and the type itself: The tradition vividly describes the machinating tyrant as theatrical, obfuscating his corrupt intentions through a rhetorical presentation of a false face. The historical type of tyrant, far from being a wooden cutout often associated with a medieval morality play, has persuasive insincerity built into its description. Thus, as Curtright concludes, "typological character could model Richard as a dramatic person who professes and plays a rhetorical style of acting" (36).

In a similar way, the author's fourth chapter on Iago is particularly revealing. Curtright isolates the highly figured speech of Iago and gives special attention to those moments of figuration in which Iago must—like an actor—convince his audience (Othello) of his (false) sincerity. Far from repeating the arguments of his study on Richard III, Curtright focuses on the delivery of Iago's speeches. Iago himself, we find out, is consciously deploying figures of "auricular defect" to personate, himself, the character of Othello's friend. Again, "type" emerges as intricately complex, as Iago must mask his flattery as friendship—much as a flatterer does—through acting. As Curtright articulates this, "an early modern performance of a persuasive and credible Iago would have ramifications in terms of audience response, which further suggests how typological character fashions a particular way for audiences to experience, or identify with, Othello's dilemma" (110). Once again, understanding the type as theatrical informs the entire play, even the metatheatrical. How well Iago performs his role implicates audiences—that is, how well Iago is performed as a persuasive actor or lifelike character will condition an audience's response.

While not always from the vantage of source or type studies, Curtright demonstrates that the distinction between the theatrical activity of Shakespeare's characters and the theatrical activity of Shakespeare's actors is underdetermined, and he elaborates how the rhetorical tradition, which Shakespeare inherited and interpreted, provides the playwright with the resources "to inscribe life-like character-effects." But he never strays from his purpose: His book is about styles of acting, so his conclusion assumes the voice of a practiced director solving a problem: "How may an early modern and theatrical understanding of persuasion's arts bear upon contemporary productions of William Shakespeare's plays?" (145). His treatment of Hamlet and direct address in the conclusion tests his thesis: Could these so-called original practices impart a naturalism that escapes the accusation of anachronism? And so, the book concludes where it began: with the contention that "formalism" and "naturalism" need not be opposed terms. We can look forward to Curtright's continued work on rhetorical styles of acting and hope to see him continue to bring together the scholarly and the theatrical.

—**JAMES DEMASI**
University of Dallas

The Disney Musical on Stage and Screen: Critical Approaches from "Snow White" to "Frozen." Edited by George Rodosthenous. London: Bloomsbury Methuen, 2017. pp. v + 257. $108.00 cloth. $29.95 paperback.

The Walt Disney Company was founded in 1923 and has been creating and globally distributing influential popular culture products for almost a century. This edited collection of thirteen essays focuses on the stage and screen musicals produced by Disney, beginning with its first full-length animated film, *Snow White and the Seven Dwarves* (1937), and ending with *Frozen* (2013). As implied by the fact that the first and last of these essays analyze musical films, the emphasis of the collection is on the latter part of its title rather than the former.

As editor George Rodosthenous notes in his introduction, the book's purpose is to understand Disney musicals not just in terms of their influence on popular culture and as political and educational tools but also as artistic innovations. The collection is organized into broad themes: "Disney Musicals: On Film," "Disney Adaptations: On Stage and Beyond," and "Disney Musicals: Gender and Race." The thematic headings are perhaps not as helpful as one might wish; three out of the four musicals grouped in the first section could easily have been placed in the final section. That the essays are also generally organized in chronological order within and across these sections is more helpful; through careful reading of the articles, an artistic trajectory of Disney musicals is formed, and overlaying that trajectory are the social and cultural shifts taking place around the musicals.

The first two essays focus on visual aesthetics and how musical theatre conventions influence how we read animated musicals. The first essay, by Elizabeth Randell Upton, provides a structural analysis of *Snow White*, discussing how the placement of songs within the film's narrative helps see beyond the "uncanniness" of the realistically rendered human characters. Next, Raymond Knapp explores the artistic shortcomings, and successes, of *Sleeping Beauty*. Both essays locate the musicals within the history of film technology available at the time of production. The last two essays in the section examine the live-action/animated hybrid film musicals *Mary Poppins* and *Enchanted*. Tim Stephenson asks why *Mary Poppins* still resonates with contemporary audiences and concludes that it is because of its often-contradictory representations of gender and gender roles. In the next essay, Paul Laird examines how *Enchanted* maintains the Disney traditions of commercialism and retrograde femininity though musical pastiche.

The section organized around adaptation is the most heterogeneous of the three, both in terms of the material covered and in terms of approaches. Geoffrey Block deploys a heavy dose of irony in his discussion of four made-for-television Disney musicals from the 1990s through the 2000s, framing the corporation as an *auteur* with an aggressive marketing agenda and products designed to reflect that changing market through nontraditional and color-blind casting. Olaf Jubin supplies a distinct international approach to his investigation of the animated stage and film adaptations of *The Hunchback of Notre Dame* in Germany and the United States. His insights into the "warring aesthetics" (112) of Victor

Hugo's original text and Disney's continual failed attempts to adapt the text such that it fit into the Disney mold illuminate both the mold and its constraints. In contrast to the travails of adapting *Hunchback*, Barbara Wallace Grossman traces out the production history of *The Lion King* from film into a "stunning realization as a daring theatrical event in which risk-taking at all levels yielded boundless rewards" (118). The section concludes with an essay that to a certain extent reads as an outlier in terms of its subject matter but nonetheless fits the broader scope of the volume. Stacy Wolf reminds us that beyond Broadway and Hollywood productions of Disney musicals are the literally thousands of productions licensed for performance by middle and high school students. Her essay explores the personal and cultural impact such productions have on students nationwide.

Of the three sections, the last contains the strongest and most critically engaged essays and will likely be the most interesting to theatre scholars. Aaron Thomas discusses the stage version of *Newsies* in terms of how its dramaturgy, choreography, and targeted marketing toward children, not adults, expands how children might grow into their own ideas about how masculinity can be performed. Continuing along the thematic thread of youth and performing gender, Dominic Symonds examines the 2006 television movie *High School Musical*, arguing that under its surface embrace of "post-feminist utopia" is a heart full of "firmly entrenched conservative ideologies" (171). In the most thought-provoking essay in the collection, four authors—Emily Clark, Donatella Galella, Stefanie A. Jones, and Catherine Young—collectively analyze how Mary Zimmerman's staging of *The Jungle Book* works to make its audience feel good about what they are witnessing onstage while it reinscribes orientalist and racist structures of power. The penultimate essay by Sam Baltimore examines how the "queer Orientalist tradition [in musical comedies], often intended as a gesture of solidarity between white queer writers and their Orientalized subjects" (206), functions to exoticize nonwhite performers. Significantly, Baltimore emphasizes how Orientalism is complicated in the live performance of *Aladdin*, where an Orientalized character initially imagined by Howard Ashman (who was both white and queer) was embodied by a heterosexual African American male star. The concluding essay by Sarah Whitfield uses Stacy Wolf's argument that Broadway musicals typically place women and female empowerment at the narrative center and teases out the limited progressive and feminist politics of *Frozen* within the competing contexts of Disney film and Broadway stage standards when it comes to princesses (and women). This last essay thus brings readers full circle, reflecting back on Upton's essay on *Snow White*, which asserted that "the association between Disney heroines and singing is very strong" (17).

Throughout the collection, patterns emerge and the articles can be placed in conversation, especially in terms of gender and the control the Disney Corporation attempts to maintain over its products. On balance, the collection is a worthwhile addition to the ever-growing scholarship on film and stage musicals and provides the start of what should be increased examinations of Disney's contributions to those forms.

—**KATHRYN EDNEY**
Regis College

Traveler, There Is No Road: Theatre, the Spanish Civil War, and the Decolonial Imagination in the Americas. By Lisa Jackson-Schebetta. Studies in Theatre History and Culture. Iowa City: University of Iowa Press, 2017. pp. xii + 245. 15 illustrations. $65.00 paper. $65.00 eBook, perpetual ownership.

At first glance, a study of theatrical representations of the Spanish Civil War on US stages in the 1930s and 1940s might seem pitched toward a specialist audience. But with this book, author Lisa Jackson-Schebetta accomplishes what the best historians do: She parlays a rigorous archival exploration of a brief yet critical historical moment into a major rethinking of the field's biggest questions. In this case, the work represents a significant expansion and realignment of the two most influential remapping projects undertaken by theatre scholars in the last two decades: those of the hemispheric Americas and of the circum-Atlantic world. Jackson-Schebetta achieves this goal by a replotting of key geographical and temporal nodes to include 1930s Spain, New York, Florida, Cuba, and Puerto Rico and by filtering the record of performance in and about those times and places through the theoretical lens of "modernity/coloniality," as developed by Aníbal Quijano, Walter Mignolo, and others. The perspective thus gained allows the author to argue that "for US, Caribbean, and peninsular Spanish theatre makers in the United States, Spain mobilized the possibility of entirely *other* worlds" (22), visions that she sees as inherently decolonial in their ability to destabilize the cultural and political borders that underpin the twinned ideologies of modernity and coloniality.

Jackson-Schebetta approaches her task via a counterintuitively inspired methodology: While she focuses on US examples, the contexts she applies to them are almost entirely those of Spain and Latin America. The result is a kind of defamiliarization that reveals new triangulations of circum-Atlantic and hemispheric cultural and political influence. A fine example is her analysis of Clifford Odets's unproduced *The Cuban Play*. While a traditional treatment might frame the work as a product of the Group Theatre's leftist domestic politics, Jackson-Schebetta charts the play as a response to the murder of Spanish playwright Federico García Lorca, filtered through Odets's experiences on a 1935 fact-finding mission to Batista-repressed Cuba.

The author's new cartographical imaginary traces the unstable edges of modernity/coloniality's fault lines (sometimes figured as "wounds," following Gloria E. Anzaldúa), particularly those of race, gender, and citizenship, whose eruptions in Spain at the inception of its imperial project situated the new power squarely in the hyphen between modernity and coloniality and whose resurfacings at the moment of empire's collapse justifies the author's centering of the Civil War experience. With chapter 1, Jackson-Schebetta takes up the gender policing of the *milicianas*, the female volunteers who fought for the republic. The threat they posed to modernist state-making and burgeoning colonial projects led to their sidelining both by the Spanish government and on US stages, where women were confirmed in their roles as mothers, wives, and lovers and portrayed as fighters only before taking up arms, or in the moment of redomestication. An exception to this trend, documented by some of the book's most compelling images, was the representation of *milicianas* by Cuban American schoolchildren at fund-raising picnics and in Labor Day parades, performances that "maintained an exteriority of modernity, a possibility otherwise" (49). Chapter 2 examines the US theatrical response to the bombing of Spanish civilians, including several radio dramas and Ernest Hemingway's only play. By infantilizing Spanish victims, demonizing their fascist attackers, and presenting US characters as saviors, these plays presented a prostrate Spain in desperate need of colonization by a Good-Neighborly US modernity. The third chapter is perhaps the author's richest elaboration of her proposed realignment of cultural imaginaries, triangulating as it does Spain, New York, and the Caribbean along vectors of multiple colonizations and diasporas. Lorca and his dramatizations of Andalusian heritage provide the through line for the chapter, linking competing Nationalist and Republican productions in Spain, the aforementioned Odets script, and *El grito de Lares*, mounted by and for Puerto Rican theatremakers and audiences in New York in support of pro-independence activists. For Jackson-Schebetta, Lorca's representation of his Andalusian home as a borderland of Spanish culture enabled his plays to cross national borders and flow through transatlantic and hemispheric networks, supporting multiple decolonizing efforts. Chapter 4 takes up issues of race, particularly a resurgent Spanish fear of the Moor and the resonance it found in the work of prominent white US playwrights like Maxwell Anderson and Irwin Shaw, as well as the experiences of African American and African Caribbean volunteers in Spain, read as performances. The author concludes that these expressions revealed both Anglo American anxieties and African American hopes about the disruptions to US modernity/coloniality that a postwar Spain might engender. With her fifth chapter, Jackson-Schebetta turns her attention to theatrical responses to the loss of Spain, analyzing grittily realistic depictions of volunteers' loss of faith but also offering a radically new reading of Paul Robeson and José Ferrer's 1943 production of *Othello*. The author suggests that experiences of exile, both external and interior, create the possibility "that *other* worlds might be imagined and perhaps realized in or through an elsewhere" (184). In her conclusion, the author briefly traces the extensions of the Spanish Civil War and its representations into the twenty-first century, from the shrouding of the United Nations' reproduction of *Guernica* during the Security Council's deliberations preceding the Iraq War to the work of the newest generation of US Latinx playwrights, including Quiara Alegría Hudes, Anne García-Romero, and Kristoffer Diaz.

This exciting and vital book will doubtlessly find its way onto the shelves of specialists interested in the political theatres of the United States in the 1930s, alongside recent studies by Barry Witham, Jonathan Chambers, and others. It is just as likely to end up on seminar reading lists, in conversation with those works by Diana Taylor and Joseph Roach that it so vitally engages.

—ANDREW GIBB
Texas Tech University

Lanford Wilson: Early Stories, Sketches, and Poems. Edited by David A. Crespy. Columbia: University of Missouri Press, 2017. pp. xi + 251. 7 illustrations. $45.00 hardcover.

Lanford Wilson: Early Stories, Sketches, and Poems, edited by David A. Crespy, is an excellent collection of work featuring eighteen short stories and twenty-three poems written by Pulitzer Prize–winning playwright Lanford Wilson. The most thrilling accomplishment of this book is that it brings to light a selection of work previously unpublished, until now; after Wilson passed away in 2011, all his papers were donated to the Special Collections Library at the University of Missouri-Columbia, where Crespy teaches playwriting. Owing many accolades to Crespy's fervent editorial labor, this remarkable collection will be received with tremendous excitement by enthusiasts of Wilson's work. Crespy begins the book with an introductory essay that offers a concise overview of Wilson's biography, including his upbringing in rural Missouri, his various travels, and his critical expansion as a writer. Readers will quickly notice that most of the selections are left undated, but Crespy asserts they were written between 1955 and 1964, a period when Wilson was still developing his voice as a young author, and years before his success as a flourishing playwright. The book's introduction also includes a preliminary analysis of each short story that draws comparisons between the characters, descriptions, and plots of these early writings and those found in Wilson's later works. The intersection between Wilson's prose and the development of his more mature dramatic dialogue establishes a clear foundation for future exploration and research by both students and scholars.

The collection is presented in five sections that organize the writings by either a common theme or a stylistic approach. Beginning with "Section 1: Six Stories," Wilson offers a nostalgic view of adolescence and the various types of people one might encounter as a young adult. He writes beautifully about topics such as a boy's remembrances of visiting his grandmother, encountering threatening neighbor children, befriending a hobo in Central Park, and noisily confronting naked apartment dwellers. With magnificently crafted character descriptions and scenarios that seem mysteriously familiar, Wilson stirs his reader's imagination while simultaneously reminding them of the innocence, and occasional pain, that accompanies youth. The most notable story in this section, "Miss Misty," is a complex, yet superbly written examination of gender identity. The story features two friends attempting to help a drag queen rehearse "masculine" mannerisms in order to appease her wealthy father. Here, before becoming a playwright known for championing the outcast and exposing the plight of gay people, Wilson, who was himself gay, reveals his early interest in openly and sincerely writing about characters struggling to cope with the social forces of oppression.

"Section 2: Travels to and from the City" includes three longer stories that explore the sentiments of independence and isolation. In both "The Water Commissioner" and "Fish Kite," Wilson presents the eye-opening adventures of young men who travel away from their homes in the country to visit, and attempt to find employment in, larger cities. Perhaps reminiscent of his own journey from Missouri to San Diego, and then eventually on to Chicago and New York City, Wilson reflects on the differences between rural and urban life, two subjects commonly found in many of his subsequent dramas. The third story in this section, "The Train to Washington," feels slightly out of place when compared to the others. This is possibly because the travels of the characters are described as something they long for rather than presented as an immediate event in which the action occurs. The story illustrates the heartbreak experienced by an eight-year-old boy when he discovers that a heated encounter between his prostitute mother and his uncle will prevent him from escaping the city to spend the summer in rural Virginia with his beloved grandmother.

The next two parts, "Section 3: Sketches of Town Life" and "Section 4: Sketches of City Life" include two micro-stories and seven pieces of flash fiction. As in the previous two sections, the division between rural and urban settings continues to be significant in Wilson's character portraits. The difference in these works, however, is that the style switches from short story to "sketch," a word used by Crespy not only to describe the extreme brevity of the works but also to demonstrate how Wilson used his initial ideas as inspiration and outlines for future plays. For example, the subject of astronomy discussed between a brother and a sister in "Fuzz on Orion's Sword" would later serve as the foundation for *The Great Nebula in Orion*, and in "Mama," readers are introduced to a cross-dressed neighbor reminiscent of Leslie Bright from Wilson's groundbreaking play *The Madness of Lady Bright*. The most obvious connections, however, are found in the characters and setting of both "Drift" and "The Rimers of Eldritch," which would later appear in Wilson's full-length play of the same name.

In "Section 5: Poems," Crespy has carefully selected twenty-three poems from the much larger collection archived at the University of Missouri. These selections compliment the rest of the book by taking the reader, once again, on a journey from Wilson's origins in rural Missouri to his establishment in New York City. The poems offer an intimate glimpse into the relationships and dreams of a writer inspired by the nostalgia of youth, the treatment of outsiders, and his deeply personal relationships with loved ones.

Overall, this newly available collection of short stories, sketches, and poems is an excellent addition to the work of one of America's greatest playwrights. The publication of these writings invites a critical conversation and fresh examination of the correlation between Wilson's early prose and his more mature dramatic dialogue. This book is a delightful treasure for anyone familiar with or interested in learning more about the various influences and writing styles of Lanford Wilson.

—JEFF GRACE
Knox College

A Critical Companion to Lynn Nottage. Edited by Jocelyn L. Buckner. New York: Routledge, 2016. pp. xii + 214. $52.95 paperback.

This much-needed collection, edited by Jocelyn L. Buckner, is a provocative introduction to a variety of Nottage's works, with a special section on *Ruined* and a dedicated chapter for each of *Crumbs from the Table of Joy*; *Mud, River, Stone*; *Las Meninas*; *Intimate Apparel*; *Fabulation, or the Re-Education of Undine*; and *By the Way, Meet Vera Stark*. This approach gives the collection focus as well as a larger vision shaped by multiple framing pieces: a concise introduction by the editor, a production history, an interview, a foreword, and an afterword. Each chapter is much more than introductory in content, providing important insights into the plays they address as well as conversations in theatre and film history and theory, Black studies, African diaspora studies, cultural studies, and feminist theatre.

Each of the contributors' essays is tightly argued around its particular play and contributes to a broader understanding of the complexity, betweenness, and crossing of borders that structure Nottage's works. Sandra Shannon's foreword emphasizes how Nottage's innovations create freedom for the playwright, her characters, and other African American female playwrights. Buckner's pithy introduction reviews the chapters and highlights three common themes: "history, diaspora, and identity" (5). Also framing the top of the collection is Scott Knowles's chronology of Nottage's works, which interweaves her production history with a few important events in the playwright's life.

Several essays address the complexity of Nottage's use of space. Jaye Austin Williams demonstrates how Nottage crafts fugitivity for black women in *Crumbs from the Table of Joy*. Williams works from theorists as diverse as Plato, Saidiya Hartman, Hortense Spillers, Frantz Fanon, and Karl Marx to find promise as well as loss and unfulfillment in the "same no-place" (21) of this form of freedom. Jocelyn Buckner's "Diasporic desires in *Las Meninas*" similarly emphasizes elision and in-betweenness, arguing that through this play Nottage enacts a "revisionist historiography in which identities are constructed in liminal space and time" (53) in response to both Eurocentric and Afrocentric notions of belonging and desire. Adrienne Macki Braconi also attends to the slipperiness and porosity of spatial boundaries in *Intimate Apparel*, analyzing in particular Maureen Freedman's stage design for the 2012 Connecticut Repertory Theatre production.

Other chapters focus on Nottage's multifaceted representational strategies. Jennifer L. Hayes examines the characters in *Mud, River, Stone* as a diverse, global chorus and argues these multiple voices inspire the audience to see many sides, and their own role, in global conflicts. By focusing on character duality, Faedra Chatard Carpenter argues that *Fabulation, or the Re-Education of Undine* recuperates the rich, complex history of Brer Rabbit, in the process challenging stereotypes, spanning geographic and temporal fissures, and creating a blackness that is a "proliferating 'work in progress'" (107). Harvey Young also highlights the multiple means of "racial role play" (115) that are critically and intentionally deployed by the black female characters in *By the Way, Meet Vera Stark*.

A special section on Nottage's 2009 Pulitzer Prize–winning *Ruined* is this collection's special strength, drawing out the relationship between the play and its relationship to activism and social transformation. Jennifer-Scott Mobley's "Melodrama, Sensation, and Activism in *Ruined*," Jeff Paden's "Renegotiating Realism: Hybridity of Form and Political Potentiality in *Ruined*," and Esther J. Terry's "Land Rights and Womb Rights: Forging Difficult Diasporic Kinships in *Ruined*" take up themes from throughout the volume as well as work together to illuminate the structure and impact of Nottage's most acclaimed play. Examining *Ruined*'s plot structure and realistic style, characters marked as clearly "good" and "bad," female heroines, music and song, and spectacular climax scene, Mobley argues that *Ruined* uses melodramatic rather than Brechtian dramaturgy to generate a more potent political response in audience members. Continuing the discussion of theatre and activism, Paden reads *Ruined*'s songs and scenes of violence through theories of performing pain to frame its oft-derided conclusion as deliberately "messy, complicated, unfinished" in a way that "dramatically calls for audience intervention" (149). This interpretation of the power of *Ruined*'s dissatisfying conclusion is even more convincing in light of Mobley's insights into the many ways the play connects with its audiences. In the collection's final piece on *Ruined*, Terry analyzes how its characters build relationships and belonging during the chaos and violence of war, "enact[ing] a performative African diaspora, or kinship as always already in the process of becoming" (161). Terry argues compellingly that this process creates space for love and kinship even for those whose entanglement with conflict, land, and body is in contradistinction to the ways in which discourses of African kinship and African diaspora structure belonging. By taking seriously the revolutionary potential of love for these characters, Terry demonstrates how *Ruined* also holds powerful political possibilities for the women of color it depicts, a vital addition to the assessment of political action generated in what we might consider the white, ally, or empowered "first-world" audiences that are at the center of Mobley's and Paden's contributions.

A Critical Companion to Lynn Nottage closes with Buckner's interview, "On creativity and collaboration: A conversation with Lynn Nottage, Seret Scott, and Kate Whoriskey," and an afterword by Soyica Diggs Colbert. The interview subjects discuss themes of history, place, home, and stereotype, as well as the working relationship of and process between Nottage and two of her key collaborators. Researchers of *Sweat* will be interested in Buckner's introduction as well as this interview, in which the playwright discusses *Sweat* and the "de-industrial revolution" (186). Colbert's afterword confirms the central theme of complexity, arguing that Nottage's nuanced representations of time and history layer with intersectional representations focused on race, class, and gender to create multifaceted, intricate works. This collection achieves Buckner's goal of expanding and complicating the current conversation, and its thorough engagement with Nottage's rich oeuvre makes it a significant contribution to the fields of modern, political, African American, *and* feminist theatre scholarship.

—STEFANIE A. JONES
New York University

Just One of the Boys: Female-to-Male Cross-Dressing on the American Variety Stage. By Gilliam M. Rodger. Urbana: University of Illinois Press, 2018. pp. 275. $28.00 paper.

In Gillian M. Rodger's first book, *Champagne Charlie and Pretty Jemima* (2010), the author traced the development of variety entertainment from the mid-nineteenth century to the early twentieth century. Exploring the class dynamics of the form's evolution, Rodger centered her study on Annie Hindle and Ella Wesner, two male impersonators whose careers brought into focus the changing relationship between class and gender, with implications regarding sexuality on the American stage.

Her latest book, *Just One of the Boys*, is an extension of this text, looking specifically at male impersonation in American variety. While Rodger again focuses on Hindle and Wesner, she introduces a number of other male impersonators, examining their performance styles, repertoires, and audience receptions to illustrate changes in variety as a whole. Rodger also expands her investigation to include male impersonators from English music hall, many of whom would also come to the United States.

Chapter 1, "Female Hamlets and Romeos," begins with an introduction to female cross-dressing on the nineteenth-century American stage. While noting that some women were performing male roles in legitimate drama, Rodger emphasizes the different attitudes audiences took toward cross-dressing in variety. Where cross-dressing on the legitimate stage was tolerated as a novelty justified by the actresses' skill, variety's perceived "low-class" status rendered it more flexible, as women were not constrained by propriety from performing cross-gendered comedy.

Hindle and Wesner make their first appearance in the second chapter, which discusses the emergence of the first male impersonators in variety. Rodger, who focuses on these two women "because together they established the performance ideal for American male impersonation that lasted until the end of the nineteenth century" (32), goes into detail about both performers' early public and private lives. While the author's description of their performance styles is interesting, it is her exploration of their private lives that I found most fascinating, especially when she teases Hindle's multiple marriages to women.

Both chapters 3 and 4 look at male impersonation in the 1870s by introducing the reader to two performers, using them to examine challenges male impersonators faced in variety. In chapter 3, Rodger focuses on the economic impact of the Panic of 1873 by presenting Augusta Lamareaux and Blanche Selwyn, who along with Hindle and Wesner found it difficult to sustain bookings in the wake of the financial crisis. Chapter 4 continues to explore the impact of the Long Depression, using male impersonators Maggie Weston and Minnie Hall to investigate the changing audience tastes. Rodger notes that while male impersonation helped Weston and Hall get their starts, they were able to sustain careers "by being flexible and by moving away from the specialization of Annie Hindle and Ella Wesner" (89).

Wesner's debut London season in 1876 serves as Rodger's entrée into an overview of male impersonation in English music halls, which are the focus of chapter 5. Citing the more established tradition of women playing male roles in English theatre, Rodger speculates that this conditioned audiences and "may have been responsible for their more feminine performance style" (106). This enhanced Wesner's popularity, as English audiences found her more masculine performance to be both novel and exotic.

Chapter 6 marks a significant shift in variety entertainment in the 1880s, as financial concerns and audience shifts drove a growing concern with "decency." This shift led variety managers to adopt "industrial models of entertainment" (115), which would eventually lead to the subspecialization of variety into vaudeville, burlesque, and other forms. While chapter 6 describes this increasing specialization, chapter 7 focuses specifically on male impersonation, returning again to Hindle and Wesner. Although both women persisted in their chosen specialty, neither was especially successful during this period, as both struggled to adapt to the new landscape. As Rodger notes, "There had never been a large number of male impersonators active in American variety, but as more comic roles for women emerged during the 1880s, male impersonation became an oddity that most funny women seemed unwilling to pursue" (132).

Rodger shifts her focus to England again in chapter 8, as a number of English male impersonators appeared on the American variety stage. The author suggests that the increasing feminization of male impersonators in variety was at least partly due to English performers such as Miss St. George Hussey, Bessie Bonehill, and Vesta Tilley. Rodger traces these changes through the end of the nineteenth century, which culminated in vaudeville performers such as Della Fox and Kitty Doner.

However, as the final chapter demonstrates, by the twentieth century, the specialty of male impersonation had all but disappeared. Rodger notes a number of reasons for this decline, from increasing opportunities for women in comedy to the concern for "decency" onstage, but it is the concern with femininity in general that seems to drive much of this change. Invoking the theory of public and private spheres, male impersonators emphasized the "danger" of women crossing into the public eye: "The . . . mannish woman closely resembled the act that these women performed on the stage, and after 1900 it became important for male impersonators to reassure their audiences that there was nothing at all mannish about them" (176).

While this text adds to the growing number of historical studies of American popular entertainment, it also highlights the difficulties that attend this kind of research. The author often remarks on the scant source materials, such as the fact that she has not yet found Hindle's death date. Similarly, while the author's attempt to trace the development of variety performance via male impersonation is an interesting approach, the overall significance of male impersonation within variety is sometimes overstated; as the author herself notes, there were never very many male impersonators in America. This text serves as a valuable resource to theatre historians investigating popular entertainment, as well as gender studies scholars interested in the performance of gender in the second half of the nineteenth century. However, it is important to remember the scope of the subject and resist the impulse to view these performers as more representative than they were.

—**FRANKLIN J. LASIK**
Baltimore Center Stage

A Theater of Diplomacy: International Relations and the Performing Arts in Early Modern France. By Ellen R. Welch. Philadelphia: University of Pennsylvania Press, 2017. pp. 302. $75.00.

Italian Renaissance intermezzi, Jacobean court masques, and ballets de cour under Louis XIII and Louis XIV all won renown in their day and continuing coverage in theatre history for their lavish spectacle, scenic innovations, and interplay of music and poetry. But there was more than aesthetic pleasure driving those court spectacles. Focusing on the French court from the early seventeenth century to 1715, Ellen R. Welch traces their evolving role in the practice of diplomacy. It is a curiously intricate history that begins even before the idea of the nation-state with borders emerged from the Treaty of Westphalia in 1648. During the formative years of nationhood, when diplomatic missions were entrusted to amateur aristocrats, a monarch could indicate disfavor by withholding an invitation to a court entertainment. As diplomacy became professionalized, foreign representatives could be likened to actors in their role-playing negotiations, even as the court ballets reveled in stereotyping national characteristics, often sending ambiguous signals: Was the portrayal intended to mock or to pay homage? In the final phase of intertwined diplomatic and theatrical performance, ambassadors behaved like celebrities, deriving personal satisfaction from the gaze of ordinary people watching them watch a public stage performance.

Beyond their familiar function as manifestations of "the ruler's magnificence" (3), court spectacles could serve strategically as tools of government. The early modern French court excelled at using spectacle and dance to achieve cultural hegemony in Europe—and in later dealing with "embassies from the Muscovite and Ottoman realms" (157). As the subject of several ballets, Europe itself was a shifting concept explored through allegorical figures like Peace, Fame, Harmony, and Discord, as well as personified nations. Frictions can occur in any relationship, and those that bridge cultural differences may be particularly vulnerable, yet there was "an almost mystical belief in poetry, music, and dance to instill concord among spectators" (7), including representatives of foreign powers who dutifully reported in their diplomatic correspondence with authorities in the home country what they had witnessed and what they understood it to mean.

Drawing upon those ambassadorial documents, private correspondence, and a wealth of other primary sources as well as focused studies in secondary sources, Welch maintains an evenhanded treatment of developments in performance activities and foreign relations throughout the early modern period. The eight chapters proceed chronologically and incorporate extended descriptions and analyses of significant court ballets. The first chapter examines the Bayonne entertainments of 1565 by which the Valois rulers of France dazzled Spanish royals and English dignitaries with a masquerade tournament, chivalric pageantry incorporating classical mythology, a pastoral banquet with folk dancing, and ever-present music to instill a pervasive sense of harmony. Diplomatic incidents at the courts of England and France in 1608–1609 are the focus of the second chapter, which theorizes concepts of diplomacy arising from incidents related to Ben Jonson's *The Masque of Beauty* and *The Masque of Queens* in London and a *Balet de la Reyne* in Paris. In chapter 3, several ballets of the 1620s and 1630s provide examples of different ways of grappling with concepts of national identity; these include *Ballet des nations* (1622), the comic *Ballet du grand bal de la Douairière de Billebehaut* (1626), *Ballet de la marine* (1635), *Ballet des quatre monarchies chrétiennes* (1635), and *Ballet de l'Harmonie* (1632). Welch's thoughtful exploration of allegory as a major component of court ballet informs her fourth chapter's coverage of Richelieu's statesmanship behind the continuing Thirty Years' War. The cardinal "commissioned three allegorical entertainments that dramatized the international conflict: the *Ballet de la Félicité* (1639), the *Prospérité des armes*, and the machine-enhanced drama *Europe, comédie héroique* (1642)" (82), and these are analyzed in terms of visual and written records of their staging as well as in responses by the diplomat-spectators. The Congress of Westphalia (1645–1649) is the backdrop in chapter 5 for a range of performative activities, notably the *Ballet de la Paix* that offered an aspirational vision of European harmony.

Most readers would particularly look forward to the chapter on entertainments at the court of Louis XIV, yet the coverage touches only lightly on the *Ballet de la nuit* and others. There is some attention to matters of hospitality in that the English court of Charles I in exile participated in three ballets at the French court. But the descriptions and documentation in this chapter seem less painstaking than elsewhere; for example, the *Gazette* that is frequently quoted in translation is nowhere to be found in the bibliography, there are omissions in the page listings for the *Gazette* index entry, and a textual reference to "Félibien's official *Relations* of the major fêtes" (149) is misleading in that Félibien's *Relation* (singular) describes *la feste de Versailles du 18e juillet 1668*. Welch hits her stride again in the final chapters, with interesting coverage of the move away from the court and toward the opera and other public stages. Diplomatic exchanges with cultures beyond the bounds of Europe brought their own influences to French ballets and plays; the *turqueries* in works like Molière's *Bourgeois gentilhomme* offer a case in point.

Copious endnotes include the original French for all the quotations that are given in English translation in the text. The two-part bibliography comprises primary source listings and secondary sources, both substantial. The ten black-and-white illustrations are low resolution but compensated by the excellent wraparound cover design in full color showing exotic figures in a 1626 ballet.

—**FELICIA HARDISON LONDRÉ**
University of Missouri-Kansas City

Must Close Saturday: The Decline and Fall of the British Musical Flop. By Adrian Wright. Rochester, NY: Boydell, 2017. pp. xx + 351. $34.95 hardcover.

Adrian Wright's *Must Close Saturday: The Decline and Fall of the British Musical Flop* was commissioned by Michael Middeke of Boydell Press. *Must Close Saturday* examines 171 (give or take a few throwaway references) theatrical flops of post-*Oliver!* London in chronological order. It's a breezy, engaging beach read of a text, and the thesis seems to be "things fail for a variety of reasons, from being overly innovative to overly conventional, overly ambitious, or just plain bad." The book also lacks a conclusion, ending abruptly with the statement "the British musical flop has always had its surprises" (255).

In the preface, Wright questions the very existence of the volume: "It was in 1977 that the *Guardian* took the trouble to ask Lionel Bart 'Whatever happened to the British musical?' . . . Bart replied, 'It stopped when I stopped. It was big when Gilbert and Sullivan were doing some; when Noel Coward was doing some. It was big when I was doing some.' I wish I had seen this brilliantly concise analysis of what happened to the British musical in the second half of the twentieth century before attempting to capture the mystery in a book of 140,000 words" (xi). Wright goes on to explain his definition of a flop (a show running under 250 performances) and then contradicts that definition by saying long-running shows that are financially successful but horrible plays should also be defined as flops (the book should extend the discussion likening the prediction of theatrical success to picking stocks). This *Hamburg Dramaturgy* of disastrous musicals features stars on their way up (Albert Finney in *The Lily White Boys*, Jane Birkin in *Passion Flower Hotel*) and on their way down (Howard Keel in *Ambassador*, Betty Grable in *Belle Starr*), the tanking of once-promising careers (Lionel Bart and Sandy Wilson, post-*Oliver!* and *The Boy Friend*), and a cavalcade of broken dreams: a crowdfunded show about Bernadette Soubirous, a biomusical about Grimaldi seventeen years in the making that stumbled through twenty-three performances, and a "smutty folly rejected by twenty-one London producers" (212) that closed in two nights. Wright details stars suffering from pneumonia and nervous breakdowns, personality clashes, lockouts, bad decisions, and a smorgasbord of quotations from scathing reviews. Occasionally, reading bad review upon review isn't entertaining and just leads to feelings of sadness for the lost livelihoods and general humiliation of all involved in a given musical flop.

While eminently quotable—"a sort of sex musical that never achieved more than half cock" (49); "a more noisy than usual British musical written for the middle aged" (52)—and enjoyable to read aloud to friends—"lyrics that rhymed 'factotum' with 'grab Hitler by the scrotum'" (175); "Godammit, those chorus boys are still thumbing their waistcoats in 2016!" (126)—*Must Close Saturday* is a bit unwieldy as an academic text. The alphabetical appendix would benefit from including one-sentence plot summaries (or even brief descriptions) of each of the flops (the book frequently reads as though it was written for people who were in the audience and/or remembered living through the included musicals being dragged by the press). It also would be helpful if the appendix included page numbers so that the reader does not have to use first the general index to find an actor or director and then the appendix of plays to find the title of the play featuring said actor and the year it was produced and then the index of plays to find the section of the book detailing what went catastrophically wrong with the production, which makes for a slightly frustrating research experience. After reading through 255 pages of flops it becomes difficult to distinguish *Wild, Wild Women* (a musical adaptation of *Lysistrata* set in the Old West and staged at a theatre restaurant) from *Saucy Jack and the Space Vixens* (defies description) or *Romance!* (best described as first world problems, the musical) from *Lust* (*The Country Wife*, with songs). There are dueling Robin Hood musicals (*Twang!* and *Robin, Prince of Sherwood*) and matchgirl strike musicals (*Strike a Light* and *The Match Girls*), questionable literary adaptations (Dickens, Fitzgerald, Hardy, Mitchell, Maugham, Shakespeare, Wells) and dreadful biomusicals (Henry II,

Winston Churchill, Oscar Wilde, Marilyn Monroe, the Rector of Stiffkey, and Edward VIII and Wallis Simpson).

The stories of some of the flops play out across multiple pages, while others barely merit a paragraph. Some flops are neglected altogether by the discussion but are featured in the illustrations. I frequently found myself wishing *Must Close Saturday* were a podcast featuring conversations between Wright and his interviewees, a picture-laden coffee table book, or a website on which one could happily spend hours lost clicking between links. But despite its flaws, *Must Close Saturday* is worth a look if only for the pleasure of reading some hysterically dreadful lyrics and fascinating bits of trivia.

—RAE MANSFIELD
University of Massachusetts Lowell

Visions of Tragedy in Modern American Drama. Edited by David Palmer. New York: Bloomsbury Methuen Drama, 2018. pp. xvi + 236. $26.95 paperback.

In *Visions of Tragedy in Modern American Drama*, editor David Palmer brings together a convocation of scholars who explore the ongoing debate about modern tragedy and its relationship to the classic definition and examples of the form. In eighteen short essays, each by a different author, the works of significant American playwrights, beginning with Eugene O'Neill and Susan Glaspell, are discussed in terms of their tragic vision, influences, and thematic concerns. In his introduction, Palmer explains the task given to the essayists: "Rather than starting with preconceived notions of what tragedy is and then forcing them down upon the works to see if they fit the mold, contributors here were asked to look directly at the plays themselves and to explore what they showed about their author's vision of the nature and sources of human suffering, the ways the self is assaulted, and the ways characters respond. From that, it was hoped, distinctive elements of the author's vision of tragedy would emerge" (7). What is so appealing about this approach is that each playwright is considered as a unique artist, engaged with the idea of tragedy in a specific way. The tragedy of Sam Shepard's alcohol- and violence-saturated families is different from the tragedy of Amiri Baraka's doomed subway rider, which is different from the tragedy of Marsha Norman's lost working-class mother and daughter and Adrienne Kennedy's chorus of fragmented selves—though all stem from distorted visions of the American dream, along with the cognitive dissonance that comes from the unrealistic expectation that it should be easily achievable.

As a reader progresses through the essays, an argument for an understanding of tragedy that is broader than a more traditional classical definition emerges, even as the expected indebtedness to classics of Greek tragedy and the work of Shakespeare is acknowledged. Can a play be a tragedy when it contains a great deal of humor? Can a play be a tragedy when the classical conception of fate does not apply but instead issues such as racism and sexism prevent characters from having true control over their lives and futures? Is there a difference between a play that contains content that would be labeled "tragic" and a play that functions in the tragic mode? Christopher Bigsby, in the foreword, attempts to define what makes a modern tragedy: "What is common is the attempt by the protagonists of these dramas to invest their lives with meaning in a context in which such meaning is neither gifted nor apparent, indeed in which they feel the pressure of unmeaning. What is common is the sense that the past pressed unbearably on the present" (xix). That past may be the disturbing history of a family or a community or even a country. The tragic mode allows dramatists to go beyond the exploration of personal psychology and to take on more universal and political themes, as essayist Jonathan Shandell argues Langston Hughes did in *Mulatto* (50).

In the final chapter, "American Theatre since 1990," Toby Zinman considers plays that are primarily about American history, rather than family dramas, and "history, as it turns out, is often about war" (213). She examines musical theatre's engagement with history and tragedy through pieces such as Stephen Sondheim's *Assassins* and Lin-Manuel Miranda's *Hamilton*, in which, as she argues, "it is America, flawed but great, that becomes the tragic hero" (215). The final section of the chapter considers recent plays that contend with the legacy of war, past and present, such as Rajiv Joseph's *Bengal Tiger at the Baghdad Zoo* and Christopher Shinn's *Dying City*. Plays like these serve a necessary purpose, "revealing the emotional truth of war" in a way that journalism can't (227), and, unfortunately, the subject continues to be as relevant as it was during the era of classical tragedy. Although Zinman, by necessity, has to limit the scope of the final chapter, I found myself wanting more in that survey of twenty-five years. Paula Vogel (*Don Juan Comes Home from Iraq*) and Lisa Peterson (*An Iliad*) are discussed at length, and there is mention of *Topdog/Underdog* by Suzan-Lori Parks, but the other dozen playwrights discussed in the chapter are male (and even in the case of *An Illiad*, Peterson's cowriter is a man, Denis O'Hare). I wondered at the absence of playwrights such as Lynn Nottage and Quiara Alegría

Hudes, whose plays about the atrocities of war and the ongoing consequences for civilians and veterans appear to fit the parameters set by the essayist.

The editor states that the book is "intended for readers with a serious interest but perhaps little background in either the concept of tragedy or American drama" (12). The essays introduce the playwrights and the ways that their plays grapple with and/or embrace the idea of tragedy. Along the way, most major theories of tragedy are introduced and explicated, so that, taken together, the essays create a good foundation of knowledge about the subject, and a reader also gains an excellent overview of more than two dozen major American dramatists and their plays. And each chapter includes references for further reading so that readers can undertake more in-depth study with ease. This accessible volume will be useful for undergraduate and graduate students, as well as anyone looking for an introduction to the genre, and may be particularly useful as a companion reading for classes in dramatic literature.

According to Zinman, "Tragedy demands more of us than tears" (213). She refers here to the audience, but these essays provide evidence that the playwrights would agree. Chapter after chapter chronicles these dramatists' intense engagement with the legacy of classical tragedy and then, later, the legacy of early-twentieth-century writers such as Tennessee Williams, Arthur Miller, Lillian Hellman, Susan Glaspell, and especially Eugene O'Neill. The book, as a whole, argues for the continued relevance of the tragic mode: the ability of plays to create an environment where empathy is demanded, where catharsis can occur, where the tension between the decisions and actions of individuals and the needs of their communities matters, where our modern drama plays out against the backdrop and demands of the American dream in all its forms.

—CHARISSA MENEFEE
Iowa State University

Adapturgy: The Dramaturg's Art and Theatrical Adaptation. By Jane Barnette. Carbondale: Southern Illinois University Press, 2018. pp. xiii + 247. $40.00 paperback.

Jane Barnette's *Adapturgy* is a welcome addition to adaptation and dramaturgy scholarship that highlights aspects of theory and practice previously overlooked or little analyzed in either field. Structured in three parts, with invaluable material on interviews and program notes the writer generously shares with her readers in appendices, the book is useful to a multitude of readers.

The first chapter carefully provides a trajectory of adaptation scholarship, clearly drawing the book's significance: Barnette presents a genealogy of adaptation studies that includes US artists and scholars. This geographical adjustment widens adaptation scholarship considerably, given that the writer's outlook interweaves adaptation studies with Northwestern University's tradition of oral interpretation and performance. The refreshing and enriching critical presentation of dominant views in the field further strengthens Barnette's introductory section. In the second chapter, Barnette exercises the same diligence for dramaturgy and clearly makes her mark as a dramaturg. The trajectory of dramaturgy education in the United States is particularly useful. In chapter 3, the writer develops her well-thought-out argument on *adapturgy*. Looking at the adaptation and dramaturgy together, she argues, provides theorists and practitioners with more ways to focus on how plays are received by their audiences.

As in other parts of the book, and adding to the pedagogical dimension seen throughout, Barnette consistently explains theoretical terms for any level of reader. In chapter 4, she breaks down "palimpsest" as she traces the trajectory of the term in adaptation studies, before turning to her case study, the Elevator Repair Service's adaptation of Faulkner's *The Sound and the Fury*. This is a fascinating and enlightening treatise on adaptation dramaturgy methodology, in its details about the process and the resulting relationship with the company's audience. My reading of this particular case study was influenced by an unusual trajectory, afforded by the book's rich paratextual material: I perused the interview *first* and *then* read Barnette's analysis; I experienced, therefore, the writer's careful weaving of the responses as she constructed her argument. This process ideally showcases the writer's mastery over her material. In chapter 5, using the film *Birdman* as metaphor, Barnette explains the case study's relevance to her overarching argument. The writer pulls together intriguing sources, but I must admit I could not clearly see how this multilayered, mediated example, which functions more as a conceptual analysis of adaptation, fits into her larger project. Still, her careful reading of a rather provocative film makes for an engaging chapter. Chapter 6, "Geographies of Adaptation," is devoted to the challenges of space and location in adaptation dramaturgy, particularly as these relate to scenic versions of novels. Barnette uses stage adaptations of *Moby-Dick* as examples of overcoming these challenges in staging an admittedly demanding source. Of great importance, the author provides often overlooked examples of collaboration between the dramaturg/adapter and director and designer team.

In chapter 7, the first in the section devoted entirely to practice, Barnette delves into the particulars of her own and Michael Haverty's adaptation of *The Red Badge of Courage*. It is interesting to see how practical experience informs

Barnette's theoretical analysis, developed earlier in the book. In particular, I was intrigued by her example of the much-contested "spirit of the source," which, as the author aptly argues, may well be found beyond the words in the "original." As part of discussing ways to interact with audiences, per her own statement, Barnette begins chapter 8 with various considerations of how adaptation dramaturgy informs casting decisions. She analyzes uses and examples of paratextual information surrounding the production, whether in the physical space of the performance or in the digital realm. Using a wide variety of examples, the writer highlights the collaborative aspect of adaptation dramaturgy. In the last chapter, titled "Postmortem Dramaturgy," Barnette returns to the important question of "why this source as theatre now," and more specifically, "why adaptation dramaturgy now" (a basic principle in her work), and summarizes her points as she argued them through a variety of examples.

In terms of structure, even though the writer clearly explains her rationale, I felt that certain heterogeneous strands in her research were pulled into her central argument with varying results. For instance, I was less convinced by the discussion on the Janus effect on dramaturgy. However, I could see how this direction could provide alternative pathways to adaptation theory, if expanded onto its own work, beyond this book's agenda. In addition, the need to tie everything together may have led the writer to reiterate in parts. Still, one of the book's most important contributions is its pedagogical value. Barnette's consistent interest in the training of dramaturgs makes this book a valuable resource for researchers, teachers, and students of adaptation and dramaturgy. Inevitably, not all parts of the book will be useful to all readers, but this is a point made by Barnette herself when she states in her introduction that her book is "both 'a theory book' about creative practice as well as a 'practical book' about theory" (2). In my view, coming from a position of theory primarily, the three first chapters are the strongest for their contribution to adaptation and dramaturgy scholarship. The rest of the book engages primarily with challenges facing practitioners of adaptation dramaturgy and can serve as useful resources for those studying the intersection between theory and practice, as well as the processes involved in adapting for the stage.

—MARIA MYTILINAKI KENNEDY
Independent Scholar

Broadway Rhythm: Imaging the City in Song. By Dominic Symonds. Ann Arbor: University of Michigan Press, 2017. pp. ix + 300. $80.00 hardcover.

A map is often a tourist's first experience of a city, a tool to navigate an unfamiliar place. But maps show only the basic outlines: streets, buildings, and major points of interest. They are static and two-dimensional, offering orientation but little sense of place. Dominic Symonds's "performance cartography" proposes a dynamic map of New York City as experienced on a series of virtual walks through the city based on some of its most famous songs. Using performance studies and cartographic theory methods, Symonds ditches the traditional paper map in favor of one that views New York from the vertical and horizontal, as well as the bird's eye: the "surge upward and plunge below" (129). Symonds's map of New York includes fire escapes, lost neighborhoods (like the portion of the West Side demolished to make room for Lincoln Center), imaginary places (like Sarah Brown's Save A Soul Mission), elevators, and subway trains. But unlike a traditional map that would simply identify *where* these structures are, Symonds digs into them to discover *why and how* they are, providing considerably more detail and nuance than Google Street View can ever hope to. The map motif, therefore, is only a starting point: The range of songs that typify the "Broadway Rhythm" makes possible endless permutations of a "map" of New York. Starting and ending points, and all stops in between, are determined by the whims of the explorer.

Symonds begins his book not with a preface but with a "Pre-amble," a scholarly itinerary of the walks he will take his readers on. His methodology is rooted in the studies of cartographic theorists J. B. Harley, Nigel Thrift, and Paul Carter, as well as poststructural scholars Gilles Deleuze and Félix Guattari. Based on the premise that New York's rich musical history is reflected in its physical attributes, Symonds suggests that we can discover musicality in its buildings, infrastructure, traffic patterns, and pace of life. "By engaging with the city," he states, "walking, mapping, dancing, or singing—we play its score, and to whatever extent that represents, constructs, or reveals, we are performing its cartography" (26). Each chapter is one potential "walk" around the city to "map" its various musical points of interest. He ends his "pre-amble" with an invitation to the first walk, invoking lyricist Dorothy Fields: "For now, grab your coat and get your hat; let's take that walk" (31). Symonds is the best of all tour guides: beginning and ending each chapter with a friendly "Come this way," then imparting meticulous historical research and thoughtful analysis.

"Walk One: A Glance at New York" delves into the city's history via the then-popular "bird's-eye view" map of 1873. This type of map—common in the nineteenth century—offered a long view of the city from its southernmost point, as if the viewer were flying into the city. As such, many streets are indistinct, but one stands out as it streaks its way north: Broadway. Symonds anchors his walk on this longest and widest of streets and narrates a history of the formation of the city's grid pattern. Although Lower Manhattan retains its original jumble of streets winding in different directions, the grid dominates the majority of the island. But Broadway defies it, slicing straight up through Lower and Midtown, then jutting west above Sixtieth Street. Symonds discusses some of the earliest popular songs about Broadway that helped to establish it as New York's most iconic boulevard. After the Civil War, Broadway began to play host to theatres and other entertainment venues, further cementing the street's cultural primacy. Symonds's analysis of "Broadway Melody" (written by Arthur Freed and Nacio Herb Brown in 1929) introduces the reader to the "gapped scale," a type of musical construction evident in many songs about New York, in which the melody spans intervals of a tone and a tone and a half. Later in the book, Symonds will map out those scales to reveal a melody line that resembles the stepped tops of New York skyscrapers.

"Walk Two: Another Hundred People" examines the clustering of musical notes and repetitions evident primarily in Leonard Bernstein's music that epitomize New York's density. Symonds observes in Bernstein's music that "the notes or buildings compete with one another in energy, force, and volume to register most prominently" (72). He cites several examples from *West Side Story*, *On the Town*, and *Wonderful Town* that demonstrate this frenetic quality.

"Walk Three: Broadway Rhythm" takes the reader below the surface to the history of building the new over the old, creating a palimpsest in both architecture and song. Using Stephen Sondheim's *Follies* and its layering of the present over the past, Symonds suggests that we can hear these layers competing through syncopation, a popular musical construct in Tin Pan Alley and Broadway songs. Just as a melody cuts across the metrical beat, reconstructions stagger over old patterns in the city's architecture. Symonds returns to *West Side Story* for much of this chapter before exploring the musical sequence "Broadway Melody" from the movie *Singin' in the Rain*.

"Walk Four: Stairway to Paradise" explores the city's architecture in building and song structure. Symonds returns to the gapped scale to demonstrate how it looks when "mapped." A history of early-twentieth-century building codes reveals that skyscrapers were stepped (tapering toward the top) to alleviate overcrowding, resulting in the iconic skyline. Symonds creates block diagrams using melody lines from "New York, New York" (*On the Town*), "Broadway Rhythm," and "I Got Rhythm" to effectively visualize the relationship between the gapped scale and the New York City skyline. He follows this with a discussion of fire escapes, as they (ironically) represent an upward escape from the confines of the buildings, and their strategic placement in musicals like *West Side Story* and *In the Heights*.

"Walk Five: Time Steps" examines how bodies moving in space create endless alternative maps and draws on theories by Henri Lefebvre and Michel de Certeau. This walk takes the reader to Grand Central Terminal and Times Square, two of New York's busiest locations. Symonds draws maps of movement through stationary spaces, including the opening sequences of the film versions of *Guys and Dolls* ("Runyonland") and *West Side Story*.

"Walk Six: So Great They Named It Twice" expands the map view to New York's national and global context, moving away from Broadway and considering contemporary popular songs like "Empire State of Mind" (Jay-Z and Alicia Keys) and "New York, New York" (from the film of the same name). While New York is synonymous with Broadway, the Twin Towers of the World Trade Center were, for the late twentieth century, symbols of New York's status as a world destination and economic power. Symonds delves into a lengthy discussion of the history of the Towers and the artistic response in the aftermath of their destruction.

Broadway Rhythm is an exciting and nuanced approach to a city through its songs. There are times when Symonds strays from his own map, devoting a bit too much space to historical studies. I would like to have seen more song examples as well; Symonds returns to *West Side Story* and Bernstein often, at the expense of other shows and composers. But Symonds's writing style and evocative redefining of the idea of the map are refreshing, warm, and lively and uncover a new look at a city that we all think we know so well.

—**ELLEN M. PECK**
Jacksonville State University

Culture, Democracy and the Right to Make Art: The British Community Arts Movement. Edited by Alison Jeffers and Gerri Moriarty. New York: Bloomsbury, 2017. pp. 263. £75.00 hardcover.

This book, as is clear from its subtitle, is about community arts in Britain—its history, its theoretical underpinnings (insomuch as it can be said to have any kind of coherent theory, a fact which the book readily acknowledges), and its legacy. While a contribution to theatre history, this book is as much about film, television, visual arts, and late-twentieth-century cultural politics as it is about performance. The multiple threads that this book weaves are all to its strength, however. The history, theory, and legacy that the various authors attempt to trace are fragmented and lacking an archive, meaning that the history is largely an oral history, constructed of memories by the very people who shaped the history. In chapter 11, Owen Kelly writes, "We think less than we think we do, and our consciousness does not contain a single coherent narrative but rather a number of contending and contradictory impressions that we arrive at retrospectively" (234). What emerges within the pages of *Culture, Democracy and the Right to Make Art* is a book that mirrors Kelly's reflection. It is a series of often-contradictory memories, attempting to make sense of a moment in history when it seemed not only that radical revolutionary politics were possible but also that artists (or at least, artists acting as facilitators within communities) would be the very vanguard of that revolution.

Editors Alison Jeffers and Gerri Moriarty have divided their book into two sections. Part one is an oral history of community arts in Britain from 1968 to 1986, divided into four chapters covering England, Scotland, Wales, and Ireland. They did not choose 1986 as an arbitrary cutoff point, however. For Jeffers, community arts began its decline in 1980 when the Association of Community Artists (ACA) became regionally, rather than nationally, focused. Some artists joined the new Association for Community Arts (AfCA), but this organization was open to anyone interested in community arts, while the ACA was specifically a platform for artists to organize. This meant "opening up of membership to include representatives of the funding bodies [which] meant that we had no place to organise when our needs did not coincide with their desires" (37). But it was the end of the Shelton Trust in 1986—an organization that created conferences and publications for community artists—that signaled the "end of any sense of coherent national organizing arts in Britain" (38).

Part two is about the theory and legacy of the community arts movement. As an example, Kelly argues that community arts did not *end* per se. Rather, technological and cultural shifts meant that community artists' work no longer made sense. For instance, Oliver Bennet, in chapter 8, discusses how some community artists, like the ones who created Vale TV in West Dunbartonshire, believed that local television held the key for revolutionary politics. The hierarchical form of television meant that studios held the means of production. Communities, these artists believed, if given the means to conceive and create their own television, would use that power to create programs that revealed deep social unrest. (It did not work out this way in practice, however. The most popular program on Vale TV was a show about the dangers of dog feces.) Once technology shifted to allow individuals to create their own content—from video to the Internet—communities no longer needed facilitators to assist them in conceiving, creating, and disseminating their own work. What Kelly argues in chapter 11 is that the spirit that animated community arts—an "active view of human beings and society" (237)—is still alive, but "the battlegrounds have shifted a few miles" (238).

While I do not agree with every artist and theorist featured in this book, I think that juxtaposing a number of divergent viewpoints is the book's strongest feature. It is an approach that mirrors the fragmented nature of community arts itself. There are a few common threads in this book, however. One of those threads is the role that government funding plays in the community arts movement. While artists need the funding to survive, is it "the duty of the state actually to subsidize those who were working to overthrow it" (173)? If the state does fund community arts, does this kind of revolutionary work become just a Feast of Fools—a performance of dissent that acts under the approval of the state? Another thread, reflected in the book's title, is the meaning of "culture" and "democracy." The state, the book argues, wants "democratic culture"—the spread of bourgeois forms of art like operas, ballets, symphonies, and art galleries, while community artists want "cultural democracy"—art by and for the people. While it is clear that this cultural democracy and, subsequently, the revolution, as imagined by community artists, never quite happened, the reasons for that are still up for debate. *Culture, Democracy and the Right to Make Art*, at its strongest, is a contribution to that debate.

—**BEN PHELAN**
Brigham Young University

*Thornton Wilder in Collaboration: Collected Essays on His Drama and Fiction***.** Edited by Jackson R. Bryer, Judith P. Hallett, and Edyta K. Oczkowicz. Cambridge: Cambridge Scholars Publishing, 2018. pp. 365. $119.95 hardcover.

In considering playwright Thornton Wilder's "collaborative" work in a variety of professional situations, this collection makes two important adjustments toward a more accurate conception of this writer's place in modern theatre history. First, it depicts Wilder as participating in a wave of collective creation in US theatre and dance that crested in the 1930s, as opposed to standing outside this broad movement, as he often has been historicized. A few essays in this book assist in this goal, most convincingly, David Roessel and Tori Novack's "'What Are You Waiting For?': Thornton Wilder, Clifford Odets, and American Drama in the Late 1930s," which offers a kind of "six degrees of separation" reading of a 1938 Theatre Arts Committee for Democracy cabaret sketch that parodies *Our Town* and *Waiting for Lefty*. Uncovering this forgotten sketch (reprinted in its entirety in the collection), Roessel and Novack connect the supposedly apolitical Wilder to the radical Odets, if not in a relationship of direct influence then at least in a relationship of shared "theatrical ancestry" (224).

Second (and related to the first adjustment), the book takes one of the most "literary" of US playwrights—Wilder, was, after all, first renowned as a novelist—and challenges assumptions about authority that traditionally accompany the concept of the modern writer: as singular, independent, and the sole determiner of a text's meaning. In other words, this collection reclaims Wilder as a theatrical writer, essentially collaborative in his process, whether he was writing the play *The Skin of Our Teeth*, the film *Shadow of a Doubt*, or the novel *The Bridge of San Luis Rey*. This adjustment to our concept of Wilder reminds readers that the "myth of the author," as Foucault would have it, is never more obvious than when it is unsuccessfully applied to the communal work of those who primarily make their living in the theatre.

The problem with this edited collection is the problem of many volumes that gather together conference papers (in this case, those presented at the 2015 Second International Thornton Wilder Conference): The effort to include so many loosely related essays results in a book that is too long and lacks the focus of a coherent whole. Editors Bryer, Hallett, and Oczkowicz do their best to sort this stack of essays into five thematic groups: Wilder in Literary and Intellectual Collaboration, Wilder in Collaboration with Dramatic Traditions, Wilder in Collaboration with Fictional Traditions, Wilder in Collaboration with Contemporary Colleagues, and Performing and Interpreting Wilder Collaboratively Today. However, the essay placement seems rather arbitrary, with many essays working as well in one category as in another.

Moreover, as a volume that embraces collaboration in the "broadest sense" of the word (viii), it would have been useful to have the contributors respond and react to one another's work—or for the editors to have brought together disparate readings of Wilder's plays for productive conversation. For example, it would be interesting to see how Macy McDonald's reading of *Our Town* as intellectually indebted to Sartre and Heidegger, culminating in the depiction of "an indefinite afterlife" employed to "torture [characters] with their own inauthenticity" (34), jibes with Howard Wolf's description of the play as one in which "light prevails over darkness" (50). A similar missed opportunity for productive conversation lies in Lincoln Konkle's description of Wilder's plays as "postmodern," in opposition "to the realism and naturalism of the late-nineteenth century theatre as developed by Ibsen, Strindberg, Chekhov, and Shaw" (14), a reading that seems juxtaposed to Sarah Littlefield's assertion that Wilder's novel *Theophilus North* was in deep collaboration with Ibsen's *A Doll's House* (197). An edited collection should not be tasked with finding consensus among its contributors, of course. Nevertheless, the many parallels and disagreements raised in these twenty essays beg for more conversation, if not within the chapters then at least within the editorial frame.

Other chapters seem like obvious candidates for future volumes on Wilder, volumes more limited in scope. For example, Oczkowicz's production history of *Our Town* in pre–WWII Poland makes the thought-provoking claim that this play's prolificness stems from "the unprecedented collaborative capacity embedded in its content and form" (254). This chapter goes hand in hand with Hansong Dan's fascinating production history of *Our Town* in China and Taiwan since the 1960s. Clearly a play with such a long history of global production deserves a volume dedicated to documenting how the work has been translated for and by cultures outside the United States and how the play may have aimed at depicting universal (even "planetary") human experience (280) yet was inevitably limited by its situatedness.

Finally, a pair of essays offers thoughtful interpretations of Wilder's collaborations with fellow renowned creative artists—and again suggests that there is enough rich material here for a full volume on the topic. Felicia Londré's description of Wilder cowriting the 1942 film *Shadow of a Doubt* for director Alfred Hitchcock considers Hitchcock's auteur mentality to be diametrically opposed to Wilder's embrace of collaboration. She quotes Hitchcock: "I, who fear being influenced by anyone in my work, was astonished that a great writer should not be afraid of another writer's influence" (125). Terryl Hallquist's chapter, meanwhile, takes up a Wilder collaboration that occurred that same year, between the playwright and director Elia Kazan prior to the Broadway premiere of *The Skin of Our Teeth*. Hallquist cleverly likens Wilder's mentorship of Kazan to that of a "mature Captain" toward "a young pilot." After all, while their play was in rehearsal, this was indeed the role in which Wilder was serving as a military officer tasked with debriefing Allied fighter pilots. These two essays are prime evidence that this volume's parts are often greater than the sum of its whole.

—SCOTT PROUDFIT
Elon University

Moment Work: Tectonic Theater Project's Process of Devising Theater. By Moisés Kaufman and Barbara Pitts McAdams et al. New York: Vintage, 2018. pp. x + 307. $18.00 cloth.

A participant says, "I begin." Something occurs. The participant says, "I end." Whatever happens in between the two phrases makes up the basis of Tectonic Theater Project's work: the Moment.

Tectonic has, for more than twenty-five years, created fascinating and groundbreaking works, telling the stories of people as disparate as Beethoven (*33 Variations*), Oscar Wilde (*Gross Indecency*), and the residents of Laramie, Wyoming (*The Laramie Project*). In *Moment Work*, they tell their own story. A combination of studio journal, history, teaching manual, and reflection, the book describes their devising and rehearsal processes and shines light on the principles underlying them. It is to their great credit that, by and large, *Moment Work* proves as eye-opening as the best of Tectonic's productions.

"Moment Work" is the term given to their approach, an outgrowth of the ideas and experiments that permeated Tectonic's founding and early work in the 1990s. The phrase does not merely refer to chronology. Rather, it involves exploring all the component elements of every unit of stage time. These vary from tangible elements like architecture, voice, and costume to more interpretive ones like tension, virtuosity, and ritual. These elements are explored through studio work singly and then combined in various ways. The goal is not just a new narrative but the discovery of new ways of creating and sharing narrative. "We do exercises about subject matter, and in tandem, we do exercises about form. The dialogue between the two is what generates the work" (22). Still, they emphasize that, although devising is often part of their work, the methods described in this book can be used with preexisting texts, as well.

The book is composed of three sections. The first identifies the predecessors from whom the company drew inspiration, describes the basic history of the group, and explains the fundamentals behind their approach to creating theatre. The second section goes in depth to illustrate the methodologies of Moment Work, and the third consists of essays by company members that shine light on particular topics related to their processes. (Although Kaufman and McAdams are identified as the principal authors, Tectonic members Leigh Fondakowski, Greg Pierotti, Andy Paris, Kelli Simpkins, Jimmy Maize, and Scott Barrow made contributions to the text, including the essays, and are listed as coauthors.)

Although it does an excellent job of laying the groundwork, the first section is the book's weakest. Short as it is, it gets rather repetitive, as the authors find numerous ways to emphasize that their theatre exists at the intersection of the literary and the performative. Perhaps the greatest flaw of the first section is a sin of omission. They do not define the term "Moment" here or in the introduction. Indeed, it does not get fully explained until fifteen pages into part 2. While its essence is strongly hinted at before that, and the term, by necessity, is an open-ended one, it would help the reader to establish a stronger understanding of the concept if the authors took the trouble to explain it at an earlier point, especially since they use the term liberally in the pages preceding its definition.

Part 2: The Moment Work Process is the heart of the book, constituting almost 70 percent of the text. The *I begin/I end* procedure is deceptively simple. This section examines the many purposes that Moment creation can serve and the many sorts of achievements that can result. Tectonic Theater Project's model is a three-stage progression. Level 1, called Making Moments, is where company members define the constituent elements of the event and explore them in increasing complexity. Level 2 finds the members creating short narratives, and level 3 deals with creating a full-length work. This portion of the book is superbly organized. Exercises that constitute the various stages of the process are explained and then described—though it would be helpful for a few of them to be described in better detail. Then Kaufman and McAdams illustrate with well-chosen examples from rehearsals and workshops. With regard to set pieces, for instance, the authors note that level 1 work often involves bringing unusual furniture choices to the studio. "Any set piece can hold unexpected discursive power, if we are willing to put aside our preconceptions and play with it" (121). Even with relatively prosaic set pieces like chairs, actors are encouraged to go beyond using them in ways that communicate setting and character traits and to discover how the furniture can be used to express stylistic and rhythmic currents within the Moment. In level 3, the authors return to the topic, describing how company members turned a seemingly simplistic piece of staging into one of the more effective visuals of *The Laramie Project*, the transformation of a line of chairs into the infamous fence to which Matthew Shepard was tied.

As the example above indicates, the pages dedicated to level 3 are of particular interest to the historian, as they provide insight into how the members of Tectonic created the works that make up their remarkable oeuvre. They provide detailed descriptions of key moments in the devising and rehearsal processes. Meanwhile, the essays that constitute section 3 of this book range in topic from interview techniques and team dramaturgy to working with college students. Each one is written clearly and purposefully and most have a sense of warmth, as if the writer is passing advice along to a friend.

Scholars and writers of documentary theatre will benefit enormously from this work, but the lessons transcend genre and style. As the authors state, "Once a moment is shared, it belongs to everyone" (63). Theatre artists and scholars of every stripe are fortunate that *Moment Work* has been shared. Now its rewards belong to us all.

—RICHARD SAUTTER
Gettysburg College

Women, Collective Creation, and Devised Performance: The Rise of Women Theatre Artists in the Twentieth and Twenty-First Centuries. Edited by Kathryn Mederos Syssoyeva and Scott Proudfit. New York: Palgrave Macmillan, 2016. pp. xx + 348. $119.00 hardcover.

Syssoyeva and Proudfit's volume is the third, self-contained study generated by an ongoing research project that explores collective creation and devising from the turn of the twentieth century to the present. Utilizing select Western practitioners and companies as case studies, this edited collection moves beyond the recording of women's contributions to collective creation to raise useful historiographical queries regarding the effect of gender on notions of authority, authorship, and attribution within group creation and its historicization.

The book is organized chronologically and divided into three sections corresponding to three historical "waves." Cognizant of the limits of such categorizations, the editors rightfully point out that this partition should be understood as porous and not as identifying rigid temporal boundaries signposting paradigm shifts. The first essay of the volume is included within the First Wave (1900–1945) section and functions as an introduction. It lays out useful terminology that will be utilized in subsequent chapters and underlines its limits. Particularly valuable is the discussion unpacking the meaning and attributes of collective creation, devising, and proto-collectivism. The remaining four essays in this unit focus on the period following the rise of the modern director and highlight women's roles in generating new theatremaking processes that remained at the heart of collective creation throughout the second-half of the twentieth century. The six chapters of the Second Wave (1945–1985) unit investigate the rise to prominence of all-female collectives and of individual female theatremakers within mixed collectives. They jointly indicate that as communitarian ethos, New Left ideals, and the 1970s feminist movement informed practitioners' utopic desires for participatory, democratic, and leaderless ensembles, women envisioned art-making beyond the traditional model adopted by patriarchal institutions. The last section of the volume covers the Third Wave (1985–present) of collective creation, which is characterized by what Syssoyeva terms its "postutopic impulse": a focus on ethics rather than ideology as the incipit of artistic creation, an interest in the creativity of the actor as a generative force and the consequent dissemination of training methods aimed at forming such performers, a return to understanding theatre as a total work of art, and a concern with intermediality (16). Together with a substantial shift from collective creation to devising, this period saw an exponential increase in the visibility of female theatre artists as well as a reappearance of feminist protest performance. Two examples of the latter are discussed in chapter 12 and chapter 20, which respectively examine Judith Malina's street protests and their connection to the Occupy movement and punk collective Pussy Riot's political interventions in contemporary Russia.

Although each essay in the collection is a stand-alone study, the volume also investigates larger questions (outlined in the introduction) underlying the historiography of women's collective creation. For example, it examines how collective creation facilitated both the emergence and disappearance of female practitioners working within collectives. While, as the book argues, collective creation made equal space for male and female artists and encouraged the surfacing of women's experience within institutional structures, it also witnessed the disappearance of women's contributions to the group. Suzanne Bing's case outlined by Jane Baldwin in chapter 2 is a blatant example of this erasure. Baldwin reveals that Bing's experimental pedagogical work was fundamental to the development of the curriculum of Jacques Copeau's Vieux Colombier School and of the actors of his Burgundy-based experimental collective creation company, the Copiaus. Through alumni of the Vieux Colombier and the Copiaus, Bing's influence spread to the emerging French mime tradition, the lineage of French collective creation, and to the curriculum of internationally renowned schools, such as Juilliard and the Old Vic. Yet, despite the far-reaching influence of her work, Bing's contributions have been erased and attributed to Copeau. Other examples illustrating the vanishing of women's contributions are analyzed in chapter 5, where Andrei Malaev-Babel discusses the obscured contributions of Russian director Alexandra Remizova to Soviet theatre, and in chapter 13, where Karen Morash proposes that Bryony Lavery's individual artistry has been undervalued as a consequence of her involvement with ensembles centering on feminist collective creation. The volume further considers the perils of the erasure of women's voices from the history of a company by exploring the tendency of historians, critics, and audiences to focus on the "group" and its "leader" in instances of collective creation, thus rendering invisible individual contributions, particularly if they are made by women. Acutely relevant are the discussions of these issues that appear in chapter 8 and chapter 10. In the former, Siobhán O'Gorman discusses the erasure of Carolyn Swift's contributions to Dublin's Pike Theatre by the press, which directly influenced how the company was historicized. Similarly, Michelle MacArthur's chapter 10 elaborates on the dangers of sacrificing complex company dynamics to create a simpler historical and mediatic narrative. In her essay, MacArthur outlines the difficulties this presents when tracing the history of two Canadian Feminist collectives: Nightwood Theatre and *Théâtre Expérimental des Femmes*.

Also addressed throughout the volume are questions of leadership within different processes of collective creation and of the impact of gendered assumptions on notions of authority. These queries are particularly resonant in chapter 6, where David Calder considers the mediated construction of Ariane Mnouchkine's role within *Théâtre du Soleil* as that of a solitary, genial leader vis-à-vis the egalitarian workings of the company that have refuted such assumption. Moreover, issues connected with women's labor, its compensation, and the economic workings of collective creation surface, for example, in Rachel Anderson-Rabern's overview of devising women-led groups in contemporary Downtown New York (chapter 17) and in Jessica Silsby Brater's discussion of Mabou Mines (chapter 7). Anderson-Rabern's analysis unearths the price that many female theatremakers must pay for the freedom to create collaboratively: modest remuneration despite awards and critical acclaim. Brater's chapter further explores women's labor within a collective. It contends that Ruth Maleczech and JoAnne Akalaitis, two of the company's founding artistic directors, resisted assumptions regarding women's labor and ensured that their collective would enact policies (such as company-supported childcare) that would enable all its members to freely participate in the creation process.

The two highlights of the volume are Victoria Lewis's essay tracing the evolution of disabled women's theatre collectives (chapter 19) and Nia O. Witherspoon's writing discussing Sharon Bridgforth's *River See*, theatrical-jazz, and the African diaspora. Through a disability studies lens, Lewis presents disabled women's collectives as spaces to explore difference, agency, and interdependence.

She thus lays bare the long-standing exclusivity of theatrical creation. Although, as she writes, "membership in the world of theatre and dance (conservative or liberal, feminist or mixed) is controlled by an unexamined standard of equality built on the intact body," there could be much to be gained by "paying attention to difference" and by "de-stigmatiz[ing] dependence and weakness" (314). If Lewis troubles an ableist understanding of collective creation, Witherspoon's chapter troubles the volume's internationalist perspective. She poignantly reminds us that "for black subjects in diaspora, creation is always already collective, and creation is always already culturally rooted," hence noting that underlying much of the discourse surrounding collective creation is a Western bias that understands creation as singular. While this collection is undoubtedly aware of its Western-centric content (and it discloses so in the introduction), it is also worth noting that the volume is is white-focused in a way that leaves out many female collective-creation practitioners of color. What is promising is that the editors anticipate an upcoming publication that will expand the exploration of collective creation beyond the geographical (and, hopefully, racial) limits present in this volume. Reframing women as "central to the emergence and development of collective creation," the collection's focused and accessible interventions are a valuable resource not just for the university classroom, theatre historians, and feminist scholars but also for devisers interested in developing a feminist, inclusive practice (3).

—**FRANCESCA SPEDALIERI**
Stony Brook University

BOOKS RECEIVED

2017–2019

Ammen, Sharon. *May Irwin: Singing, Shouting, and the Shadow of Minstrelsy*. Urbana: University of Illinois Press, 2017.

Arjomand, Minou. *Staged: Show Trials, Political Theater, and the Aesthetics of Judgement*. New York: Columbia University Press, 2018.

Aronson, Arnold. *The History and Theory of Environmental Scenography*. Second edition. New York: Methuen, 2018.

Barker, Harvey Granville. Colin Chambers and Richard Nelson, eds. *Granville Barker on Theatre: Selected Essays*. London: Bloomsbury, 2017.

Bennett, Susan, and Sonia Massai, eds. *Ivo Van Hove: From Shakespeare to David Bowie*. New York: Methuen, 2018.

Blank, Paula. *Shakesplish: How We Read Shakespeare's Language*. Stanford, CA: Stanford University Press, 2018.

Boyd, Amanda Weldy. *Staging Memory and Materiality in Eighteenth-Century Theatrical Biography*. New York: Anthem, 2018.

Brauneck, Manfred, and ITI Germany, eds. *Independent Theatre in Contemporary Europe: Structures, Aesthetics, Cultural Policy*. Bielefeld, Germany: Transcript Verlag, 2017.

Bredeson, Kate. *Occupying the Stage: The Theatre of May '68*. Evanston, IL: Northwestern University Press, 2018.

Cahill, Alex. *The Formation, Existence, and Deconstruction of the Catholic Stage Guild of Ireland*. Newcastle upon Tyne: Cambridge Scholars, 2017.

Dadario, Will. *Baroque, Venice, Theatre, Philosophy*. New York: Palgrave, 2017.

Damodaran, Sumangala. *The Radical Impulse: Music in the Tradition of the Indian People's Theatre Association*. New Delhi: Tulika, 2017.

Davies, Rachel Bryant. *Victorian Epic Burlesques: A Critical Anthology of Nineteenth-Century Theatrical Entertainments after Homer*. New York: Bloomsbury, 2019.

Day, Stuart A. *Outside Theatre: Alliances that Shape Mexico*. Tucson: University of Arizona Press, 2017.

Ducomb, Christian. *Haunted City: Three Centuries of Racial Impersonation in Philadelphia*. Ann Arbor: University of Michigan Press, 2017.

Ellinghausen, Laurie, ed. *Approaches to Teaching Shakespeare's Plays: English History Plays*. New York: Modern Language Association of America, 2017.

Enders, Jody, ed. *Holy Deadlock and Further Ribaldries: Another Dozen Medieval French Plays in Modern English*. Philadelphia: University of Pennsylvania Press, 2017.

Farfan, Penny. *Performing Queer Modernism*. New York: Oxford University Press, 2017.

Ferdman, Bertie. *Off Sites: Contemporary Performance Beyond Site-Specific*. Carbondale: Southern Illinois University Press, 2018.

Gibb, Andrew. *Californios, Anglos, and the Performance of Oligarchy in the U.S. West*. Carbondale: Southern Illinois University Press, 2018.

Goodman, Jessica. *Goldoni in Paris: La Gloire et le Malentendu*. Oxford: Oxford University Press, 2017.

Grene, Nicholas. *The Theatre of Tom Murphy: Playwright Adventurer*. New York: Bloomsbury, 2017.

Johnson, Odai. *London in a Box: Englishness and Theatre in Revolutionary America*. Iowa City: University of Iowa, 2017.

Jones, Chris. *Rise Up! Broadway and American Society from "Angels in America" to "Hamilton."* New York: Methuen, 2019.

Lemon, Rebecca. *Addiction and Devotion in Early Modern England*. Philadelphia: University of Pennsylvania Press, 2018.

MacDonald, Laura, and Willaim A. Everett, eds. *The Palgrave Handbook of Musical Theatre Producers*. New York: Palgrave, 2017.

McAvinchey, Caoimbe, Lucy Richardson, and Fabio Santos, eds. *Phakma: Making Participatory Performance*. New York: Bloomsbury, 2018.

Montez, Noe. *Memory, Transitional Justice, and Theatre in Postdictatorship Argentina*. Carbondale: Southern Illinois University Press, 2018.

Nathans, Heather S. *Hideous Characters & Beautiful Pagans: Performing Jewish Identity on the Antebellum American Stage*. Ann Arbor: University of Michigan Press, 2017.

Ney, Charles. *Directing Shakespeare in America: Historical Perspectives*. New York: Arden Shakespeare, 2019.

Pangallo, Matteo A. *Playwriting Playgoers in Shakespeare's Theater*. Philadelphia: University of Pennsylvania Press, 2017.

Richlin, Amy. *Slave Theatre in the Roman Republic: Plautus and Popular Comedy*. Cambridge: Cambridge University Press, 2017.

Senelick, Laurence. *Jacques Offenbach and the Making of Modern Culture*. New York: Cambridge University Press, 2017.

Shandell, Jonathan. *The American Negro Theatre and the Long Civil Rights Era*. Iowa City: University of Iowa Press, 2018.

Shannon, Sandra G., and Sandra L. Richards, eds. *Approaches to Teaching the Plays of August Wilson*. New York: Modern Language Association of America, 2016.

Shimazaki, Satoko. *Edo Kabuki in Transition: From the Worlds of the Samurai to the Vengeful Female Ghost*. New York: Columbia University Press, 2016.

Smith, Matthew Wilson. *The Nervous Stage: Nineteenth-Century Neuroscience and the Birth of Modern Theatre*. New York: Oxford University Press, 2018.

Wood, Michael. *Heiner Müller's Democratic Theater: The Politics of Making the Audience Work*. Rochester: Camden House, 2017.

Wright, Matthew. *The Lost Plays of Greek Tragedy*, Volume 2: *Aeschylus, Sophocles, and Euripides*. New York: Bloomsbury, 2019.

CONTRIBUTORS

GUILLERMO AVILES-RODRIGUEZ is a theatre and performance studies PhD candidate at UCLA and a lecturer in theatre and the Chicana/o Studies Department at California State University, Northridge. His article "Darning *Zoot Suit* for the Next Generation" is in the Spring 2019 issue of *Aztlán: A Journal of Chicano Studies* and "Theatre and Transit: A Transit-Oriented Site-Specific Triptych" is featured in *TheatreForum*. He is the creator of *Meet Me @Metro*, a site-specific, transit-oriented theatrical extravaganza.

SEAN BARTLEY received his PhD in theatre studies at Florida State and is a lecturer in the Department of Music and Theatre at California State University, Bakersfield. He holds a BA in theatre arts management from American University and an MFA in dramaturgy from the joint program between the American Repertory Theatre Institute for Advanced Theatre Training at Harvard University and the Moscow Art Theatre School. His research centers on contemporary American site-based, ambulatory, and immersive theatre practices. His work has been featured in *TDR: The Drama Review*, *Theatre Journal*, *PARtake: The Journal of Performance as Research*, and *Borrowers and Lenders: The Journal of Shakespeare and Appropriation*.

DAVID BISAHA is an assistant professor of theatre history and theory at Binghamton University, State University of New York. David's research specializes in the history of scenic design in the United States and in the more recent history of immersive and participatory performance. His book project, titled *American Scenic Design and Freelance Professionalism*, is a history of modern scenic design praxis among twentieth-century artists in New York City. At Binghamton, David teaches theatre history and acting/directing theory in the MA and BA programs.

ELIZABETH COEN is a researcher who examines the role of theatre and performance in nation building. She is also a freelance dramaturg and coeditor of LMDA's journal *Review*. She holds a PhD from the University of Washington in theatre history, theory, and criticism.

PENELOPE COLE received her PhD from the University of Colorado at Boulder, where her research focused on the work of Scottish female playwrights. A lifelong teacher, she most recently held a faculty position in the Honors Program at CU Boulder delivering courses in performance studies and directing a study abroad program in Edinburgh, Scotland, using the Edinburgh Festival Fringe as a classroom. Her directorial work engages and integrates the audience in challenging and unexpected ways, whether in a traditional theatre or a found location. Most recently, she staged a new translation of Leonid Andreyev's *The Black Masks* in a converted nineteenth-century mansion in Denver. She is currently an independent scholar engaging in a wide variety of research and writing projects, including the production of a bill of solo performances at the 2019 Fringe. Her work has been published in the *Journal of Irish and Scottish Studies*, *Theatre Research International*, the *Journal of Dramatic Theory and Criticism*, and *Theatre Survey*, among others.

MICHELLE GRANSHAW is an associate professor of theatre arts at the University of Pittsburgh. Dr. Granshaw's articles have appeared in *Theatre Survey*, *Nineteenth Century Theatre and Film*, *Popular Entertainment Studies*, *Journal of American Drama and Theatre*, *Theatre Topics*, and the *New England Theatre Journal*. Her book, *Irish on the Move: Performing Mobility in American Variety Theatre*, is available from the University of Iowa Press.

RAND HARMON is a theatre director, producer, and a creative entrepreneur, as well as a scholar investigating the conceptual practices of leading site-based theatre creators in the United Kingdom and the United States. In 2007, Harmon founded Specific Gravity Ensemble in Louisville, Kentucky, and as artistic director, he conceived and produced their popular three annual *Elevator Plays* festivals, as well as four other acclaimed site-based productions. Harmon is an assistant professor of theatre studies at the University of Northern Colorado.

BRIDGET MCFARLAND received her PhD in English and American literature from New York University. She teaches in the Expository Writing Program at NYU.

ERIN B. MEE is the founding artistic director of This Is Not A Theatre Company, with whom she has conceived and directed the site-specific pieces *Pool Play 2.0*, *A Serious Banquet*, *Readymade Cabaret*, *Ferry Play*, *Subway Plays*, *Festival de la Vie* for the Avignon Festival, and *Versailles 2015/2016*. She is the author of *Theatre of Roots: Redirecting the Modern Indian Stage*, and her born-digital Scalar article "Hearing the Music of the Hemispheres" won the ATHE-ASTR Award for Best Digital Article in 2016. She is an assistant arts professor in the Department of Drama at Tisch, NYU. www.erinbmee.com.

DANIELLA VINITSKI MOONEY (University of Pennsylvania) is a PhD artist/scholar trained in experimental and classical methods through the NYU Tisch School Experimental Theatre Wing and the Royal Academy in London. She currently dramaturgs with PlayPenn and is a contributor to the new Routledge anthology, *Physical Dramaturgy: Perspectives from the Field*. Daniella's manuscript, *Field of Mars Revisited: The Opera/Installation/Performance of GAle GAtes*, is a study of the defunct immersive company through the lens of the avant-garde.

COLLEEN RUA is an assistant professor of theatre and performance studies at the University of Florida. Her work in immersive theatre includes conceiving and directing *An Awfully Big Adventure* and *Alice in Wonderland* with student devisers. Her scholarship also includes work in Latinx Theatre, and her manuscript *Coming Home: Latinx Figures on Broadway* explores the place and significance of the Latinx character regarding the search for and construction of "home."

RYAN TVEDT earned his PhD in theatre and drama from the University of Wisconsin-Madison. He has taught at universities in Kazakhstan, Russia, and South Korea, and currently works as a legislative advisor in the US Senate. He would like to acknowledge research support for this project in the form of a fellowship provided by the Center for Russia, East Europe, and Central Asia at the University of Wisconsin-Madison.